112598

Living by the Sword

Living by the Sword

America and Israel in the Middle East 1968–87

STEPHEN GREEN

faber and faber
LONDON · BOSTON

First published in 1988
by Faber and Faber Limited
3 Queen Square London WC1N 3AU

Photoset by Parker Typesetting Service Leicester
Printed in Great Britain by
Mackays of Chatham Ltd Kent
All rights reserved

© Stephen Green, 1988
Maps prepared by Joseph Robinson

British Library Cataloguing in Publication Data

Green, Stephen, 1949–
Living by the sword.
1. Israel – Foreign relations – United
States   2. United States – Foreign
relations – Israel
I. Title
327.5694073   DS119.8.U6
ISBN 0-571-15047-0

For my mother, who finds something good
in almost everything.

Contents

List of Maps

Acknowledgements

Several people gave me frequent advice and encouragement during the researching and writing of this book: John Fialka, Sue Dangler, Mark Bruzonsky, Muna Hamzah and most of all, my wife Gisa. Others were kind enough to review chapters or portions of chapters and to comment, including Art Weber, Clyde Mark, D. J. Kiely, Les Janka, Robert Dillon, Donald Neff, Thomas Pianka, Robert Kubal, Gerry Funk, Ned Redican and Talcott Seelye, among others.

Valuable materials and information were provided by Michael Dunn, Israel Shahak, Jean Jacques Surbeck and Leslie Schmida.

Attorneys Richard Sobol, Michael Trister and Richard Cassidy helped me to convince the State Department and the Defense Intelligence Agency to comply with the requirements of the Freedom of Information Act. In the case of DIA particularly, this was not easy.

The staff of the Norwich University Library, Vermont, again cheerfully, repeatedly provided valuable assistance with reference materials, military periodicals and inter-library book loans. I'm indebted to Wilma and Bruce Coon, Paul Heller, Ann Turner, Margaret Partlow and Jacqueline Painter.

Some of the most important assistance I received came from persons whose current positions in government and industry would be abruptly affected by the revealing of their names. I say it admiringly – friends of Israel in Washington reward their like-minded colleagues and punish their perceived enemies with singular efficiency.

Finally, I wish to acknowledge the unwitting assistance of Mortimer Zuckerman, Irving Kristol, Conor Cruise O'Brien,

Amos Perlmutter and Wolf Blitzer among others who, without realizing it, repeatedly convinced me of the importance of persevering.

ONE

Introduction

Not long ago, I had lunch in Washington, DC with a friend of many years. I had always considered him to be one of the very few real gentlemen I'd ever known – considerate and moderate in all things. I couldn't recall ever having seen him show anger. Now, he was nearing the end of a long career with US intelligence in and on the Middle East. We arranged to meet at a particular hotel restaurant we had both frequented years ago, when we saw each other often.

At the table, staring out a nearby window, he told me that he was leaving his life's work in a state of confusion and doubt, wondering whether he had been serving the right side. I was startled. When he looked back, he said, at how the Soviet Union and the United States had operated in the Middle East in the last thirty-five years, he had come to the conclusion that the Soviets had been more ... responsible. He shook his head slightly as he grasped for the word; it was obvious that he did not enjoy saying this.

'We just haven't exercised any restraint, and they have,' he said. When he had taken his first field assignment in the early 1950s, Israel was a small, struggling country. Survival was really an issue then, and the thrust of American foreign policy in the Middle East was to achieve peace in order to ensure that survival.

Now, he said, Israel had the fifth or sixth most powerful army in the world, the third largest air force, and nuclear weapons with five or six different delivery systems, all provided directly or indirectly by the United States. No longer, in terms of US policy, was Israel seen as a homeland, a refuge. More and more in Washington, Israel was seen as a 'strategic asset', a kind of huge, docked aircraft carrier pointed at the Soviet Union. In the process, we had made of Israel an immediate, serious threat to the national security of each of its Arab neighbours.

We'd got entangled in the cold war, or something, and we'd just lost sight of what our primary objective was over there. He was still looking out the window. There will be another war, he said, and it will involve a new generation of weapons. 'It's all offence now . . . missiles, chemical–biological warheads . . .' He then looked at me. 'We have driven the Arabs to seek strategic, maybe even nuclear weapons,' he said. 'They have no choice . . . and the Soviets have none either; they must help the Arabs defend themselves.'

We had intended this as a kind of reunion, a chance to 'catch up'. But after the conversation of the first few minutes, neither of us was really enthusiastic about exchanging news of wives and children. I had never seen the man without his gentle optimism. Whatever the news of the moment, he had always been able to put it in perspective. Now, it seemed that it *was* the perspective, the long view, that disturbed him.

When my friend had first committed himself to the covert defence and projection of US interests in the Middle East, American goals there were principled, and they were clearly stated. In 1950, Britain, France and the United States stipulated in the Tripartite Declaration their 'unalterable opposition to the use of force between any of the [Middle Eastern] states'; they pledged to regulate arms shipments to the region, and guaranteed the territorial integrity of the states-party to the conflict.

For a time, these concepts guided the way in which America related to the countries of the region. In the 1950s and early 1960s, Presidents Truman, Eisenhower and Kennedy exercised restraint on arms sales to the region, and otherwise conducted the country's business in that region as if peace between Arab and Jew were the primary objective of US Middle East policy.

Then under President Lyndon Johnson, this principled objectivity was transformed into unreserved support to one side in the conflict. This departure in American Middle East policy occurred during and immediately after the Six Day War in 1967.

In the fighting itself, the US provided covert material and direct operational assistance.[1] Just as important, however, was US diplomatic support in the United Nations which delayed cease-fires on the various fronts and allowed Israel the precious time to complete the conquest and occupation of portions of three Arab states. US intelligence had accurately predicted the lop-sided outcome of the war, but the assistance had been provided anyway, perhaps in a misguided effort by the Johnson White House to break nineteen years of stalemate in the Arab-Israeli conflict. The Israelis would be allowed, even assisted, to take territory as 'bargaining chips' to force the Arabs to the negotiating table.

The size of the territory under Israeli administration quadrupled in the Six Day War of 1967. In one sense, the additional land brought new security. Chaim Herzog, former Director of Israeli Military Intelligence, took great comfort in his country's new military position after 12 June 1967. The occupied Golan Heights now provided a twenty-mile-wide buffer between Israel and Syria. The acquisition of the West Bank of Jordan eliminated Israel's vulnerable thin waist, and permitted Israeli Defence Force (IDF) deployments along the 'natural' border of the Jordan River. The Israeli occupation of Sinai, according to Herzog, meant that 'the electronic warning period given to Israel in respect of an air attack from Egypt had increased fourfold, to sixteen minutes'.[2]

However, many in Israel thought of the occupied lands as territorial bargaining chips that would finally force the Arabs to negotiate with Israel on her terms. Said Herzog:

> The conclusion of the Six Day War ... created an atmosphere, particularly in Israel, indicating that an end had been reached in the wars of Israel with the various Arab countries ... the imminent opening of peace negotiations was envisaged. From a military point of view, Israel was now in a much stronger position than it had ever been and, in the eyes of most Israelis, this fact enhanced the prospects for peace negotiations. This time Israel would be negotiating from a position of strength.[3]

This was also apparently the view of the Johnson White House. Barely one day after the beginning of the war, presidential aide Walt Rostow had sent Lyndon Johnson a memo in which he suggested, with obvious relish:

> If the Israelis go fast enough, and the Soviets get worried enough, a simple ceasefire, i.e. without a return to pre-war borders might be the best answer. This would mean that we could use the de facto situation on the ground to try to negotiate not a return to armistice lines but a definitive peace in the Middle East.[4]

With hindsight, Washington's and Tel Aviv's expectations in the immediate post-war period appear remarkably naïve. There was little if any understanding of the Arab point of view, from which the new map of the Middle East and the prospect of long-term Israeli military dominance in the region looked a bit different.

The IDF, which had raided Syria in battalion strength several times in the 1950s, and had stormed the Golan Heights at the end of the Six Day War, now stood thirty miles from the gates of Damascus. Only twenty miles stood between Israeli forces on the Jordan River and downtown Amman. Egypt, which had experienced full-scale invasions by the IDF in 1956 and 1967, now looked through the opposite end of Chaim Herzog's telescope and saw, larger than life, Israeli soldiers digging in on the Suez Canal, sixty miles from Cairo. More important, within days of the end of the Six Day War, Egypt knew that the Israeli Air Force (IAF) was repairing and expanding the captured Sinai air bases at Bir Gifgafa and at several other locations. Cairo now had less than four minutes' warning time for an Israeli air attack, a concern which, as we shall see, was somewhat more justified than was Herzog's fear of air raids from Egypt.

Israel annexed Jerusalem in stages in the weeks after the fighting stopped, and began a process of dispersing Jewish settlers into the traditionally Arab communities of the occupied territories. Moshe Dayan, Israel's popular Defence Minister during the war, called it 'creating facts'. Not surprisingly, it was a time of euphoria in the Zionist homeland. Almost a billion dollars had been received from private sources in the US. Foreign exchange reserves had risen dramatically (by over 30 per cent) in just a few days during the Six Day War. The old city of Jerusalem would be a marvellous tourist attraction. Israel now had its own oilfields. There were several hundred million dollars in captured Arab (Soviet) weapons to sell.[5] Within days of the end of the war, the US agreed to the sale of planes and tanks to Israel that would not only replace its losses in the war, but would substantially upgrade its offensive capabilities *vis-à-vis* the neighbouring Arab states.

The Arab states bordering Israel had two options following the June 1967 hostilities. They could of course negotiate peace with Israel from a position of complete military helplessness. The likelihood of this happening diminished rapidly in the days and weeks following the war as Israeli Defence Minister Moshe Dayan and Foreign Minister Abba Eban made statements reflecting official inflexibility on the matter of the return of the occupied territories. Bargaining chips don't work when the side holding them decides that it wants to make the bargain *and* keep the chips. Nor did it appear that the international community was prepared to intercede as 'facts' were being created. After urging the passage of Security Council Resolution 242 in November 1967, which called for 'withdrawal of Israel armed forces from territories occupied in the recent conflict', the Western nations backed off, and agreed to accept the changed map as it stood. Effectively, the possibility of peace negotiations had been closed off, as there appeared to the Arab states to be little they could negotiate for, except surrender.

The alternative, of course, was to re-arm for the next round. Newly dispossessed Palestinians swelled the ranks of the Palestine Liberation Organization and related groups, and began the organizational and fund-raising activities that would soon lead to a wave of terrorism in the Middle East and Europe. The governments of the Arab confrontation states had 'friends' they could turn to. Defeated Arab armies in the Six Day War had carried Soviet arms, and the Soviets were ready, anxious and able to assume the posture of saviour and to salvage the reputations of their weapons at the same time. How to do that? More and better arms, of course. Less than a week after the fighting had stopped, the Soviets began air shipments of new weapons to Egypt. Among them were anti-aircraft missiles, modern fighters and other weapons far more advanced than those previously provided to Egypt, Syria and other Soviet clients in the region.

The Johnson Administration had intended to drive the Arabs to the bargaining table, and had instead driven them into the arms of the Soviets. By early 1968, the terms of the twenty-year-old Middle East conflict had changed, and would never be the same again. Both superpowers were now directly involved in the conflict, on opposing sides.

Israel, without the size or population or natural resources of her Arab neighbours would be obliged in the next twenty years to pay a very high price for the land it occupied in 1967. There would be other wars, and each would involve increased risk, as technology improved the speed and power of modern weapons systems. Even in peacetime, Israel as an occupying power would be obliged to augment and maintain its police and security forces. Finally, Israel would become a forward projection of US efforts to thwart the increased Soviet presence in the region. The aircraft carrier, to use my friend's analogy at that lunch meeting, had docked.

The occupation and settlement of Arab lands necessitated a new US-Israeli security relationship, for it meant a continued state of war with the Arab Middle East. It also meant huge Israeli military budgets in the years to come, a decision to push ahead with a nuclear weapons programme and a succession of increasingly conservative governments in Israel willing to demonstrate military power in the region again, and again, and again. The question was, would the aircraft carrier become a source of strength and security to the homeless Jews who had sought refuge in Israel after the Second World War, or would it become a focus of regional hatred and a potential target of ever more threatening weapons of mass destruction?

In *Taking Sides*, the volume which preceded this book, I used original source materials from the National Archives and several presidential libraries, together with documents obtained under the Freedom of Information Act from US Government agencies, to examine little-known episodes in US-Israeli relations in the period 1948–67. Somewhat to my surprise, it was frequently possible to convince government officials to declass-ify relevant materials from this earlier period.

The present volume deals with the period 1968–87, however, and predictably, when the focus of the requests shifted to events and people still in the news, fewer and fewer documents could be pried away. This was particularly true as my research was being undertaken during an administration in which the vast majority of those who work in Washington as presidential appointees are firmly, deeply committed to the proposition that government is none of the people's business. Fortunately, how-ever, many of the participants in these later occurrences were available for interviews, and it was therefore far easier (than had been the case with *Taking Sides*) to whipsaw back and forth between the available documentation and the recollections of those who lived these events.

Some people were overjoyed when I contacted them, and seemed to have been waiting for years to 'get the story out', as they knew it. In other instances, I was the last person in the world the individual wanted to hear from. The following pages reflect both types of conversations. Many aspects of US-Israeli co-operation have not been attractive or honest or honourable. And the ugly side of our relationship did not, as the reader will soon discover, begin with schemes to sell arms to Iran.

TWO

A Terrible Swift Sword:
the Introduction of the Phantom F-4E
into the Middle East, 1968-9

When, just after dawn on 5 June 1967, the Israeli Air Force began the rolling attacks on Egypt, it concentrated first on the airfields. And later that morning when the war spread to Jordan, Syria and then Iraq, the same tactic was used. War is not a sporting event, and the IDF Command was determined that when Arab ground forces were engaged, Israeli soldiers would have air support and their enemies would not.

The specific targets at the Arab air bases were planes, radar stations, barracks, command centres and the runways themselves. On the latter, the Israelis dropped special, French-designed 1,200-pound bombs fitted with two sets of rockets, one which retarded the weapon's forward momentum when released, and one which drove it directly down into the runway surface where the warhead detonated.[1] One hundred and eighty-three planes participated in the initial wave of attacks, and 164 in the second wave, and from the first moments they were remarkably successful. In all, Egypt lost 309 of its 340 serviceable combat aircraft that day, along with almost a third of her pilots. The entire Jordanian Air Force, some thirty planes, was destroyed, as was the bulk of the Syrian Air Force, which lost fifty-seven planes. Iraq lost ten planes. Within a few hours, Israel had become, as one Israeli General Staff officer put it, 'the only air power in the Middle East'.[2]

The war was effectively over, as it had become a contest between Israeli planes and Arab ground forces, in open terrain. It is very, very difficult to shoot down a high-speed fighter bomber with a tank, but the latter is easy prey for the former. Unchallenged air superiority is one thing in Vietnam where there is heavy jungle cover, and quite another in the deserts of the Sinai.

In the months immediately following the Six Day War, the Soviet Union went through the motions of replenishing the devastated Arab Air Forces, sending a total of 200 MiG 19s and 21s to Egypt, Syria and Iraq, along with SU-7 fighter bombers. Indeed, by mid-1968 the air forces *and* armies of these 'confrontation states' had been re-supplied to about the levels prior to the Six Day War.[3] The principal problem from the Arab standpoint was that aircraft do not an air force make. The training, cohesion, morale and command-control structure of the Israeli Air Force were far superior to those of the Arabs.

Ze'ev Schiff, quoting General Ezer Weizman in *A History of the Israeli Army*, advances an explanation for this:

> The talent of the nation is to be found in the Israeli Air Force. We are a sensible and talented people. Jews cannot avoid this fact. The evidence: our contribution to culture, to science and the world of the spirit. Within the military these talents can be fully utilized . . . The aircraft more than anything else is a tool of war. The use of it demands considerable intelligence. In order to activate such a complex weapons system things must be done at maximum speed. For this, the operator must have special traits and talents. Here, the Jewish people stands out more in its talent, and therefore we are more capable than the enemy . . . Half of the scientists in the world are Jews! In other words, our Air Force is an expression of the basic character of the Israeli Jew.[4]

One does not have to accept theories of racial superiority to acknowledge that the Israeli Air Force was the predominant air force in the Middle East in the late 1960s. And without question, part of the reason for that was superior hardware. Israel simply had better planes than the Arabs, and Soviet re-supply efforts after the Six Day War did nothing to alter this fact.

In January 1968, the US Defence Department (DoD) prepared a detailed assessment of relative Arab-Israeli air strength, in preparation for Israeli Prime Minister Levi Eshkol's impending visit to the United States. The White House knew that the primary purpose of the visit was a formal request for America's top-of-the-line fighter bomber, the F-4 Phantom.

Predictably, Eshkol would try to justify the request by reference to recent Soviet plane shipments to the Arabs. President Johnson asked DoD to comment on the strategic balance. The response:

> Although the USSR has replaced a major portion of the Arab aircraft losses, the Arab effective capability is still far below that of Israel and in our judgement will remain so for some time to come. While some qualitative improvement is to be expected, the Arabs will not be able to improve their communications, organization, maintenance capabilities, target intelligence, command and control, confidence and morale to the degree where their air forces will pose a serious threat to Israel in the foreseeable future, despite increased USSR assistance.[5]

Virtually all Israeli combat aircraft in the Six Day War had been French: sixty-five Mirage IIICs, twenty-five Mystères and twenty-five Super Mystères constituted the core of the force. A French arms embargo on Israel, declared during the Six Day War, precluded replacement or upgrading of these, but in late 1967 and early 1968, the US agreed to sell Israel forty-eight American A-4 fighter bombers. DoD concluded that with the addition of the A-4 Skyhawk long-range attack aircraft to its arsenal, the Israeli Air Force was in fact better off, relative to the Arabs, than it had been even at the beginning of the Six Day War. For this reason, said DoD, 'We can safely postpone our future review of the situation until after mid-1968'.[6]

One important factor in this calculation was DoD's recognition of a rather fundamental problem of the Arab air forces: they hadn't the planes to reach Israel:

> The offensive (attack) capabilities of the Arab air forces are limited, and considerably inferior to those of Israel. Arab fighter aircraft generally have a very limited radius of offensive action in a bomber role. This significantly curtails Egyptian offensive capabilities. No Egyptian fighter aircraft, including the SU-7 and MiG 21 can fly a lo-lo-lo mission from Cairo to Tel Aviv (a radius of approximately 250 nautical miles) with even a minimum (1,000-lb) bombload. (The Israeli A-4H could carry, in comparison, over 2,000 lbs of bombs on such a mission.)[7]

In sum, said the Defence Department, the A-4H fighter bomber which had just been provided to the Israelis was 'considerably superior in attack capability' to any Soviet plane available to any of the Arab air forces. General Ezer Weizman, writing at about this time in *The American Zionist*, pointed out that in effect the territories occupied during the June War had reversed the Arab-Israeli strategic military position – Israel was now 'at the gates of Cairo and Damascus', while the Arabs were 'hundreds of miles' from Israel's heartland. 'Our situation was never better,' he concluded.[8]

It was at this time and in this context that Israel requested and received from the Johnson White House permission to purchase the fastest, most versatile, most advanced interceptor/fighter bomber in the world in 1968: the McDonnell Douglas F-4 Phantom, a plane which had been in production for only five years. Moreover, at a time when the US was engaged in a full-scale war in South East Asia, and many USAF units were using obsolete planes and awaiting delivery of the F-4, the Israeli Air Force specifically requested the most advanced version, the deep-strike, nuclear-capable F-4E. The then Israeli Air Force Commander, Mordechai Hod, informed the Defence Department that the IAF wanted the F-4E 'with as few modifications as possible'.[9]

On the eve of Eshkol's visit, the DoD proposed to the Israelis that they purchase the F-5 interceptor fighter which, in combination with the Skyhawks already committed, would provide the Israeli Air Force with both defensive and offensive capabilities far superior to that of the combined Arab air forces.

The Israelis dismissed the F-5 idea. They refused, in fact, even to test fly it: their objective was not defence. They wanted a fighter bomber, not an interceptor. To President Johnson, DoD addressed a warning:

> The F-4 can carry a much greater payload than the A-4H, and its performance is superior to the A-4H in all respects . . . considering the overall capability of the Arab air forces, including the lack of versatility of their light and medium bombers, the F-4 would provide a strikingly superior capability for the Israelis.[10]

In the end, after all the background data and advice, the decision was the President's: yes or no to a giant escalation of the Middle East arms race.

A Texas decision

The setting, the occasion, was a highly publicized meeting between President Lyndon Johnson and Prime Minister Levi Eshkol at the LBJ Ranch in Texas, perhaps best remembered in America for the 'photo opportunity', in which Johnson showed Eshkol, and the world, his appendectomy scar. Behind the clowning, however, the meeting involved some very hard bargaining on substantive matters.

The American President's primary objectives were a strong statement of support by Israel for the 'free world's' effort in Vietnam, an Israeli agreement to sign the Nuclear Non-proliferation Treaty (NPT), and a commitment from the Israeli leader that he would maintain a flexible position on then ongoing UN-sponsored Middle East peace negotiations, and would avoid the hasty annexation of territories occupied during the Six Day War.[11] He got no statement on Vietnam, no agreement on NPT, and two days after Eshkol's return to Tel Aviv, Israel 'expropriated' portions of occupied Jerusalem, over the vehement objections of then US Ambassador to Israel, Walworth Barbour.[12]

Eshkol's primary objective was to get a firm American commitment to sell Israel fifty F-4Es, and to have them delivered as quickly as possible. He got it.

After the meeting, Johnson publicly maintained that he had only promised to give 'active and sympathetic consideration' to the request for the planes. In fact, Lyndon Johnson agreed to provide the planes on an accelerated time schedule which included discussions on the desired configuration (type of armament, etc) and completion of a plan for Israeli pilot instructor and navigator training within weeks of the last official barbecue at the ranch.[13] Officials who attended the Texas summit, including Israeli Ambassador Ephraim Evron and Presidential Assistant Harry McPhereson, have since admitted that the planes were firmly but privately committed at the meeting.[14] Levi Eshkol himself stated one year after the meeting that indeed a firm commitment had been made.[15]

The Lyndon Baines Johnson Library in Austin, Texas,

contains numerous memoranda by White House and Defence Department staff indicating that Johnson did *not* make a firm commitment at the January 1968 meeting with Eshkol. I can only conclude that these persons were not 'on board' as to the private commitments Johnson had made to the Israeli leader. Certainly, a great deal of action in reliance upon a positive decision commenced shortly after Eshkol left Texas.

Moreover, Lyndon Johnson made his decision in the face of almost unanimous opposition from his advisers. The Pentagon's Office of International Security Affairs, the CIA, the State Department and even White House staff members, all argued against the sale in briefing papers prepared just prior to the Texas meeting.[16] At the State Department, for example, periodic lunchtime meetings, called 'open forums', provided a channel for dissenting views on a wide range of policy matters. In the weeks prior to the Texas meeting, a paper opposing the F-4 sale was produced by some thirty-three foreign service officers, and presented to Joseph Sisco, Assistant Secretary for Near Eastern Affairs. Then eleven of the paper's authors demanded and got a meeting with Sisco to express their frustrations. It was not a cordial affair, and afterwards several of the junior FSOs involved were reprimanded. At least one was fired.[17]

What followed the Texas decision was a nearly year-long public debate on the sale, 'full of sound and fury, signifying nothing', as production of the Israeli planes and training of Israeli support personnel proceeded quietly. It will be remembered that 1968 was a presidential election year, and Johnson's delay while giving the matter 'sympathetic' consideration (as numerous White House press statements put it) allowed him, and then Hubert Humphrey when Johnson withdrew from the race, to derive maximum political benefit from the issue, without providing an occasion for negative reaction from Arab governments, European allies concerned about the Middle East arms race, and the many US military officials who did not want such an advanced weapons system in the hands of a non-NATO country. Negotiations there were, but they dealt with price, financing arrangements, delivery dates and training schedules, and not whether Israel would in fact get the planes.

Throughout the election year, candidates vied with each other in their support for the sale. The public announcement that a decision had been made was issued by the White House at a time calculated to achieve maximum political effect – four weeks before the date of the election.

The Pentagon (International Security Affairs office), the CIA and the State Department, all of whom had argued against the sale in the briefing papers done in preparation for the Texas meeting, continued to oppose it even after the decision was made public. Middle East specialists at DoD now proposed an extended delivery schedule for the planes, citing the lack of any military justification for the sale in terms of Israel's security and a corresponding immediate need for the planes in Vietnam, and warning in position papers that the Soviet Union would be forced to respond in kind with new advanced weapons systems for the Arabs.[18] It was a warning which, as we shall see, later proved to be remarkably accurate.

Most of the news fit to print

Whether meaningless or not, the public debate on the F-4 sale did have its comic aspects. In January 1968, shortly after the Texas meeting, a *New York Times* editorial argued against the sale, warning darkly of a 'tit-for-tat expansion of [Middle East] arsenals'.[19] In July, the *Times* still thought that shipment of F-4s to Israel almost certainly would 'set off a new round in the Middle East arms race'.[20] Even in September, the *Times* did not see a need for the sale, in terms of Israeli national security, correctly quoting DoD officials to the effect that:

> Egyptian forces have not been restored to their pre-war strength, either in quantity or quality. The Soviet re-supply effort practically stopped months ago.[21]

But 1968 was an election year, and by late summer/early autumn the candidates were in full flower. Incumbent Jacob Javits was involved in a hotly contested Senate race in New

York State and, campaigning in Sullivan County, solemnly assured cheering audiences that sale of the F-4 Phantom aircraft to Israel was

> 'imperative' because of the heavy flow of Soviet weapons to Syria and Egypt, which he said had now achieved full military strength since last year's defeat by Israel's forces.[22]

The delivery of these aircraft must be immediate, said Javits, as the continued shipment of the latest Soviet aircraft to the Arab states threatened to 'disadvantage' Israel.

Democratic presidential candidate Hubert Humphrey, addressing a convention of the Zionist Organization of America in New York the next month, stated that sale of the F-4s to Israel was necessary to 'maintain a balance of power in the area'.[23] Republican candidate Richard Nixon had beaten Humphrey to the punch, having assured the convention of his support for the sale several days previously.

The *New York Times*, in reporting these speeches, dutifully noted that 'American [military] officials doubt that Soviet aircraft shipments have been as great as Israel contends.' To Messrs Javits, Humphrey and Nixon – candidates all – the professional assessments of the US Defence Department on this subject were about as relevant as those of the Bolivian Air Force. The threat was there, by God, and each of these men knew his duty was to meet it.

By 1 October, even the *New York Times* was beginning to see the light. Reporter Peter Grose quoted 'Israeli sources' to the effect that a new, secret Soviet arms deal with Egypt would soon bring '200 modern fighter planes' to the region. Six days later, two separate *Times* articles quoting 'observers in Beirut' and 'officials in Washington' raised the spectre of a major Soviet–Egyptian arms sale. On 10 October the White House instructed the State Department to begin negotiations with Israel on the sale of the F-4s.

Three years later, with the decision now apparently taken, the *Times* carried yet another article on the Soviet deal, this one on page 1, detailing the specific combat aircraft which the Russians had allegedly agreed to provide to Egypt. The article cited 'pro-Israeli informants whose previous reports have proved strikingly accurate', and ended with a paragraph which has to be one of the great masterpieces of innuendo in the history of modern journalism:

> The Soviet Union is reported to be helping the Egyptians build a 12-division army, but so far, it is said, there are no credible reports that Moscow has supplied guided missiles capable of striking Israeli population centers. Moreover, there are no reports that the Soviet Union has stored tactical nuclear weapons on Egyptian soil. If such weapons are present in the area, it is noted they are probably stored aboard Soviet warships.[24]

When you are committed to providing 'all the news that's fit to print', you certainly have to get out there and beat the bushes to find it.

Predictably by December, the *New York Times* had managed to wrench its liberal, anti-arms-race editorial position around to one supporting sale of the F-4s. The facts had been found to suit the new position, of course. Said the *Times*:

> The arms race, since 1955, has seen more than \$2 billion of Soviet weapons delivered to the Arab states, far more than the United States has shipped. Since the June 1967 war, Arab arms losses have been substantially replaced by Moscow, particularly in jet aircraft. The Israelis, who lost more than 40 combat planes, thus had a strong case for American deliveries.[25]

What a difference three short months (and one US election campaign) can make in the Middle East strategic balance! It is not hard to understand why, upon occasion, the US military and intelligence communities take journalistic criticisms very, very lightly.

Nuclear flimflam

When Lyndon Johnson left the presidency and retired to his ranch in Texas to write his memoirs, one of the achievements of which he was most proud was the four and a half-year-long effort of his administration to stop the spread of nuclear weapons. He recalled 'the glare of television floodlights' in the

East Room of the White House on 1 July 1968 as representatives of the Soviet Union, Britain, the US and over fifty other nations signed the Treaty of Non-proliferation of Nuclear Weapons (NPT). Nations without nuclear weapons formally agreed not to make them or receive them from others. Nations that had 'the bomb' agreed to work toward effective arms control and disarmament, and to ensure access by non-nuclear states to the full benefits of the peaceful uses of nuclear power. Recalling 'four years of painstaking and complicated diplomatic effort', Johnson thought that the NPT was 'the most difficult and most important . . . of all the agreements reached with Moscow' in his five years plus as president.[26]

At the time of the signing of the NPT, five nations – the US, the Soviet Union, Britain, France and China – had successfully tested nuclear weapons. Several other nations, India, Pakistan and Israel among them, were thought to have nuclear weapons programmes in advanced stages of development. Naturally, this latter group was the focus of the Johnson Administration's most intense hopes where the NPT was concerned.

Among the countries in the 'nearly nuclear' club, the White House probably had the most information about Israel's programme:

- In mid-1968, the CIA informed the administration that tracings of weapons-grade uranium had been found near the Dimona nuclear reactor in Israel.
- The Atomic Energy Commission (AEC) and the FBI were in the midst of a full-blown investigation of the Nuclear Materials and Energy Corporation (NUMEC) of Apollo, Pennsylvania for diversion of enriched uranium and leaks of classified nuclear weapons-related documents to Israel. This investigation would result, the following year, in a recommendation by the FBI Director that all classified contacts between AEC and NUMEC be terminated, and that the security clearances of NUMEC's President, Zalman Shapiro, be lifted.
- The Defence Department had detailed intelligence reports from the US Air Attaché in Tel Aviv about Israeli testing of a short range ballistic missile of a type, size and cost that could only be intended to carry a nuclear warhead. The White House had tried unsuccessfully the previous year, in September 1967, to get Israeli Air Force chief Ezer Weizman to discuss the matter candidly.[27]

17

On the basis of this and (no doubt) other evidence for an Israeli nuclear weapons programme at a very advanced stage, Lyndon Johnson tried for a time to use the F-4 Phantom as a bargaining chip with the Israelis, to convince them to slow down or stop the programme and to sign the NPT. Both at the Texas meeting with Eshkol and in subsequent discussions on training, delivery schedules, etc, Johnson and his staff pursued the matter.[28] Without success.

Israel's answer to Johnson, and to each successive US president who has waved the NPT in the air, has been a resounding 'No!' That in itself is not surprising: neither India nor Pakistan, the two other near-nuclear powers in 1968, have agreed to sign. And India has taken the next step, and actually tested its own nuclear device in 1974.[29] What is a bit odd, given his strong commitment to a policy of nuclear non-proliferation, is that it was Lyndon Johnson who gave Israel its first dependable nuclear weapons delivery system!

Back in 1965 the test of Israel's short-range ballistic missile – it was actually a French Dassault MD 620 missile modified slightly by the Israelis – had not gone well. The problem was accuracy. In October, 1965 then IAF Commander Ezer Weizman came to the US with a shopping list of weapons, and surprised his hosts by asking for the F-4, a plane originally developed for the US Navy and first flown by them in 1960. The version of the plane which had been modified for the USAF, known as the F-4C, had only been delivered six months earlier in March 1965, and was intended (and equipped) as an interceptor, a 'defensive' aircraft.

The object of Weizman's desire however, was, as we have seen, the F-4E, a version of the plane which, in October 1965, was only on the drawing boards, and would not even be delivered to the US Air Force until October 1967! The F-4E was superior to earlier types in several respects: it had more powerful engines, an internally mounted General Electric Vulcan 20 mm cannon, and a new fire-control system. Finally, it was wired and harnessed for delivery of 'theatre' nuclear weapons.[30] A special attitude and reference computerized bombing system – known as the AN/AJB-7 – was designed for use in nuclear strike missions. The E version was versatile – it was an interceptor, but it was also the fastest, most sophisticated, most deadly deep-strike fighter bomber in the world – a plane which, at the time of Weizman's visit, the US Air Force was waiting for, pleading for, in Vietnam. Weizman nevertheless wanted the F-4E, and nothing but the F-4E, and specifically requested that the plane be 'nuclear capable'.[31] The answer he received, in 1965 at least, was 'no'.

When Levi Eshkol arrived in Texas in early 1968 to renew Israel's quest for the Phantom jet, he again specifically requested the E version, and asked that the nuclear delivery paraphernalia not be removed from the plane. At issue here were wiring 'bundles' under the skin of the plane, attached to a 'black box' which contained the hard and software that computed the parabolic trajectories necessary when nuclear bombs were dropped, or more accurately, lobbed. Finally, special racks or 'harnesses' were fitted to the F-4E, to carry the enormous weight and size of a nuclear bomb.

This time, Johnson not only agreed to sell the E version, but it is unclear what if any precautions were taken to ensure that the planes would not carry nuclear weapons. The *New York Times* later reported that Israel was merely asked to agree that their Phantoms wouldn't carry nukes.[32] Robert Kubal, who was at the time the Israel desk officer in the International Security Affairs (ISA) office at DoD, recalls that 'theoretically' the equipment unique to strategic deliveries was to have been physically removed. The wiring could not be stripped, after the planes rolled off the production lines at the McDonnell Douglas factory in St Louis, as this would have been too expensive a process, but the 'black boxes' and special bomb racks were, according to Kubal, 'supposed' to have been removed.[33]

They weren't. The first four of Israel's Phantoms were delivered on 5 September 1969, and by December of that year a full squadron of twelve had been delivered. These planes went with everything – wiring, computers and harnesses.[34] Whatever agreement Lyndon Johnson thought he had, whatever DoD's theoretical understanding about the neutering of the planes, Israel had a state-of-the-art delivery system for its nuclear weapons less than nine months after Johnson left office.[35] Nonproliferation indeed.

THREE

Whose Desert Will Bloom?
The East Ghor Canal Raids, 1968–70

On 3 September 1969 Joseph Sisco sat in his office at the State
Department, preparing for an urgent meeting with the 'chargé'
of the Israeli Embassy in Washington. Sisco was Assistant
Secretary for Near Eastern Affairs, a job which in the best of
times leaves one little opportunity for anything but crisis
management. On this day, his staff were not just busy: they
were angry.

The Israeli Air Force had just destroyed a section of the East
Ghor Canal in Jordan, a project which was by far the largest
and most important single US contribution to Jordan's development effort. Sisco was about to meet with the Israelis to plead
with them to allow repairs on the Canal. Thomas Scotes, one of
his aides, had been asked to prepare a memorandum summarizing the extent of damage, and the expected impact of the
raid upon US interests in the region.

The problem, said Scotes in his report, was that the water
flow in the Canal had been severely reduced, endangering not
only crops but long-term investments such as banana and citrus
trees. The project area in the Jordan River Valley produced
almost 40 per cent of the agricultural production of the country,
exclusive of the West Bank of Jordan, which had been occupied
by Israel during the Six Day War. 'The Canal', concluded
Scotes, 'is extremely important for Jordan's viability.' But the
theme to which Scotes returned again and again, was the damage that was being done to US interests:

> We believe it is imperative that we make another attempt to
> persuade the Israelis to permit the repair of the Canal before
> irreparable damage is done, not only to the crops, but to Huss-
> ein's pro-American position as well . . . the project has served as a

model of how US Government aid can induce progress and modernization while buttressing a friendly state. Therefore, we urge the Israelis in the strongest terms to permit the Canal to be repaired because to do so is very important to US interests.[1]

Israel maintained that it was carrying out such attacks in retaliation for Palestinian border crossings and acts of violence carried out from Jordanian soil, Scotes said, and to this extent, the bombings were intended as a 'message' to King Hussein to control strictly the Jordanian side of the cease-fire lines. But even in this context, Scotes believed the continuing attacks to be counter-productive:

> any leverage that Israel seeks to exercise by preventing the reopening of the Canal will be lost once damage [to trees] reaches the irreversible point . . . The persons who would suffer thereby would not be the *fedayeen*, but the innocent farmers whose lands would have to be abandoned . . . The only winners would be the extremists who would bring greater pressures to bear on Hussein for a further escalation of violence on the cease-fire lines.[2]

Technicians of the Natural Resources Authority of the Jordanian Government had tried a few weeks previously to repair the Canal, and had been driven back by small-arms fire from the Israeli side of the border. Searchlights and gunfire had even prevented efforts to make repairs at night.[3] United States Agency for International Development (USAID) officials responsible for the project had ceased visiting the Canal because of the danger.[4] The future of the project, therefore, rested on Joseph Sisco's ability to convince the Government of Israel to allow repairs to be made as quickly as possible.

One might think, given the extensive US economic and military aid to Israel at the time, that a positive response to Sisco's request for repairs would be a foregone conclusion; and one would be wrong. And one might assume that while Israel would continue to hit military targets in Jordan (in response to guerrilla attacks) American protests would at least end the concentrated attacks on the Canal itself, if only to avoid potential American casualties. Again, one would be wrong. From that point on, the ironies are compounded.

Making *our* desert bloom

The primary issue here may not have been terrorism, but water. The 1967 war had, in terms of Israeli water policy, solved one problem and created another. One-third of Israel's pre-1967 water consumption was ground water stored in aquifers beneath the West Bank, and tapped by extensive drilling on the Israeli side of the 1949 armistice line. Now, Israeli soldiers occupied this important reservoir. That, from an Israeli perspective, was the good news.

The 1967 war had created, however, some 323,000 new Palestinian refugees, according to United Nations figures, and the vast majority of these individuals clustered just outside Israel's borders in Jordan, Syria and Egypt. As a group, quite naturally, they were angry and bitter, and their camps and communities were fertile ground for organizations seeking volunteers for guerrilla attacks into Israel. Of these refugees, 178,000 had fled to Jordan, and a majority of these had, in turn, settled in the Jordan River Valley, adding both legitimacy and urgency to the Jordanian Government's claim on the use of the Jordan Valley's limited water supplies.[5]

For almost two decades the United States, Great Britain and the UN had tried to develop a regional plan for an equitable apportionment and utilization of the Jordan River (and tributary) water resources, among the various riparian countries. Israel had long argued for diversion of a substantial portion of these resources to the Negev Desert, some hundred miles away in southern Israel. Syria and Jordan had favoured retention of the water for use in the region of origin. The embodiment of the US/British/UN 'regional' approach had been the 'Main plan', drafted in 1953 by Charles T. Main working under the auspices of UNRWA. Intended as a synthesis of previous Arab and Israeli schemes for utilization of Jordan River water, the plan in its final form was acceptable to neither side. Arab governments opposed it primarily because it allocated 33 per cent of the total water resources of the Jordan Valley to Israel, in whose land 23 per cent of that water originated. Israel opposed it because the plan contained no provision for diversion of Jordan waters to the Negev.[6]

Even before the plan was finalized, Israel unilaterally began to construct its Negev diversion canal at B'not Yaakov in the Israeli-Syrian demilitarized zone created after the 1948 war. Arguing convincingly for a regional approach to the region's water problems, President Dwight Eisenhower reacted by cutting off all US aid to Israel.[7] Temporarily, Israel halted its diversion project, only to recommence it in 1956. Seven hundred million cubic metres of the Jordan's waters were then diverted, amounting to 60 per cent of the river's total flow.[8]

The effect of channelling water out of the Jordan River just south of Lake Tiberias was to lower the level and raise the salinity of the main portion of the river between Tiberias and the Dead Sea, greatly reducing the amount of irrigation water available in the rich Jordan Valley. The salinity problem was exacerbated in the early 1960s (while the West Bank was still in Jordanian hands) when the Israelis started to pump saline water and sludge from the bottom of Lake Tiberias into the Jordan River at a point just above the Israeli-Jordanian armistice line.[9] Effectively, Israel had ruined the Jordan River for irrigation purposes. For the Hashemite Kingdom of Jordan, whose economy was largely based upon agriculture, these actions were damaging, and might have been destabilizing, had it not been for the construction of the East Ghor Canal.

In August 1958, two years after Israel's diversion of the river, the US mounted its largest single contribution to Jordan's development effort, at a cost of around $15 million, siphoning water out of the Yarmuk River north and east of its confluence with the Jordan, and transporting it south in a canal running more or less parallel with and just east of the Jordan River. When water began to flow in East Ghor, therefore, it reduced the amount of water available for Israel's diversion to the Negev. In the first stage of the East Ghor project, completed shortly before the Six Day War, 43.5 miles of main canal and 250 miles of lateral canals irrigated over 3,000 farms covering 30,000 acres of land.

The East Ghor Project, however, included much more than the construction of canals, and was in effect a complete reorganization of the project area's economy. Landholding patterns were changed and a large number of subsidiary projects were completed, including dams on the side wadis, farm to market roads, fruit and vegetable processing plants, agricultural research stations, public health facilities and reforestation. Agricultural credit and extension services were established.[10]

East Ghor had a dramatic impact upon farm income in the Jordan Valley, raising it from $1.2 million in 1959–60 to $9.5 million in 1965–6. Moreover, the effect of these increases was disproportionately large upon Jordan's foreign currency earnings because the Jordan Valley enjoyed a six to eight-week advance in harvesting period over neighbouring countries, including Israel, and the project area's produce therefore commanded high prices abroad. USAID, which administered the American assistance to the project and provided technical assistance, estimated that farm income from the East Ghor Project area would reach $20 million in 1970–1.[11]

During the 1967 war Israel had spared the Canal itself in the fighting on the Jordanian front. Presumably military targets were then far more important. The new refugees created by that war, however, now clustered just outside Israel's borders in the Jordan Valley, hoping for the opportunity to return. Some had been twice displaced; once in 1948 from land that had become Israel, and again in 1967 from what was now the occupied West Bank of Jordan. Many of the refugees settled in the East Ghor Project area itself, the Canal offering hope in the short term as a source of employment and food production.

Israel thus had a new reason to dislike East Ghor besides the fact that it reduced the flow in the Yarmuk, a main tributary of the Jordan River, for the project area now harboured and sustained people who promised to become a genuine security problem to Israel's border communities, and to Israelis in the West Bank.

The manufacture of terrorists

In the months just after the Six Day War, the Jordanian–Israeli border was relatively quiet, but by October 1967 the number of 'terrorist incidents', as they began to be called, picked up considerably. Initially, these were crossings into Israel and the occupied West Bank by bands of Palestinians, some with the purpose of attacking Israeli soldiers and communities, and, at least in the case of the West Bank crossings, others merely involving people who wished to return to houses and farms abandoned during the intense fighting in the war.

At this stage, the US position on these incidents was that the saboteurs/guerrillas/terrorists, whatever they were called, were hard-liners within the Palestinian community who were operating on their own without assistance from the Jordanian Government. Hal Saunders and John Foster, who worked in the White House at the time on Middle East matters, wrote to presidential aide Walt Rostow:

> Our view is that Hussein himself is doing his best to stop the terrorists who move across Jordan from Syria. The Israelis disagree and say that Hussein could not possibly be unaware of Jordanian military complicity. They cite such events as Jordanian artillery joining in one Jordan River fight between Israelis and terrorists, while we think the Jordanians were probably just replying to anti-terrorist shells that landed in Jordan.[12]

Civilians who were caught in this particular exchange no doubt had difficulty remembering that the shells heading west were terrorist shells, whereas the ones heading east were anti-terrorist. It is the kind of distinction that can be made far more clearly sitting behind a desk in a comfortable chair, gazing at a map.

Saunders and Foster were, however, accurately reflecting reports emanating from Jordan from both diplomatic and intelligence communities, concerning the genuine efforts King Hussein's Government was making to reduce guerrilla activity along the border with Israel. The US Ambassador in Amman at the time, Harrison Symmes, and the CIA station chief, Jack O'Connell, both recall making numerous strong representations to their respective superiors in Washington, to the effect that the King was trying his best to deal with the numerous Palestinian guerrilla organizations, and to prevent crossings back into the occupied West Bank by members of the enormous Palestinian community in Jordan.[13]

In February 1968, after a particularly heavy artillery exchange that caused extensive damage in the Israeli villages of Kfar Rupin and Maoz Chaim in eastern Galilee, the IDF responded with tanks and planes. As one Israeli historian recalls,

> The retaliation was directed primarily against Jordanian villages east of the river, which served as forward bases for the terrorists, but command posts and concentrations deep inside Jordanian territory also came in for a beating in what turned out to be the largest IDF operation since the Six Day War.[14]

In fact three refugee camps at Karameh, Shumeh and Ghor Nimrin took the brunt of the Israeli attack, causing a 'mass exodus of refugees from the Jordan Valley'. In addition, for the first time the Canal itself was damaged, though not put out of commission.[15]

By early March the IDF was planning a major strike against the increasingly active Palestinian guerrillas. Yasser Arafat, who had emerged as the first among equals of the leaders of the various militant Palestinian groups, had in early 1968 established headquarters at the refugee camp in Karameh, about fifteen miles north of the Dead Sea. The previous November, a number of children from this particular camp had been killed by Israeli fragmentation bombs and mortars, and Arafat chose the site for its propaganda value.[16] But Karameh was less than a mile from the occupied West Bank and the nearest Israeli forces, and presented a tempting – indeed predictable – target for the IDF.

For several weeks the Israeli Government proposed, and the US Government discouraged, a major strike on Karameh, complete with massed tanks, helicopters, paratroop drops and infantry units in battalion strength. Within Prime Minister Eshkol's cabinet, Foreign Minister Eban argued strongly against the attack on the grounds that

> its scope was exaggerated, its target was unsuitable, it unnecessarily endangered the lives of uninvolved refugees, and its political risks were disproportionately high.[17]

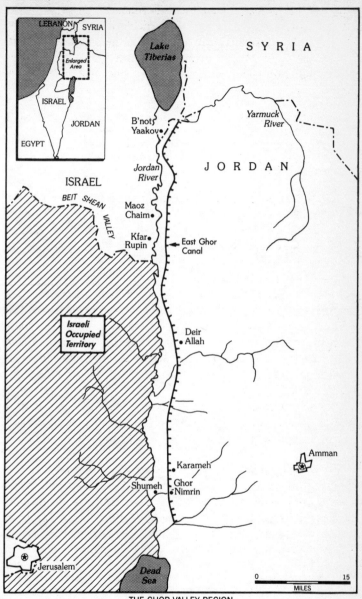

THE GHOR VALLEY REGION

On 18 March, however, an Israeli school bus struck a landmine planted by Fateh, the major PLO group, resulting in several dead and wounded children and adults. Three days later, the IDF struck at Karameh.

At least four distinct versions of what happened at Karameh exist: Palestinian, Israeli, Jordanian and American. What *is* agreed is that both Palestinian and Arab Legion (Jordanian) forces knew beforehand exactly when, how and by what route the IDF was going to attack. There is also agreement that both PLO and Arab Legion forces fought like tigers, causing enormous – and unexpected – Israeli casualties (twenty-nine dead, ninety wounded) the majority of which were apparently caused by Legion artillery. Finally as US officials and Abba Eban had predicted, the operation was a spectacular, near perfect failure in terms of its obvious purpose. Former Israeli Deputy Foreign Minister Gideon Raphael has summarized the results admirably:

> One thing appears certain: the Karameh operation was more of a boost than a blow to the terrorist organizations. It did little to stop the recurrent incursions but much to swell Arafat's ranks. The Israeli Ambassador in Washington, Yitzhak Rabin, reported to the Prime Minister that the Karameh action had produced a worldwide reverberation for the cause of the Palestine liberation movement.[18]

What has not until now been revealed is that it was a US Government official who informed the Jordanian army exactly when and by what route the expected attack would come.[19]

At war with a canal

The Karameh raid did have one intended effect: it drove many farmers out of the East Ghor Project area, creating the first farm labour shortages in the four years since water had begun to flow in the Canal. On 11 April, the Canal was actually cut for the first time, as Israeli artillery targeted the raised concrete flumes that radiated out from the main Canal. Following this particular attack, IDF soldiers began to fire on the Jordanian and Palestinian farmers who had stubbornly remained to work in the irrigated fields, forcing them to move their families into the highlands. Through the summer of 1968, however, the farmers returned to work, 'commuting' down from their highland camps in the morning, working the fields, and returning in the evening. Towns in the Jordan Valley were largely deserted, but sufficient numbers of workers remained to begin construction of a six-mile extension of the main Canal.[20]

In August and December 1968, and again (repeatedly) in January–March 1969, Israeli planes and helicopters began to raid targets in the 'interior' of Jordan, particularly rail and highway bridges and refugee camps. Civilian casualties were heavy. Even the outskirts of Amman were bombed.[21] The UN Security Council and, finally, even the US Government formally condemned these attacks. To a representative of President Nixon visiting Amman, King Hussein complained that the objective of these Israeli attacks was no longer that of reigning in or punishing terrorists, but rather the toppling of his government and destabilization of his country.[22]

Officially, Israel was bombing infrastructure targets in Jordan to pressure the King and his government to bring maximum pressure on the guerrillas, that is, to use the Arab Legion to prevent border crossings and terrorist acts. In February the commander of the IDF's Northern Command, Lieutenant General David 'Dado' Elazar, toured Israeli villages in the Beit Shean Valley which had been the object of Palestinian attacks in previous months. He explained the IDF's (i.e. the Israeli Government's) rationale behind large-scale military responses to small-scale guerrilla attacks:

> The IDF actions are more conducive to quiet than extended restraint is. If our people can't live in peace, then neither will the people on the other side of the border.[23]

The point, said Elazar, was 'to make life bearable for us and unbearable for them'.

Shortly after Karameh, however, a pattern emerged in the IDF attacks which indicated that more was involved here than 'an eye for an eye, a tooth for a tooth', or 'teaching Hussein a lesson'. The new focus of Israel's attacks occurred, perhaps not entirely coincidentally, shortly after Prime Minister Levi Eshkol's death (on 26 February 1969) and the assumption of his office by Golda Meir.

On 11 April, the Canal itself was pin-pointed by Israeli artillery. Specifically, large concrete overhead flumes were hit and destroyed. The main Canal was for the first time completely cut, and the flow stopped. IAF planes followed on 22 April, again bombing the main Canal and destroying road-building equipment. On 23 June, an entire section of the Canal was demolished by Israeli commandos, and Jordanian Natural Resource Authority (NRA) technical personnel were fired on when they approached the break to assess the damage. USAID officials who were in Jordan at the time recall that NRA Director Omar Abdullah Dokgan would walk to the Canal-side with a loudspeaker in his hand, shouting to the Israelis to please stop the shelling.[24] Repairs were not made until 1 July.

Quite simply, Israel was at war with a canal, and it was a war it was predictably winning:

> On 10 August, Israeli aircraft again cut the Canal. By this time, according to Natural Resources Authority (NRA) estimates, only 20,000 persons were still living in the Valley out of 350,000 there before the June war. Repairs on the Canal were not completed until 29 September and substantial agricultural losses were incurred, particularly of banana and citrus production.[25]

Following the August bombing, the Israeli Government disclosed to the press that there had been a secret deal made between Israel and Jordan to permit Canal repairs after the previous (June) attack. Jordan was to curb Palestinian commando operations and, in return, the IDF would refrain from firing on repair teams, so the water system could be restored and the fields and trees irrigated. According to the Israelis, the arrangement had broken down when new commando raids occurred. The Jordanians said they had promised only to try their best to prevent the crossings. In the meantime, the Canal again lay in ruins.[26]

In the United States, these repeated attacks did of course

create certain problems for those American institutions dedicated to promoting Israeli interests. On Sunday, 24 August, the *New York Times* carried a feature piece on the Canal ('Irrigation Helps Jordan to Bloom') which must have shocked those who had followed the East Ghor Canal story in the months since the Israeli attacks had begun. The *Times* even revealed that the Canal had been built with the help of the United States! This would have been a bit of a surprise to avid *Times* readers since previous articles on the Canal raids, on 24 June, 13 August and 19 August, had provided copious background detail on the East Ghor Project, but had neglected to mention that the (bulk of the) funding had come from USAID, or that American engineers and technicians were working on the project even as it was being attacked.

In fact, prior to June 1969 the *Times* had not once covered Israel's frequent attacks on the Canal in any way. The raids were non-events for the *Times* editors. USAID and State Department officials who reported on such attacks in April 1968 and in March, April and early June 1969 must have wondered why the attempted destruction of one of America's largest development projects in the Middle East by a presumed ally, was simply not news. Or at least, it was not news 'fit to print'.

The *Times* did let its readers down gently, however, in that 24 August article which revealed US support for the Canal. It provided an explanation as to how the damage might have occurred:

> The East Ghor Canal has been damaged twice [sic] by Israeli gunfire, although the Valley farmers admit that the Israelis do not generally fire indiscriminately on farms and agricultural or irrigation projects. But if a farm or a canal happens to be in the line of fire between Israeli batteries and what they believe are guerrilla targets, a salvo of shells is likely to destroy the work of months or years.[27]

Some days things don't work out well, even when you have the very best of intentions.

The *Times* may have received some complaints about its provocative coverage of the Israeli attacks, for it soon returned to its previous practice of concealment of US funding for East

Ghor. On 23 and 24 September 1969 the paper carried two articles on an Israeli-Jordanian agreement for repair of the Canal, worked out through the mediation of the US State Department. Assistant Secretary Joseph Sisco's meetings with the Israeli chargé in Washington had, finally, borne fruit. Readers of the two *Times* articles, however, might have wondered what interest the US Government had in the matter, as neither article mentioned US funding or involvement of any kind in the East Ghor Project.

Ungrateful Skyhawks

Alas, what had been fixed was broken again in early 1970, as the attacks resumed in spite of US protests to the Israelis, and the US role in negotiating Canal repairs. The American Embassy in Amman informed the State Department on 30 January 1970:

> Most recently . . . Israeli aircraft destroyed a section of the Canal on New Year's Day, 1970, and no repairs have been attempted. At present, the Jordan Valley seems more dangerous than ever before and several civilians including farmers and [Government of Jordan] officials, have been killed. There is no work on development projects, most [Government of Jordan] civil servants have been withdrawn from the Valley and little farming activity is done outside the Deir Allah area which lies farther from the Jordan River than other project area lands.[28]

As it happened, this was to be the last major Israeli attack on the Canal. USAID, which had planned further involvement in the purely agricultural aspects of the effort in East Ghor, had instead been effectively driven from the project by early 1970. USAID technicians and officials were told to stay away from the project area, and no further American funding was provided.[29] But in March 1970 the US State Department successfully mediated intense, indirect negotiations between Israel and Jordan which resulted in a cessation of the Israeli attacks. According to Joseph Sisco, who was personally involved in these negotiations, 'we made it very clear [to the Israelis] that

31

we attached considerable importance to this project'. In the end, even without USAID, the Jordanians persisted, and European technicians and Gulf State funding gradually replaced American support. Today, the Canal has been extended almost all the way to the Dead Sea, the amount of land irrigation has nearly doubled since 1970, and the Jordan Valley plays an even more important role in Jordan's still largely agriculture-based economy. By almost any standard, the East Ghor Project was and is a brilliant development success.

But Israel's repeated attacks on the Canal angered and embittered many American officials who were involved with Middle East matters. Tom Scotes, Foreign Service Officer who wrote the briefing memo for Joseph Sisco, recalls 'anger at the working level' at the State Department, 'as we saw the Canal being destroyed in front of our eyes'. Like Ambassador Symmes and USAID official Richard Dangler, Scotes believed that Israel's concentration of attacks upon the Canal itself reflected 'more concern about water levels than about refugees or terrorism'. [30] The crossings by Palestinian guerrillas provided a convenient excuse for something Israel wanted to do anyway.

There was another aspect to the raids which enraged not only State but the Defence Department as well: Israel used American A-4 aircraft repeatedly to destroy the Canal. Eyewitnesses to the attacks clearly recall the distinctive profile of the A-4 Skyhawk, as well as the delta-winged French Mirage, during the bombing and strafing runs.[31] The Office of International Security Affairs at the Pentagon was aware that US planes were being used in the raids, and for a time considered delaying the delivery of the F-4 Phantoms which Israel was, in the summer of 1969, about to receive.

Delay was not considered politically feasible, however, and so America delivered the first four of Israel's F-4E aircraft on Friday, 5 September, the day after Joseph Sisco met with Israeli officials to plead for time to repair an American development project which had been damaged by the last planes the US sent to the IAF. By 1969 the US – Israeli relationship had begun to develop some bizarre characteristics.

FOUR

The War Israel Did Not Win: the War of Attrition, 1969–70

Less than one week after the end of the Six Day War, the Soviet Union established an air bridge to begin the re-supply of the devastated Egyptian armed services. To bolster Egyptian morale, Soviet Army Chief of Staff Marshal Matvei Zakharov arrived in Cairo with a large delegation of senior officers to plan further assistance. Soviet President Nicolai V. Podgorny followed, arriving on 21 June 1967 for formal talks with Egyptian President Gamal Abdel Nasser.

While wishing to reassure Nasser of the Soviet Union's commitment to rebuild Egyptian military strength, Podgorny emphasized the importance of moving quickly toward a peaceful settlement with Israel. Nasser responded that a settlement could only be achieved once Egypt had military parity with Israel. Egypt, like Israel, did not wish to negotiate from a position of weakness. Said Nasser to his guests:

> We in Egypt have been the victim of aggression both in 1956 and in 1967 because the US and the West considered us in both instances as aligned to the Soviet bloc, in as much as we rejected colonialist stances and policies. Our policies were, in fact, based on our national interests and the principles of non-alignment which allow for friendship with the Soviet Union. Now we have seen Israel attack us and occupy our territories, with the consent of the United States. With the growing US support to Israel we feel it is not logical to maintain neutrality between those who strike us and those who help us. We wish to deepen and strengthen Egyptian–Soviet relations with the aim of eliminating the consequences of Israeli aggression.

This stolid, logical structure was followed by a statement which, in retrospect, foretold the major events of the Arab–Israeli confrontation in the succeeding years, known as the

33

'War of Attrition', events which would lead directly to the October war of 1973. Said Nasser to Podgorny:

> if we cannot drive the Israelis from Sinai peacefully we shall resort to war. Yet this is not your responsibility, it is exclusively ours. We could, however, ask you to help in the air defence of Egyptian territory. Israel may attempt to cross the Suez Canal and penetrate deep into Egypt. Confronting such an attack should be the responsibility of our joint defence systems.[1]

Israel had just two weeks to savour what was perhaps the most decisive military victory in the history of modern warfare. On 1 July 1967 Egyptian and Israeli troops exchanged mortar and artillery fire across the Suez Canal. On 8 July the IDF called in air strikes to respond to a particularly intense Egyptian artillery barrage, and by 14 July the air forces and navies of both sides were actively engaged in fighting all along the Canal front. Israel's Minister of Defence, Moshe Dayan, was quoted by the state radio service (Kol Israel) as saying that 'the Canal fighting practically amounted to war'.[2] The War of Attrition had begun.

Women and children first

From the outset, a curious pattern developed along the front: Egyptian forces would attack Israeli patrols, outposts and fortifications, and the IDF would respond with attacks on Egyptian civilian centres along the Canal, notably Suez City, Ismailia and Port Said.

On 14 July, for example, following an exchange of artillery fire in the Port Taufiq area, the Egyptian Air Force surprised the Israelis by attacking an armoured column crossing between IDF strongpoints on the eastern side of the Canal. The Egyptian High Command later claimed to have destroyed numerous tanks, half-tracks and trucks. The IDF responded with artillery and air attacks upon Egyptian Army positions, but also upon the central sections of the cities of Ismailia and Suez. Two civilians were killed, and forty-six injured. An eyewitness recalls seeing 'dead and dying horses and people in the streets'.[3]

Egyptians were not the only non-combatants involved in this particular battle. The IAF attack in Ismailia struck a hotel in which were observers from the United Nations Truce Supervision Organization (UNTSO). Coincidentally on that same day, 14 July, UN Secretary General U Thant in a report to the UN General Assembly accused Israeli troops of repeatedly looting the United Nations Emergency Force (UNEF) headquarters in Gaza, north-east of Ismailia on the Mediterranean coast. After the buildings were looted, said U Thant, UN vehicles were driven off in front of UNEF representatives who were 'unable to secure any effective action by the responsible Israeli authorities to prevent it'.[4]

During July to October, Israeli destroyers and motor torpedo boats (MTBs) jousted with Egyptian MTBs along the Mediterranean coast while the war heated up on the Suez Canal. In July the Israeli destroyer *Eilat* caught two Egyptian patrol boats about sixteen miles off the Sinai coast west of El Arish, and sank them both. Thereafter the Egyptians, who had sustained heavy naval losses in the Six Day War, were careful when and where they exposed themselves, not least because of the total Israeli control of the air over the Sinai coast.

On 21 October, however, the 2,500-ton *Eilat*, in the company of several Israeli MTBs, ventured too close to Port Said harbour, and was sunk by three SS-N-2 Styx surface-to-surface missiles fired from two Egyptian Komar-class missile boats of Soviet origin.[5] Forty-seven Israeli sailors died and ninety-one were wounded. Military historians noted the event as the first use of missiles in the Arab-Israeli conflict, and the first occasion in history in which a warship had been sunk by missile fire.

Ismailia, Suez City and smaller population centres along the Canal had been struck repeatedly by Israeli planes and heavy guns since the Six Day War in June. Thousands of civilians had fled westward toward Cairo and other Nile River communities. Now, in anticipation of Israeli retaliation for the sinking of the *Eilat*, the exodus became a flood. On 22 October, the *New York Times* reported that 75 per cent of the population of Ismailia, 60 per cent of that of Suez City, and many families from Kantara and other smaller towns along the Canal, had either lost their homes or abandoned them in the face of the attacks. A total of 350,000 people had left, said the *Times*, despite initial Egyptian Government discouragement. Cairo was already overcrowded.[6]

The Egyptian civilians who fled the Canal zone knew their enemy well. The *Eilat* was of course a military target, and had herself recently sunk two Egyptian naval vessels. The retribution when it came, however, was directed at civilian targets. On 24 October, concentrated Israeli artillery and air attacks destroyed a refinery and factory complex outside Suez City. Oil storage tanks created a spectacular blaze, visible at a distance of forty miles. Cement, brick, petrochemical and fertilizer plants were also hit, and some 80 per cent of Egypt's refining capacity was eliminated, in what must be considered one of Israel's most successful military operations of the entire War of Attrition.[7]

The Egyptian Government estimated that eight civilians were killed and sixty wounded, figures that must be considered conservative in view of the Government's official policy of discouraging the exodus toward Cairo.[8] The Government left little doubt regarding its feelings about the targets Israel had chosen, however. In New York, Egypt's Permanent Delegate to the UN, Mohamed Awad el-Kony denounced Israeli military operations 'conducted against civilians and industrial installations, not against military targets'. He railed against the continual shelling of Suez City and its residential areas resulting in, he said, 'extensive human losses'.[9]

For about nine months after the attack on Suez City, the Canal front was relatively quiet, with only sporadic shelling. On 8 July, 1968, however, Suez City was again hit in an artillery exchange. The Egyptian Government estimated forty-three civilians killed, seventy injured and 150 houses destroyed.[10] And in September the level of fighting along the Canal rapidly increased. Egyptian forces had deployed massed artillery recently received from the Soviet Union – over six hundred guns and rocket launchers – and enjoyed a considerable advantage over the opposing Israeli forces in terms of ground-based firepower.

On 26 October, the Egyptians caught the IDF off guard in a particularly heavy exchange, killing fifteen soldiers and wounding thirty-four, including some who were playing volleyball and football behind their positions. This was the largest single daily casualty toll for the IDF since the sinking of the *Eilat*. For the first time, the Egyptians had used heavy Katyusha rockets, and with devastating effect. Once again, the refinery and downtown Suez City took the brunt of the Israeli response. Minister of Defence Moshe Dayan was touring the battlefield at the time, and later recalled:

> From our stronghold near the Canal, I could see the city of Suez through field glasses as though it were laid out on the palm of my hand. The first row of houses was in ruins, but behind it I occasionally spotted figures dashing from one point to another. Beyond the city black smoke rose from the burning oil tanks, and at anchor in the port were vessels which had been hit. I turned my field glasses toward the main entrance to the port from the Gulf of Suez. The last time I was here, I had noticed the two huge stone lions which adorned the principal quai of the Canal. I now saw that one of them was shattered. Though they were dark red in colour, I fervently hoped they were examples of modern art made out of concrete and not ancient Egyptian statues formed from Nubian sandstone.[11]

Dayan's statement reflected a considerable sensitivity to the international conventions pertaining to the protection of cultural property in the event of armed conflict, signed by Israel at The Hague in May 1954. His statement and the actions of his army, however, evidenced a commensurate insensitivity to the provision of the Hague Convention of 1907, and the Fourth Geneva Convention of 1949, regarding the protection of civilians in time of war. The latter was signed by Israel in 1951.[12]

A caveat is in order here. Because the cease-fire line that ended the June 1967 war was on the Suez Canal, abutting Egyptian population centres and over a hundred miles from the nearest Israeli community, and because Israel had undisputed control of the air space in between (i.e. over the Sinai), obviously Israel did have the capability to strike Egyptian cities while Egypt did not have the ability to respond in kind.

Doubtless the latter would have done so had the means been at hand, if only to make the IDF reflect before it bombed civilians. The fact remains, however, that in this period Israel repeatedly violated internationally accepted standards of behaviour in respect of treatment of civilian non-combatants in time of conflict, and Egypt did not. By early 1969, around half a million refugees had fled Egyptian cities and towns along the Canal.[13]

The canal war expands

During the early stages of the War of Attrition, Israeli troops stationed in the Sinai tended to take their Egyptian opposite numbers very lightly. It was understandable, given the swiftness of Israel's total victory in the Six Day War. It was easy to forget that in that war, Egyptian soldiers had fought without air cover in open terrain. In the halcyon days of July 1967 a *New York Times* correspondent visiting Israeli troops along the Canal reported this conversation between an IDF artillery battery commander and his head quarters, when he came under fire:

> 'Shall I return the fire?' he asked.
> 'No, I shouldn't bother. They won't hit anything anyway.'

By mid-1968, however, Egyptian artillery and rocket performance had Israeli troops smiling less and taking cover more often. The morale of the Egyptian Army rose steadily if slowly during this period.

It was the development of the Egyptian commando forces that provided the greatest surprise at this stage of the war, however. Small units began crossing the Canal at night, first just looking, then planting land mines on the roads connecting Israeli strongpoints, and then ambushing patrols and attacking small outposts.

Colonel Sami Biblawy, the Egyptian commander of one of those units based in Ismailia, recalled:

> We needed to build our self-confidence that we can do it; and we had to learn how to do it. So we did it many times between 1967 and 1970. If you ask anyone who participated in these raids, he

will tell you that it was fun, because each time you will have more confidence in yourselves, when you go to the Israelians and you come back without even a scratch. And it was night; and you can know the directions by night, and you can lead your people by night. It was nice to do it once and twice and the third time, and so on, so on. Maybe it wasn't too effective, but it was for us very, very useful because we have our self-confidence back. Some of us never lose this confidence in the Six Day War, but some lose it, and they get it back by this kind of thing.[14]

Military historian Edgar O'Ballance would later observe that the commando units had been 'the really sharp tip of the rather flaccid Egyptian spear' in the War of Attrition, 'well-trained, aggressive and capable'. They had, he judged, 'many more successes than the Israelis would admit'.[15]

A 26 October, 1968 artillery exchange was the largest of the war, and literally drove the Israelis underground. The IDF was taking unacceptable losses, and there ensued a protracted debate in the Israeli Defence Ministry between proponents of a mobile armoured defence set well back from the Canal, away from Egyptian artillery, and those who proposed to harden and strengthen the Israeli defensive position into a line of linked fortifications right along the Canal. The latter prevailed.[16]

A series of daring Israeli commando raids provided the opportunity for construction of the forts. In the last few months of 1968 the IDF used huge French Super Frelon and SUD 321 helicopters, each capable of carrying thirty soldiers, to strike deep into the Upper Nile region of Egypt, destroying bridges, electrical transmission stations, high tension lines and agricultural irrigation projects. Air strikes accompanied and supplemented the work of the commandos. The objective was to create such economic pain and disruption that Gamal Nasser would reconsider his massed artillery barrages on the Canal.

Indeed what the raids demonstrated was that the Aswan Dam itself and/or downtown Cairo were not beyond Israel's reach. Very soon, the IAF would show just how real the threat was.

Concerned and embarrassed by the raids, the Egyptian Army temporarily suspended the shelling along the Canal, and concentrated on the installation of new Soviet air defence missiles, primarily SAM-2s, and on the formation of a national militia whose mission it would be to protect vital transportation, utility and communications infrastuctures. On the other side of the Canal, the IDF commenced the construction of a series of individual fortifications, spaced two to five miles from each other over virtually the entire length of the east bank. Made of reinforced concrete and built into the (protected) eastern side of large ridges with a commanding view of the Canal, thirty-five of these elaborate bunkers were linked by mobile armour patrols, and supported by far larger bases of armour and artillery deployed well behind the ridges, out of sight of the Egyptians.[17] The entire system of defensive fortifications was completed in 1969, and became known as the 'Bar Lev line', after the name of Israel's Chief of Staff Lieutenant General Chaim Bar Lev.

Inevitably the deep-penetration commando raids and the construction of the fortifications served to make the occupation of the Sinai even more intolerable for Gamal Nasser and his people, and the IDF appeared to be digging in for a long stay. Having experienced three thousand years of foreign domination under the Nubians, the Assyrians, the Persians, the Romans, the Arabs, the Mamelukes, the Ottoman Turks and the British, and having only broken this cycle in the 1950s, the Egyptians were not inclined to submit to Israeli occupation and military domination in the 1960s.

In March 1969 President Nasser announced in a speech to the Arab Socialist Union what he called the 'liberation' phase of the War of Attrition, and the Egyptian artillery boomed again, signalling the beginning of sixteen months of virtually unbroken fighting along the Canal. Nasser was not unmindful of the sacrifice he was asking of his people. The totality of the Israeli victory in the Six Day War in 1967, the phenomenal success of the Israeli commando raids in late 1968, and the IAF's unchallenged air supremacy, soon to be augmented by fifty F-4 Phantoms from the United States (the sale had been announced publicly four months previously), all augured badly for the 'liberation' of the Sinai by conventional military means. But Nasser believed that there would be a limit to the amount of punishment Israel would accept as a price for staying on the

Canal – a nation of over thirty million people could simply absorb more punishment than a nation of less than three million – hence the theory of a 'war of attrition'. Moreover, such a war, as Chaim Herzog later observed, was calculated to play to one of Israel's few military weaknesses:

> Basing themselves on the assumption that the Israeli armed forces have always shown their true strength in a war of movement in which speed and maneuverability are of the essence, the Egyptians came to the conclusion that the Israel Defence Forces would be at a disadvantage in a static war of attrition, in which maneuverability was of little value and in which Egypt possessed a marked superiority over Israel in the main weapon for such a war, artillery.[18]

For about six months through the middle of 1969, the war evolved pretty much as Nasser had anticipated. The Israelis continued their daring airborne commando raids into the Upper Nile Valley, striking again at Nag Hamadi in April, and at Suhaj in late June. Along the Suez Canal, both sides mounted elaborate commando operations which seemed to grow in size and scope with each passing month. One such Egyptian raid inflicted heavy damage on an armour staging area well behind the 'Bar Lev line'. Artillery exchanges along the Canal were heavy and frequent, and caused high casualties on both sides.

By late July 1969 it appeared that attrition was having the intended effect. Israel could not afford the material and human losses involved in static trench warfare along an exposed front 150 miles distant from its borders. For Egypt a stand-off was victory. Israeli Defence Minister Dayan decided in late July, therefore, to use the IAF as a form of 'flying artillery' systematically to destroy Egyptian radar stations, anti-aircraft guns and missile batteries, and supporting facilities. Once Israeli planes were unchallenged in the air, they would wreak havoc on the Egyptian front line. In its later stages, the War of Attrition thus became an air war.

At first, the Egyptians attempted to oppose the IAF with interceptor aircraft, and to respond with their own air raids into the Sinai, using Soviet MiGs and Sukhoi bombers recently absorbed into the Egyptian Air Force. But in the air, the tables were turned: the Egyptians began to take unacceptable losses. 'Attrition' was a game that two could play. On one single day 11 September, 1969, Egypt committed 102 aircraft to raids over the Sinai, and lost eleven. The IAF lost one plane in the operation.[19]

Unable to challenge the Israelis in the air or to reach the many airfields, including those from which Israel was launching its attacks, the Egyptian Army was obliged to sit and wait for Israel's 'flying artillery', and defend as well as possible with anti-aircraft guns and missiles.

Israeli victories, real and hyped

On the ground, Israel escalated the scale of its commando operations to that of small invasions, in an effort to humiliate Nasser and his army into giving up the incessant attacks on the Bar Lev line, and to demonstrate to the Soviets that the IDF could hit and even capture their best equipment, anywhere in Egypt.

A few of these raids were virtual media extravaganzas. On 9 September, 1969, for example, several hundred Israeli soldiers crossed the Gulf of Suez to El Khafayer, Egypt and sped fifty miles south with tanks and armoured personnel carriers to a point near Ras Zafarana, thence crossing the Gulf to occupied Sinai. It was a land, sea and air operation involving continuous air cover, and requiring over ten hours to complete.

The Israelis destroyed military posts and radar installations as they surged down the coast. Over a hundred Egyptian soldiers were killed, and several Russian armoured vehicles were captured, including a T-62 tank which had been 'in service' in the Soviet Army for only four years. The IDF suffered only minor losses in the raid: one soldier wounded and one plane lost.

The operation was a remarkable success from any standpoint, and within a few hours of the invasion force's return, the IDF had held a news conference, and statements about the raid had been issued by Prime Minister Golda Meir, Defence Minister

Moshe Dayan and IAF Chief of Staff Mordechai Hod, among others. A senior officer of the General Staff exulted:

> We have posed a problem for the Egyptians. What are they going to do about a situation where an enemy force can land on their territory and operate for ten hours, most of it in broad daylight, and withdraw safely.[20]

Defence Minister Dayan, speaking on Israeli television, described the operation as complicated, ambitious, and 'even acrobatic at times'.

The *New York Times* covered the raid in great detail in a page 1 article by correspondent James Feron, filed, of course, from Jerusalem. Maps and satellite photography were used to show the scope of the raid, and the article even carried a photograph, credited to Associated Press, of a 'hit-and-run' attack conducted during the assault. Was the AP photographer taken on the operation, or was the photo, like the account, provided by the IDF?

One wonders about the last matter because, with all its detail, the *New York Times* article contained several important, perhaps strategic omissions. The motorized Israeli assault force was equipped with Soviet tanks and APCs captured from Egypt during the Six Day War, and still painted with Egyptian markings. The Israeli soldiers were selected as Arabic speakers, and outfitted in Egyptian uniforms. Many of the casualties were taken when an Egyptian troop convoy, believing the Israelis to be a fast-moving Egyptian armoured unit, moved off the road to allow them to pass. The Israelis machine-gunned them as they sped by.[21]

It was certainly not the first or the last time that the Hague Conventions were violated in the long history of the Arab–Israeli conflict, though it may have been one of the more flamboyant instances, in the sense that few countries violate the conventions and then give press conferences about it. Article 23 of the Hague Regulations Respecting the Laws and Customs of War on Land, of which Israel was a signatory in 1969, state that it is 'especially forbidden':

> To make improper use of a flag of truce, of the national flag or of the military insignia and uniforms of the enemy, as well as the distinctive badges of the Geneva Convention.

Hopefully, the distorted version of the affair in the *New York Times* resulted from nothing more than the poor journalistic practice of relying upon a single involved, and therefore partial, source – in this case the IDF. The alternative is that the *Times* was accomplice to a flagrant violation of international law.

Legal or not, the Ras Zafarana raid was a severe shock to Nasser, who was reported to have suffered a mild heart attack when he heard of the operation. Over fifty senior military officers, including the Egyptian Army chief of staff and the commander of the navy, were replaced before the end of the month.

As noted earlier, the IAF began in August and September to concentrate its air attacks on Egyptian air defence installations, with telling effect. By early November, Israeli officials were claiming to have destroyed all Egyptian ground-to-air missiles along the Suez Canal.[22] Indeed, most historians of the War agree that by December Israel had not only suppressed Egypt's air defences, but had destroyed or otherwise silenced most Egyptian artillery units as well.

An Israeli military historian later summarized the situation along the Canal at the end of 1969:

> By December, the whole Egyptian front was shattered and the IAF enjoyed complete mastery of the air. Effective resistance from the Egyptian air force had ceased; Egypt's dispersal of her defences in the face of recurrent Israeli commando raids further reduced military pressure on the Bar Lev line and forced her to abandon any thoughts of an immediate crossing into Sinai. Egypt was clearly on the defensive, and a defensive war negated the fundamental objective implicit in her launching of the War of Attrition. Egypt's strategy of combining political pressure with military attrition in order to compel Israel to retreat lay in ruins ... Israel's success in checking the Egyptian campaign and recapturing the initiative was clearly reflected in the steady decline of the casualty rate during the second half of 1969. The IDF's losses on the Egyptian front were 106 dead and wounded in July, 65 in August, 47 in September, 56 in October, 39 in November and 30 in December. During the same period, Egypt lost 32 planes and Israel lost 4.[23]

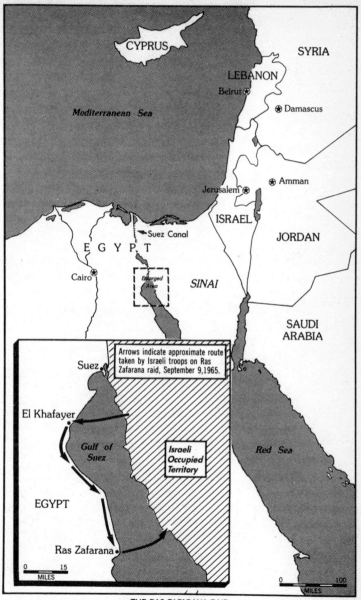

THE RAS ZAFARANA RAID

The road not taken

In late 1969 Israel and her Arab neighbours had an opportunity to end two and a half years of almost constant conflict between them. Israel's remarkable military victories in the Six Day War had been consolidated. The Syrian front had been relatively quiet since the cease-fire. Most Palestinian refugees in Jordan had been driven away from the border areas in the East Ghor Valley. And along the Suez Canal, Nasser's attempt to make occupation of the Sinai unacceptably expensive for Israel had failed, at least for the time being. Military success appeared to give Israel an opportunity to negotiate from a position of strength, an opportunity to be magnanimous.

The framework for peace was certainly there – several diplomatic initiatives had been floated in 1968–9. Following the passage of Resolution 242 in November 1967 by the UN General Assembly, Gunnar Jarring of Sweden had been appointed as the Secretary General's special envoy to the region, and he had begun to shuttle between Tel Aviv and Cairo. From the outset, however, Jarring found Egypt unwilling to consider any negotiating process involving Israel until the latter had withdrawn its troops to pre-Six Day War lines.

Israel's problems with the Jarring mission were even more fundamental, in that he was unable to determine whether Israel even accepted Resolution 242, which provided the framework for his mission. In February 1968 the US Government, through US Ambassador Walworth Barbour, urged Israel to be 'more specific and forthcoming' with Jarring, and complained that Israel's negotiating position was simply not understood by the State Department.[24] One particular aspect of the Israeli position that frustrated Jarring was the fact that Israel claimed to be a land without borders, that is, it had no negotiating position on what might be 'secure and recognized' borders, in the language of Resolution 242. When, on one of the first of his shuttle visits, Jarring asked Israeli Foreign Minister Abba Eban for clarification on this point, he was told that Eban 'was not in a position to draw a map now'.[25]

It was not a promising basis for peace negotiations. One side,

Egypt, wanted the other to surrender its best cards – the occupied territories – before talks even began; and the other side, Israel, would not state its demands or even, in a territorial sense, identify itself. Through most of 1968 Jarring made little if any progress. His mission was suspended in October.

The next major diplomatic effort involved 'Big Two' and 'Big Four' power talks based upon an initiative taken by the Soviet Union in December 1968. Periodically during 1969 US and Soviet representatives discussed the conflict in meetings which never really involved the principal parties, Israel and Egypt. Israel's attitude towards these talks was described by (then) Deputy Foreign Minister Gideon Raphael, in his memoirs:

> Of course, we did not contest the necessity of the two principal nuclear powers to maintain their lines of communications intact, but we doubted whether the Soviet Union was willing to play a positive role in the resolution of the Middle East conflict. There were two keys, we argued, which could unlock the deadlock in the Middle East. One was global, held by the United States. The other was regional, held by Israel. Nothing could happen internally in the area against Israel's will, because of its military preponderance. All that the United States was asked to do was to hold on firmly to its key and resist the Soviet Union in its attempt to turn it, while keeping Israel's arm strong enough to deter any regional aggression.[26]

In October 1969 during the culmination of the Soviet–US talks, US Secretary of State William Rogers presented to the Russians a detailed plan for a peace settlement between Israel and Egypt. But when Rogers announced his proposals publicly in December, Israel and the Soviet Union rejected them outright, and Egypt declined to react formally until further clarification was received regarding Israeli withdrawals from Jordan and Syria.[27]

In the end, however, it was Israel's reluctance to specify its territorial demands which doomed any possible accord with Egypt. And the Nixon Administration, for which Secretary of State William Rogers most definitely did not speak on matters Middle Eastern, supported this posture behind the scenes. In his analysis of Henry Kissinger's White House years, Seymour Hersh describes this unfortunate, convoluted situation:

Even without a direct role, Kissinger's influence was enormous – and negative. The national security adviser constantly urged the President to discourage the State Department from going ahead with any initiative that called for Israel to give up some of its occupied lands in return for a peace guarantee.[28]

That influence had been particularly evident during Golda Meir's first visit to the US as Prime Minister, just weeks before the announcement of the Rogers plan. Mrs Meir had come to Washington, according to Gideon Raphael, (a) to discuss additional arms purchases, and (b) to avoid discussion of peace plans, whether Rogers's, the Soviets', the Israelis' or anyone else's. Raphael described the results of this first meeting:

> She deduced from her talk with the President, who evoked hopes of a satisfactory response to Israel's defence requirements, that the political issues were not of primary presidential concern. These were left to Secretary Rogers.[29]

The Knesset and the Israeli press and public, noted Raphael, tended to judge the success of prime ministerial missions to Washington by their achievements in the field of military procurement. Ben Gurion had returned from his talks with President Kennedy with a promise of Hawk missiles. Eshkol had brought home the Phantoms. On her next visit to Washington, Golda Meir would bag additional F-4s and sophisticated munitions for them. In the meantime, recalled Raphael, the motto at the Israeli Foreign Ministry was 'the time has not yet come to draw maps'.[30]

There were other, *ad hoc* efforts to bring about negotiations, efforts involving international organizations, European and Third World government officials, and even private citizens who offered their mediation services. The war along the Canal in 1968–9, and the increasingly direct involvement of the Soviet Union in the conflict no doubt generated much of this activity. Mahmoud Riad, Egypt's Foreign Minister at the time, recalled one such intervention proposed by NATO Secretary General Joseph Luns in New York in October 1969 during the UN General Assembly session:

> Luns, Joseph Luns the Secretary of the NATO, he came also to me and said the same thing. I said 'All right, you do the

mediation, and the credit will go to you if you can reach a peace agreement.' And then next day he said 'Eban is saying, maximum security for Israel, minimum change in borders.' I said 'I accept!' He was so happy. You know he's tall and he jumped. Very happy. 'Do you really mean that?'

I said 'Of course, I mean it. But maximum security for Israel – this I can sign on paper without even reading it. I leave to Eban to put whatever he likes on this, but only what I'm asking, you know, that the same measures he asks for Israel they will also be given to me. The same measures. If, for example, he wants a demilitarized zone on our side, he should give me also a demilitarized zone on his side. If he needs forces from the UN to be on our side, of course, they should be also on his side. So we'll have the same. We also are scared; we also have the right to be afraid that they may commit an aggression. So he's right to have this feeling we may threaten him, but we also feel the same thing. So let us have both of us the same measures and I give him the full right to write whatever he wants with this.'

He said 'This is fair enough!' I said 'Fine, good; there is no problem. Half of the problem is now solved . . . Now we come to the question of borders. Well, please ask Eban to bring me just a small map with the proposed changes, I may accept them. If I accept them, I can assure you within four weeks we can sign a peace treaty.'

He went and came, went and came and I invited him in Cairo. I said 'Luns, where is the map?' And Luns said 'You know Abba Eban is a very good man. But he has a very bad government. They refused to give him the map.'[31]

Bombing for peace

By early January 1970 Israeli casualties along the Suez Canal front were at their lowest level since the beginning of the War of Attrition.[32] The Egyptian Army's ability to inflict punishment had been effectively destroyed, as had any semblance of an air defence system in the Canal zone. Internationally, there was enormous pressure for a peaceful settlement, or at least for some negotiation process toward that end. It was curiously at this moment that Israel chose to commence strategic, deep-penetration bombing raids on Egypt's heartland beginning, on 7 January, with the area around Cairo. Initially the targets selected were military installations. A war that

·appeared to be dying was suddenly escalated.

Years later in his memoirs Moshe Dayan would recall that the Israeli Government's reasons for the deep-penetration bombing were 'to put pressure on the Egyptians and to compel them to maintain a cease-fire'. At the time of the decision, however, he had been more candid. When asked in a radio interview in Jerusalem in late January whether the aim of the attacks was to humble Nasser before his people and topple his regime, he had responded that he 'would not shed tears' if Nasser's Government fell.[33] Ezer Weizman, who was Transport Minister at the time (and former IAF chief) also confirmed that the demise of Nasser figured prominently in cabinet discussions at the time, on whether or not to bomb.[34] Yet another reason for the bombing was provided by Israeli Ambassador to Washington Yitzhak Rabin, who since the previous September had been urging Dayan and others in Golda Meir's cabinet to step up the war in the interest of encouraging further military aid from the Nixon Administration, which he was convinced supported escalation as a means of militarily embarrassing the Soviets.[35]

In fact, the reason for the bombing may have been a good deal simpler than all that. One is reminded of the old penology cliché that 'crime is 10 per cent motive and 90 per cent opportunity'. In December 1969 Israel had received and completed the absorption of its first squadron of twelve F-4E aircraft and, in the words of one historian of the war, the decision to bomb

was not a complex set of calculations, but simply the ability to perform the operation. It is difficult for the side which is at a relative disadvantage at the existing level of violence to confine its efforts at that level if it has a potential advantage at a higher level ... In this specific case, Israel's acquisition of the Phantoms gave her a potential for far greater superiority at a higher level of violence than the one she already enjoyed at the tactical level of the Canal War. The temptation to escalate was, accordingly, considerable.[36]

There was an immense irony here. Two years earlier, in December 1967, when Yitzhak Rabin had been IAF Chief of Staff, he had travelled to Washington to convince US officials of

Israel's need for new F-4 Phantoms – the plane which Prime Minister Eshkol would subsequently formally request at the Texas barbecue with President Johnson. In a meeting with the US Joint Chiefs of Staff Chairman, Earle Wheeler, Rabin had maintained that 'airpower was the key to a credible Israeli deterrent'. Without a distinct airpower advantage, said Rabin, 'Israel is forced on to a posture of pre-emption as the only choice for survival.'[37] General Wheeler was most impressed with Rabin's point, said so for the record, and later became the single most vociferous and important advocate for the F-4 sale within the Johnson Administration.

The US agreed to sell Israel the planes in the hope that having them, it would not have to use them. Israel used them on strategic bombing missions literally within days after assembling the first squadron – precisely because it had them.

Not all US Defence officials were as naïve as General Wheeler. Robert Kubal, Israel desk officer at DoD's Office of International Security Affairs, recalls that at about this time he and his superior at ISA sat down with Israeli defence and air attachés in Washington, just after the deep-penetration raids began. The IAF was abusing the equipment, said the Americans: the Phantoms had not been intended for offensive use. In response, the Israeli Defence Attaché asked 'What could happen? We're only bombing Egyptians.'

Kubal found the response 'not a little arrogant', and responded that two things could happen. First, based upon (then) recent US experience in Vietnam, the F-4s 'were so quick' that close-in bombing raids in heavily populated areas could result in many civilian casualties. Second, said Kubal, the Russians were almost certain to be provoked into a response that would serve neither Israeli nor US interests.

The Israeli Defence Attaché answered that Israeli pilots were better than US pilots, and no civilians would be killed by mistake. As for the Russians, he said 'We know them better than you do, because a lot of our people came from the Soviet Union. The Russians won't do anything.'[38] The gentleman was wrong, dead wrong as we shall see, and in the seven months which followed, the Israelis managed with great effort and at great cost to snatch a stalemate from the jaws of victory.

Even before the raids began, Israeli F-4s repeatedly streaked over downtown Cairo and the Nile delta at supersonic speeds breaking windows and intimidating the population. The bombing itself began on 7 January, lasted for just over three months, and involved 3,300 sorties. An estimated eight thousand tons of bombs were dropped on Egypt during this period.[39] In January, the IAF bombed factories at Kanka, ten miles north-east of Cairo, and the following month returned to bomb a metal factory at Abu Zaabal, two miles north of Kanka. Eighty civilians were killed in the second attack. Both incidents were said by the IAF to have resulted from accidental releases of bombs. In January, February and March military factories were hit at Helwan and at Digla, near Cairo. On 8 April, an elementary school was hit at Bahr al Baqr, fifteen miles west of the Suez Canal, killing forty-six children.[40]

It has always been the contention of the Israeli Government that these casualties were 'accidental'. If that is true, then accidents occurred very frequently during the period of the deep-penetration raids. Colonel Thomas Pianka, Assistant US Army Attaché at the US Embassy in Tel Aviv at this time, maintains that a high percentage of Israel's targets were infrastructural: transportation, industrial, utility and communication facilities – what air force professionals call 'counter-value targets'. In densely populated Egypt, the Israeli Government must have realized (if only because the US Defence Department told them so) that choosing such targets greatly increased the risk of civilian deaths.[41]

It was shortly after the bombing of the elementary school that the raids were terminated. Israeli military leaders, even those who strongly supported the raids in 1969, could see that they were clearly counter-productive. Ironically, this was because they achieved their intended result – the humiliation of the Egyptian people. The idea, of course, was to show the Egyptian people that their government could not defend them, in hopes that they would overthrow Nasser and accept a peace agreement – or at least a cease-fire – on Israeli terms. Instead, the immediate lessons learned were: (a) that Gamal Abdel Nasser's policy of confrontation with Israel was a legitimate response to a government that would resort to indiscriminate bombing, and (b) that massive Soviet aid was necessary to protect the nation, even if this meant basing agreements, large numbers of advisers and other distasteful reminders of past centuries of foreign domination of Egypt.

Meeting in Moscow

On 22 January, two weeks after the raids began, Gamal Nasser flew to Moscow with Mohamed Heikal, his close friend and Minister of Information, to plead for a Soviet-manned air defence system with which to defend his country. In the Lenin Hills outside the Soviet capital, the two met with Soviet Premier Leonid Brezhnev, Defence Minister Marshal Andrei Gretchko, KGB Chief Yuri Andropov and Soviet Naval Chief Admiral Sergei Gorshkov. From the beginning, it was apparent that there were in the Soviet leadership two different assessments of the significance of the deep-penetration raids. The military appreciated the significance of the new Israeli tactics, while the civilian leadership did not, or at least wished to minimize the matter.[42]

Brezhnev began the first official meeting with the Egyptians by pooh-poohing the raids, which he said had only 'tele-visionic', not strategic significance. Nasser pushed ahead, presenting his extensive list of weapons needed to defend Egypt, including new advanced fighter aircraft and air defence missiles. Obviously, said Nasser, the air defence batteries would require extended training of the Egyptian missile crews, most probably in the Soviet Union. During their absence, Nasser said, he wanted Soviet crews to come to Egypt to 'stand in' and defend the cities while the crews trained abroad.

Brezhnev was visibly taken aback at this suggestion, knowing as he did of Nasser's extreme sensitivities about the posting of Soviet soldiers on Egyptian soil, and launched into a tirade at this point, lecturing Nasser on the importance of exerting leadership and mobilizing the Egyptian Army to defend his homeland. The provision of a Soviet air defence system with Soviet crews, he said, would internationalize the conflict and thus would carry grave consequences for superpower confrontation.

Nasser was furious. The Soviet Union had previously provided Egypt with Scud missiles, he said, and at that time had insisted that Soviet crews accompany the missiles, install them, and remain to control their use. Egypt, said Nasser, had accepted this arrangement. Now the United States had provided Israel with F-4 aircraft, and the planes were being used to strike deep into Egypt, even to Cairo itself. Did the Soviet Premier think, asked Nasser, that the US had not specifically approved this new escalation of the war? Was the war not already internationalized?

The US, said Nasser, was trying to expel the Soviet Union from the Middle East, and to this end had provided Israel with the weapons with which to defeat Egypt, an outcome which would make the US master in the Middle East.[43] He would not accept that as president but, Nasser told his Soviet hosts, he also had to accept reality. Therefore, he would return to Egypt and resign, asking the Egyptian people to appoint a president who would be willing to accept the US as master of the Middle East.

Admiral Gorshkov now set a trap for Nasser. If we send the air defence missile crews as you request, he said, they will need air cover. We will have to send planes and Russian pilots, and they in turn will need air bases. The Soviet Navy Mediterranean Fleet would have to provide medium-range support, and thus ports would be necessary. Smiling, Gorshkov said that as a military man, Nasser could surely appreciate that the air crews could not be sent by themselves.

But it was Gorshkov's foot, and not Nasser's, that was in the trap. Nasser said that he understood that such support services would be required, and that many Soviet technical personnel would be necessary to provide it. Right at that moment, said Nasser, he could commit to the Soviet Air Force the huge new Egyptian military base at Geanaklis, thirty-seven miles southwest of Alexandria. The Egyptian Air Force would vacate the facility, he said. Nasser knew that the Soviets had long coveted the base. The details of access to the port and other required facilities, he said, could be worked out later.

Gorshkov, Brezhnev and Marshal Gretchko now began to talk excitedly among themselves in Russian, while Nasser and Mohamed Heikal waited patiently. Finally, Brezhnev announced that further consultations would be needed, and that the request would be put aside for discussion at a later time. The meeting had ended. Interestingly, at no time during the session had the Soviet officials questioned the basic, critical premise that the deep-penetration raids had direct US approval. Throughout the meeting, Heikal had noticed that Marshal Gretchko had been 'doodling' on a notepad. Now, as all rose to leave, Heikal saw what Gretchko had been drawing – pyramids. It was a good omen.

Nasser and Heikal returned to their *dacha* for the evening. The next morning, the driveways in the Lenin Hills began to fill with large black Zis limousines. The politburo came; it seemed that every marshal in the Soviet Army came. Then the word arrived. A second meeting with the Egyptian visitors would be held at 4 p.m.

Nasser, Heikal and Brezhnev were chatting and waiting for the others to arrive when Marshal Gretchko came through the door. Shaking hands with Brezhnev, Gretchko looked over the Premier's shoulder and gave Nasser a slight wink – it was the next sign that the trip would end in success.

Brezhnev spoke first. A far-reaching decision had been reached, he said. The Soviet Union would send the air defence missile crews, pilots, planes, ships and support personnel. The peace of the world would depend upon the skilful handling of this matter. The mood in the room then became buoyant. Brezhnev asked Nasser to be sure that Gretchko did not get too much sun down there in the sand among the pyramids.

Heikal was so overjoyed that he failed to notice that Brezhnev had risen from his chair and circled the table. Suddenly, he felt a large hand on his shoulder. 'Comrade Propaganda,' said Brezhnev. It was an appellation that was used derisively in Egypt, and Heikal hated it – but he was too happy to object. This must be kept a secret as long as possible, said the Premier. Of course, I would not write about it, said Heikal. No, of course you would not, said Brezhnev, but I would like you to co-ordinate with (KGB chief) Yuri Andropov here, to ensure that the matter be kept secret as long as possible. Obviously the US would discover such a huge operation, said Brezhnev, but we should work to delay that moment as long as we can.

Later that evening, Heikal and Andropov met as instructed. Heikal began, suggesting that the agenda should include how to cover the operation from Western eyes, and how to deny the thing when it was finally discovered. There is no agenda, said Andropov, as we simply cannot conceal such a huge amount of hardware and number of people. What we should do is leak information ourselves about the operation, he said, so we can control it. All we have to do here is decide when and how to leak. Nasser will kill me, Heikal thought to himself. The two had had a running, half-serious discussion for months about Heikal's inclinations as a journalist dominating his obligations as government information minister. How will we leak it, asked Heikal? You leave that to us, said Andropov.

Indeed, Nasser was angry at the outcome of the 'co-ordination'. The following morning, however, Nasser and Heikal met yet again with Brezhnev and Andropov. The latter took the lead, and spoke at length with Brezhnev in Russian. Finally, Andropov turned to Nasser and made his case. The moment the first ship left Odessa, he said, the Americans would know that something was up. Thereafter, any serious attempt at hiding the operation would merely serve to heighten the Americans' suspicions, and to make them ascribe even more importance to the matter than it already had. It would be better to let them know up-front how Russia was responding to Israel's escalation of the war.

Later in Egypt when the rockets arrived, there was no effort to conceal them. When the planes arrived, the Soviet pilots spoke to each other over their 'plain language' radios in simple Russian. In this way did the Soviet Union come to the

Middle East, boldly, defiantly. And that was just the beginning.

The response

In April to September 1970 the Soviet Union sent 15,000 soldiers and missile crewmen to Egypt, and the number of civilian technicians and advisers doubled to 5,000. Eighty SAM-3 Goa missile launchers with 160 missiles arrived, giving the Egyptians a needed defence against low-level attacking Israeli planes. Fifteen T-shaped hardened concrete shelters for the Goa missiles were constructed at seven-and-a-half-mile intervals down the west bank of the Suez Canal. ZSU-23-4 four-barrelled, radar-controlled anti-aircraft guns were deployed around the missiles – weapons which previously had been used only by Soviet and Warsaw Pact forces. One hundred and fifty MiG 21J interceptors, with extended range and far better performance characteristics than any previous Egyptian aircraft, were brought in together with over 250 Soviet pilots to fly them.

Alexandria and Port Said virtually became Soviet naval ports. Tupolev TU-16 strategic reconnaissance aircraft were imported and based at Aswan to provide early warning of Israeli attacks in the southern Red Sea area. Soviet Picket destroyers were stationed off the Sinai coast to furnish early warning of Israeli air activity in the north. The Soviets took over the complete operation of three Egyptian military airports, and managed three others. Camouflaged and/or underground shelters were constructed at all military bases. Advanced Soviet low-level radar, code-named 'Low Blow' and 'Flat Face', were installed with Soviet operators. New Sukhoi SU-7 fighter bombers were brought in to supplement those already in the Egyptian Air Force. Crash training programmes were established to enable Egyptian personnel to operate and maintain these and other new Soviet weapons systems, including tactical helicopters, tanks and armoured personnel carriers.[44]

For the first time, Egyptian TU-16 reconnaissance aircraft

with Soviet crews began regular overflights of US Sixth Fleet operations in the Mediterranean. *Aviation Week and Space Technology* concluded, in the midst of this build-up, that in effect the Soviets were 'developing a vast military air base structure on the North Africa littoral', and that, 'NATO's southern flank, long considered secure, is now exposed to the Soviet naval squadron.'[45]

For weeks after Nasser's visit to Moscow, Israeli leaders continued to assure US officials, the news media, and anyone who would listen, that Moscow would not dare to become directly involved, fearing a Vietnam-like entanglement in Egypt.[46]

In May, however, Israeli Defence Minister Dayan publicly acknowledged the Soviet/Egyptian build-up, but insisted that Soviet pilots would never actually fly air defence missions for Egypt. In fact, by the end of March, some sixty to eighty Russian pilots had already arrived, and by early April they were flying missions.[47] There are two possibilities here: either Dayan was 'misrepresenting' the facts in order to minimize the Soviet reaction to the bombing, or he did not have the facts, and the IDF had very, very poor intelligence on Egyptian/Soviet military activity.

The latter possibility should not be dismissed. In early 1970 the US provided the IAF with a C-97 Stratocruiser aircraft modified to conduct electronic intelligence. In return, Israel turned over to the Americans a captured Soviet SAM-3 anti-aircraft missile. The C-97 was specifically requested by Israel, and obviously met a felt need for 'elint' on Egyptian/Soviet military activity on the Canal front. In the spring of 1970, however, the C-97 was itself shot down by a SAM-2. The aircraft had twenty-two stations, at least twenty of which were filled at the time. It was the first time the IDF had suffered female casualties in combat, and represented a major blow to IAF intelligence.[48]

In an editorial in *Aviation Week and Space Technology* in May 1970, Robert Hotz summarized the changed situation in Egypt.

The new Soviet moves in the Middle East have strategic implications far beyond the earlier supplies of arms and advisers. They have tipped the strategic balance against the Israeli forces in the air and on the ground. By taking over the air defence of the Cairo–Alexandria areas, the Soviet pilots have freed the Egyptian air force to concentrate on air strike missions against Sinai.[49]

In late June the Soviets moved twelve improved SAM-2 missile batteries forward to the Canal zone, and on 30 June shot down two Israeli F-4s. A third IAF plane, an A-4 Skyhawk, was downed by anti-aircraft fire. Four Soviet MiG 21s with Soviet pilots were also shot down in dogfights that day, but neither side acknowledged the fact, the Israelis not wanting to provoke the Soviets, and the Soviets embarrassed at the performance of their pilots. Nevertheless, the missiles were a challenge the Israelis could not ignore, and during the month of July 1970 a new phase of the War of Attrition flared up, this time pitting the IAF's F-4 aircraft with their advanced electronic counter-measure (ECM) pods against Soviet SAM-2s and 3s arranged with redundant slant-range coverage. The ECM pods warned Israeli pilots when a homing missile had been fired and, ideally, diverted the projectile by confusing its radar guidance system. On the other hand, the redundant missile coverage meant that at certain times during an attack mission, the Israeli pilots might be obliged to face two different types of missiles. In addition, the Russians used the tactic of 'ripple' firing, launching an entire battery of six missiles in a short, staggered time sequence so that pilots had to deal with several missiles at one time.[50]

The IAF again began to concentrate its attacks upon missile batteries, to the exclusion of other targets along the Canal. The Egyptians, and presumably the Russians, took enormous losses among their crews and technicians as Israeli F-4s furiously attacked the missile 'box', a particularly heavy concentration of missile batteries placed along the Cairo–Ismailia road. The presence in Egypt of the Soviet pilots also became a factor in the fighting, and a further limitation on the range and scope of Israeli air attacks:

The Israelis tried one or two tentative probes in the air towards the Nile Valley, but each time Soviet fighters took off to intercept them, and the Israelis withdrew. Egyptian air space beyond the 25-mile limit from the Canal was effectively barred to them,

so instead they hammered away at the concrete emplacements
being constructed in the SAM box.[51]

In July Israel lost seven planes, as Soviet and Egyptian technicians and missile crews replaced virtually overnight the missile emplacements which the IAF had, at some risk, destroyed
the previous day. By the first week of August 1970, it was
apparent that the Soviets were prepared to commit an unlimited
number of missiles, launchers, radars, etc. The IAF did not, on
the other hand, have an unlimited supply of planes and pilots.
Militarily, the War of Attrition had become a stalemate. In a
remarkably short time Israel, by escalating the level of violence
and forcing a response from the Soviets, had managed to turn
the military situation to its own disadvantage. For the first time
in the history of the Arab–Israeli conflict, on an important,
volatile military front, Israel did not have total air supremacy.

In the previous month (June) US Secretary of State Rogers
had proposed a second 'Rogers plan' which involved a ninety-
day truce along the Canal, during which UN mediator Jarring
would facilitate indirect talks among Egypt, Jordan and Israel.
During these ninety days, neither side would strengthen its
positions in a thirty-two-mile-deep zone on either side of the
Canal. Initially, this proposal received the same cold reception
as that given the first Rogers plan. But in late July, with the
stalemate apparent to all concerned, first Egypt and then Israel,
under enormous pressure from the Nixon Administration,
accepted the plan. The cease-fire was set to take effect during
the night of 7 August.[52]

Yitzhak Rabin, who was then Israeli Ambassador in Washington, has written of the wrangling between Henry Kissinger
and Golda Meir over the second Rogers plan, that 'We were at
one of the low points in Israeli–US relations.' But that hardly
explains the bizarre incident which occurred in the days just
prior to the cease-fire. In order to provide an agreed 'base line'
of military emplacements as at 7 August, the US proposed to
take high-altitude, high-resolution photographs of the entire
Canal zone, on both sides. Through the Israeli Defence Attaché
in Washington, 'a senior personage in Israel's defence establish-

ment' not only rejected the US proposal, but threatened to shoot down the American planes if they attempted to take the photographs.[53]

On 8 August, less than twenty-four hours after the commencement of the cease-fire, the Government of Israel issued its first formal complaint that the Egyptians and Soviets had 'massively' violated the terms of the cease-fire by moving additional missiles and launchers forward into the standstill zone near the Canal. The official American reaction to these accusations came from the State Department. The US Government was said to have 'insufficient evidence' on the reported Egyptian violations, and had reached 'no conclusions'.[54] This remained the official US position for three weeks, while the Israeli Government fumed.

According to Whetten the US had launched a reconnaissance satellite on 22 July expressly to cover the Suez Canal area, and also conducted regular overflights before and after the cease-fire with SR-71 and/or U-2 aircraft. It is likely, therefore, that US protests of 'inconclusive' evidence of Egyptian/Soviet violations were merely games that intelligence agencies play. The IDF was being made to pay for its threats. Parenthetically, the US overflights and satellite reconnaissance not only confirmed wide-scale Egyptian/Soviet violations of the cease-fire, but frequent Israeli violations as well, in the form of major additions to the Bar Lev line of fortifications, particularly in the area east of the Bitter Lakes.[55]

Perfect failure

There are policy decisions which are flawed in that they do not bring about the intended result; and then there are policy decisions which are perfect failures in that they achieve precisely the opposite of the intended effect. Israel's decision to undertake deep-penetration bombing in Egypt in early 1970, and the Nixon Administration's decision to support the bombing, fall into the latter category.

Israel's objectives in the deep-penetration bombing, and in

the War of Attrition generally, were to oblige the Egyptian Army to keep the cease-fire established at the end of the Six Day War, to consolidate the Bar Lev line and maintain air superiority over both sides of the Canal, to demonstrate to the Egyptian people that Nasser's Government could not protect them and was not worthy of their support, to demonstrate to the other Arab nations that Nasser's policy of confrontation was not effective and, finally, to demonstrate to the Soviets that Egypt was an undependable military ally.

American objectives, that is to say Henry Kissinger's objectives, in the war were rather less complex than were Israel's. The US merely wished to keep the Soviets out of the region and, if possible, to find a way to discredit Gamal Abdel Nasser.

By September 1970 nearly 20,000 Soviet soldiers and advisers were integrated into what had become, for all intents and purposes, the joint Egyptian–Soviet armed services. Israeli pilots were confronted with a missile barrier that was far more sophisticated than anything faced by US pilots in Vietnam: the Israeli Director of Military Intelligence, Major General Aharon Yariv, described it as 'one of the most advanced missile systems in the world'.[56] Between five and six hundred missiles were in place on the western banks of the Canal, providing coverage that reached fifteen to twenty miles into the airspace over Israeli-occupied Sinai – sufficient to cover a crossing of the Canal by Egyptian troops. There was disagreement as to how much of this barrier had been erected before and after the 7 August, 1970 cease-fire. But there was no disagreement that it was erected after, and only after, the brutal deep-penetration bombing of January to April 1970.

Former Egyptian Army Chief of Staff Lieutenant General Saad El Shazly has written that under cover of the missile barrier, 'the work of preparing a new assault could proceed'.[57] The road to Yom Kippur had begun. Moreover, the War of Attrition had improved the morale and training of the Egyptian armed forces, in particular that of the commando units which would lead the crossing of the Canal three years later.

Gamal Abdel Nasser may never have been more popular with the Egyptian people than he was in the last few months of the War of Attrition. His policy of relentless military confrontation with Israel had, in the eyes of many Arabs, been vindicated. Upon his death in late September 1970, millions of Egyptians poured into the streets of Cairo. But the reaction was almost the same in other Arab capitals, and throughout the entire Muslim world.

Finally, the War of Attrition and the excesses of the deep-penetration bombing colour Israeli–Arab relations even today, almost a decade after the Camp David agreements. In particular, it was the experience of the bombing in January to April 1970 that made Egyptians empathize so strongly with the Iraqis in 1981, the Lebanese in 1981 and 1982, and the Tunisians in 1985, in spite of the fact that Israel was in this period Egypt's 'peace partner'.

There is a thin line between fear and hate among adversaries, and while fear and humiliation were the objectives of the Israeli Air Force in its operations over Cairo, etc, in early 1970, hate may have been what was finally achieved. In 1984, Colonel Sami Biblawy, who saw constant action along the Canal as an Egyptian commando in 1967–9, recalled his strongest impression of the War of Attrition:

> Remember when they shoot the elementary school in the Azi? We are not very good in publicity. If we shoot one child in Israel, they will make a very big thing of this incident . . . if you went to the elementary school, you will find children's bodies and their books and papers and everything with blood everywhere. And we can't do anything. If we judge the Israelian soldiers by the same basis which you judged the criminals of the Second World War, they would be all criminals of war.[58]

It does not matter whether Biblawy is justified in his accusations: indeed it is almost inconceivable that this particular bombing was anything other than a tragic accident of war. The point, however, is that this interview occurred fourteen years after the event and five years after Egypt signed a peace agreement with Israel, and it was a vivid, emotional recollection.

The F-4 Phantom is a blunt instrument of political engineering, especially when it is used on a people whom you do not understand.

FIVE

The Last Flight of 5A-DAH, 1973

Wednesday, 21 February 1973. Flight 114 landed in Benghazi in the morning at 0922 hours, eight minutes ahead of schedule. The plane, a Libyan Arab Airlines Boeing 727, had had following winds virtually all the way across the Gulf of Sidra, on the flight from Tripoli. The layover was scheduled for one hour, and included a complete crew change for the flight on to Cairo.

Pre-flight procedures were carried out routinely. Nineteen thousand kilos of JP.I fuel were loaded. One hundred and four passengers boarded, as did three fresh flight crew members and six cabin attendants. Lightning had struck the aircraft in flight two days earlier, but no maintenance action had been taken, and all equipment appeared to be operating normally. The pilot in command was handed the meteorological documentation, projecting weather for the flight: the plane would have following (westerly) winds of 30–40 knots for the climb, 100 knots for the cruise, and 30–50 knots for the descent into Cairo International Airport.

In fact, the winds which the plane would experience that day would be considerably stronger: 30–100 knots during the climb, 135 knots on the cruise, and 100–115 knots during the descent, which would not occur as planned at Cairo International Airport. There was a fast-moving low-pressure system centred near Tel Aviv, with a warm front extending southeastward.

The navigational aids available for the flight that day were NDBs (non-directional beacons) at seven locations, and VORs (VHF omni-directional radio) beacons at four airports across northern and central Libya and Egypt. With the exception of

63

the NDB and VOR at Cairo International, all were operating normally. Cairo NDB was, however, not radiating satisfactorily, and Cairo VOR was emitting signals irregularly. This was not part of the pilot's briefing that morning.

The passengers were settled in their seats at 1030 hours. Almost half were women and children. There were two infants-in-arms on board. For several of the passengers, this was their first flight. The cabin crew was experienced and quite used to this, however: three of the six, including the chief steward, were French nationals working for Libyan Arab Airlines under contract from Air France.

As the plane taxied for the runway, the tower at Benina airport, Benghazi, was given its first SIGMET (significant meteorological briefing) for the trip: 'Sand forecast Cairo . . . reducing visibility to 1,000 metres or less, intensifying moving east.' The aircraft became airborne from runway 33L at 1040 hours and, in the usual way, Benina tower originated a departure message to Malta air control, and to Cairo air control. Cairo did not receive the message. As the plane rose over the runway, its registration numbers could be seen painted on the underside of the wing: 5A-DAH.

During the plane's climb, air traffic clearance was received for each stage through to the planned cruising altitude. Initially, 5A-DAH maintained the required track, passing over the Labraq NDB at 1054 hours, as per the flight plan, and making its first turn. The stronger-than-reported westerly winds pushed the plane on at this point, however, and by the time it reached its next marking point, Sidi Barrani NDB, the plane was five minutes ahead of schedule as against the precomputed, zero-wind flight plan.

The plan called for 5A-DAH to pass south of Cairo, and to approach the International Airport from the south-west. At 1144 hours, about the time the plane should have turned left for its final approach run, however, clouds enveloped nearby Qarun Lake. Had the lake been visible, it might have provided a visual check on the plane's position. High winds completed the picture, pushing the plane along at a groundspeed of 650 knots. By the time 5A-DAH passed over the Nile south of

Cairo, it was fifty miles off course and heading for the Gulf of Suez. Beyond the Gulf lay occupied Sinai and Israel's Bar Lev line.

Co-pilot Younis, a Libyan national, was now flying the plane. At 1146 hours, Captain Bourges, a French national, began to notice strange readings on his instruments. Cairo Airport VOR, now working again, should have been radiating straight ahead of the plane, but was instead abeam on the left side. Bourges commented on this to Flight Engineer Nandin, who was also French and was the third person in the cockpit. For eight minutes, Bourges and Nandin discussed their navigational problem and endeavoured to check their actual position using various instruments. It was a conversation which only the two of them could understand, however. Co-pilot Younis was busy flying the plane and did not in any event understand French. He'd been trained by Air France, but entirely in the English language.

Bourges and Nandin knew something was wrong, but not exactly what. Captain Bourges considered turning back and said so at one point, but as he and Nandin tried to get their bearings, no action was taken.

'After all,' Bourges reasoned, 'we're being monitored from Cairo.'
'Yes,' Nandin agreed.
'Then we can't have an abeam [reading from] Cairo at present. That's all.'

The winds aloft had by this time increased, and the plane shot east and north at a ground speed of 660 knots. At two minutes before noon, Cairo tower radioed 5A-DAH to ask its heading. The co-pilot responded, adding that he was having difficulty reading Cairo's VOR signal. Now, sensing that there was a problem, Cairo tower radioed:

Lima November 114, stick to the beacon, you are diverted from the airways.

But LN 114 had already crossed the Gulf of Suez and was heading fast, not for Cairo International, but straight for Bir

Gifgafa, the Israeli Defence Force's most important air base in occupied Sinai.

By now, Captain Bourges and his flight engineer were frantically trying to determine their whereabouts, using other, nearby directional beacons. But co-pilot Younis, responding to a second query from Cairo tower, was apparently still unaware of the problem. He reported that the aircraft was fifteen miles from the airport, and was maintaining its proper heading. Cairo tower cleared 5A-DAH to land on runway 23, and passed the plane on to Cairo approach control.

Meanwhile at Bir Gifgafa, the progress of 5A-DAH was being carefully, and anxiously, tracked on radar. At 1156 hours two Israeli Air Force F-4Es lifted off to intercept the unidentified aircraft. Climbing fast, the two fighters drew up behind the airliner at 1201 hours. Visibility was good, although all three aircraft were flying under cloud at this point. The IAF section leader immediately identified the intruder as a Libyan Arab Airlines Boeing 727. He then stationed his plane to the rear and right of 5A-DAH, just behind the wingtip. His number two – the other fighter – drew up just behind the left wing of the plane.

In the passenger section of the airliner, a stewardess announced that the plane would be landing in Cairo in a few minutes. Mr Elsterie, sitting in a right aisle seat near the rear of the aircraft, leaned across two friends in the seats to his right. It was Elsterie's first flight in a jet aircraft, and one of his very first flights ever, and he wanted to see Cairo from the air. What he saw instead was an Israeli fighter level with and just beyond the extended wing of the airliner.

Steward Jean-Pierre Burdiat later recalled the pandemonium that erupted in the cabin when the fighters were first seen – several passengers got up and rushed to the windows, as the cabin crew loudly demanded that they be seated for the expected landing. Both cabin crew and passengers immediately recognized the six-pointed blue star of the Israeli Air Force painted below and behind each fighter's cockpit. Stewards and stewardesses endeavoured to calm the passengers, telling them there was no danger: 5A-DAH was, after all, a civilian airliner

on approach and (so far as they knew) about to land at Cairo
International Airport.

It was shortly after noon, just before the interception, when
Captain Bourges finally realized what the problem was, telling
Flight Engineer Nandin that the plane had flown past Cairo. At
this point, 5A-DAH was either directly over Bir Gifgafa or fast
approaching it. Co-pilot Younis suddenly became aware that
fighters were approaching the plane from the rear, and advised
Captain Bourges accordingly. Bourges, in turn, informed Cairo
tower that his aircraft was having 'some problems' with its
heading, and was being trailed by 'four MiGs'.[1] As he did this,
he swept 5A-DAH into a left-hand turn, heading it back toward
Cairo, and levelling off at about 6,000 feet altitude. The air-
speed was reduced slightly, and Bourges requested a radar fix
from Cairo tower.

As 5A-DAH completed its turn, the Israeli section leader
brought his F-4 Phantom forward, so that his cockpit was even
with and just to the right of the airliner's cockpit. The time was
1204 hours. The section leader made hand signals, pointing
down and to the rear of the three aircraft, presumably at the Bir
Gifgafa air base. In the cockpit of 5A-DAH, someone saw the
Israeli pilot's signals, and commented:

> We've come close, ah yes old chap. But you have nothing to do
> with it. Ah, ah no, but I don't understand that language.

At this point, the Israeli fighters moved away from the airliner,
or at least out of eyesight, and Captain Bourges, involved with
his instruments, asked his companions 'They are still behind,
eh?' During this sequence of events, the plane descended
slightly and its landing gear was briefly lowered, and then
raised.

At 1205 hours Cairo tower informed the captain that its
directional beacon was again working normally, and suggested
that 5A-DAH climb back up to 6,000 feet so as to receive the
signal better. The plane accordingly began a gradual ascent at
1206 hours and as it did so, the two Israeli fighters moved back
into flanking positions just beyond the airliner's wings. Again,
the Israeli section leader signalled with his hands, pointing to

the ground. Co-pilot Younis replied this time with his own hand signals, pointing straight ahead. None of the cockpit crew had yet seen the Star of David on the fighters' sides.

A few seconds later, at 1206.22 hours, the first shots were fired, as the section leader sent a burst of tracer bullets (or rockets) across the nose of the airliner. Seconds later 5A-DAH began to descend again, tripping an alarm, a safety mechanism which indicates that the engines have been throttled back while the landing gear is not extended. Within seconds – certainly less than a minute – the Israeli section leader returned on a strafing pass, firing into 5A-DAH's wing tips, and roaring past the cockpit. The second fighter fired a burst at the other wing. The cockpit crew, who could not see their wing tips, were apparently unaware that they had been struck.

At 1208 hours, less than two minutes after the firing began, 5A-DAH locked on to the Cairo ILS (instrument landing system). For the first time in almost half an hour, the flight crew knew exactly where they were in relation to Cairo International Airport. But it was too late. At 1208.19 hours, the two Israeli F-4s again roared past 5A-DAH, firing rockets and/or sustained bursts from their Vulcan cannons into the passenger cabin, engines and wing area of the airliner, where the fuel tanks are located. As the Israeli Section leader peeled away from this pass, he could see smoke and/or fuel spewing from the plane. For the first time, finally, the flight crew saw enough of their attackers, or saw them for a sufficiently long time, to be able to identify them. Shouted the co-pilot, 'It's an Israeli fighter, an Israeli fighter!' as the plane began to descend.

Inside, the cabin wall lining burst into flames. As the fire spead, most of the passengers remained in their seats, praying, but cabin attendants had to calm some of the passengers, particularly the children, who were hysterical. Number 1 and 2 engines ceased operating, causing loss of the plane's flight controls. The starboard wing began to sag. Steward Jean-Pierre Burdiat saw a second burst of gun and/or rocket fire through the passenger cabin during the descent.

The flight recorders and DME (distance measuring equipment) ceased operating when engines 1 and 2 failed at 1209.15

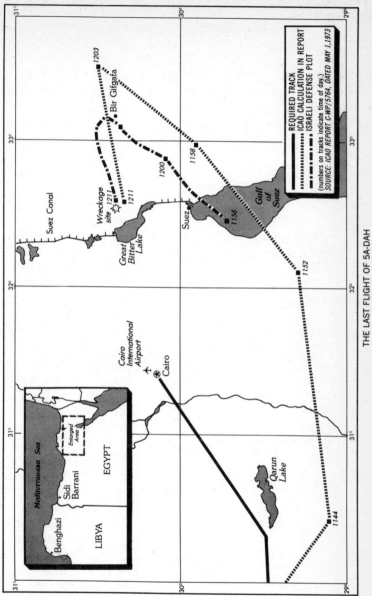

THE LAST FLIGHT OF 5A-DAH

REQUIRED TRACK
ICAO CALCULATION IN REPORT
ISRAELI DEFENSE PLOT

(numbers on tracks indicate time of day.)
SOURCE: ICAO REPORT C-WP/5764, DATED MAY 1, 1973

Suez Canal

Wreckage site 1211

Great Bitter Lake

Bir Gifgafa

Suez

Gulf of Suez

1203
1200
1211
1158
1156
1152
1144

Cairo International Airport
Cairo

Qarun Lake

Mediterranean Sea

Benghazi
Sidi Barrani

LIBYA
EGYPT

Enlarged Area

hours. The passenger cabin continued to burn as the plane descended, because none of the cabin attendants dared to get up to seek the fire extinguishers. Captain Bourges managed, however, to keep the plane aloft, flying right wing low, for an additional two minutes. Just prior to impact, it is 'probable' that there was an explosion in the starboard wheel-well area. Then the right wing and fuselage struck the lip of a sand ridge, breaking into pieces. The main portion of the passenger cabin turned slightly to the right, flipped over, came to rest in a generally upright position, and continued to burn. It was 1211.25 hours when the plane's clock stopped. Bourges, Nandin and five of the six cabin attendants were dead.[2] One hundred of the 104 passengers, men, women and children, were dead. The last flight of 5A-DAH was, mercifully, over.

Every detail of this account, every single detail of this account, is taken from the International Civil Aviation Organization (ICAO) Working Paper entitled 'Report concerning the Libyan Arab Airlines Boeing 727–224: 5A-DAH (Sinai – 21 February 1973)'[3] The report runs to ninety pages, and contains the results of a fact-finding investigation carried out by a special ICAO team of specialists, a minute-by-minute reconstruction of the flight, transcripts from the cockpit voice recorder and from tapes of Cairo approach control, maps, and interviews with the Israeli section leader, with Jean-Pierre Burdiat, and with two surviving passengers.[4]

Deep sorrow, *inter alia*

Within a very few hours of the fall of 5A-DAH, the Israeli Government knew from examination of the wreckage that (a) the plane had no bombs, soldiers or armed terrorists, not even a spy camera, and (b) Israel had a major public relations problem on its hands. The situation was made worse by the fact that coincidentally, just hours before 'the Libyan plane incident', as it would come to be known, the IDF had carried out combined air and sea raids on alleged Palestinian guerrilla bases in refugee camps north of Tripoli, Lebanon, killing numerous civilians in the process.

An initital communiqué by the Israeli cabinet stressed the efforts that the IAF pilots had made to contact the airliner before 'intercepting' it. Shortly afterward, Israeli Prime Minister Golda Meir issued a statement which foretold what would become Israel's official position in the days ahead:

> The Government of Israel expresses its deep sorrow at the loss of life resulting from the crash of the Libyan plane in Sinai and regrets that the Libyan pilot did not respond to the repeated warnings that were given in accordance with international procedure.[5]

Israel Galili, Minister without Portfolio, followed with a communiqué claiming that repeated efforts had been made to contact the airliner over a fifteen-minute period. IDF Chief of Staff Lieutenant-General David Elazar, in a late-night meeting with the cabinet, said that the Libyan plane had overflown 'a most highly sensitive Israeli military area and behaved in a manner that aroused suspicion and concern about its intentions'. That same evening, the then Transportation Minister Shimon Peres advanced the following propositon:

> There are international principles regarding the penetration of the airspace of another country whether deliberately or by error. To the best of my knowledge, Israel acted in accordance with those procedures.[6]

Peres did not indicate which specific international principle required that the plane and its passengers be destroyed.

Official US reaction to the downing of the plane was swift and vague. President Richard Nixon arranged for the delivery of the following 'message of condolence' to Colonel Moammar al-Qaddafi, Libya's head of state:

> I have heard with [excised] dismay reports of the shooting down of a [excised] civilian Libyan airliner which has resulted in a tragic loss of life. Accept Mr President my deepest condolence at this moment of loss.[7]

Secretary of State William Rogers sent a similar message to the Libyan leader, indicating that he was 'saddened' by 'the loss of some seventy lives'. A State Department spokesman, asked to elaborate on the administration's feelings about the incident, said he had 'no further comment'.[8] Neither Nixon's nor Rogers's messages mentioned who had shot down the plane. Apparently in Washington, as in Tel Aviv, the official sorrow and dismay were restrained.

The day after the downing of the plane, the US Embassy in Tel Aviv telexed a report to the State Department summarizing Israeli Government and press reaction to the affair. Generally, both had 'justified the forcing of the plane down', but, said the classified report, 'justifications have been somewhat contradictory'.[9] In the days and weeks that followed, Israel's explanation for its role in the demise of 5A-DAH and her passengers would in fact simply disintegrate, as cockpit and air control recordings were examined and made public, and then a full investigation was undertaken by the ICAO.

Getting the story 'right'

Central to Israel's version of and justification for the attack was the claim that the F-4 pilots had followed accepted international procedures for the interception of aircraft violating another country's airspace without prior permission. The Israeli Government press office statement issued on the evening of 21 February, just hours after the downing, stated:

> It has been established beyond all doubt that the pilots of the Libyan plane had noted the repeated warnings according to international aviation usage. The pilot of the Libyan plane even acknowledged that he noticed the warnings and interception signals, but nevertheless refused to heed those warnings.[10]

Specifically, the signals that were supposed to have been made and acknowledged were (a) the hand signals pointing down to Bir Gifgafa, which the IAF section leader made twice when his plane was cockpit-to-cockpit with 5A-DAH, and (b) the tipping of the fighters' wings from a position in front of the airliner, to instruct the latter to follow the fighters into a nearby airport.

Each signatory nation is required by the Chicago Convention to establish and publish its own aircraft interception procedures (AIP) and to ensure that these conform to ICAO advice on the subject. Israel's AIP was published in January 1972, and did indeed conform to established procedures. Nowhere in it, however, are hand signals mentioned.[11] Furthermore in the cockpit recording either Captain Bourges or the co-pilot (the ICAO investigation team did not determine which) clearly states that he does not understand that 'language', that is, whatever pointing or gesturing the Israeli section leader was doing.

As for wing-tipping, there is simply no evidence in the ICAO investigation report, other than the self-interested testimony of the section leader, that the Israeli planes did in fact move ahead, that is, in front of 5A-DAH, as the Israeli AIP requires, and tip their wings. On the contrary, there is at least circumstantial evidence in the transcripts that the Israeli planes never positioned themselves in front of the airliner, in that the fighters were never identified as Israeli planes until they began strafing passes; until, in fact, *after* the fatal bullets/rockets were fired at 1208.19 hours. Only at 1209.11 hours does co-pilot Younis shout 'It's an Israeli fighter, an Israeli fighter.' Prior to that moment, the attackers are identified on the transcript only as 'Egyptian MiGs'. Had the F-4s followed correct procedures prior to shooting, Captain Bourges, who had served in the French Air Force, and co-pilot Younis, who had served in the Libyan Air Force, would surely have identified them as Israeli, as had the civilian passengers who glimpsed the fighters out the side windows.[12]

A second and related claim made by Israeli military officials just after the event was that following the fighters' attempts to signal 5A-DAH, Captain Bourges had shown aggressive intent by turning back toward Egypt and the Canal. At a press conference with Defence Minister Dayan on 22 February, Israeli Air Force Commander General Mordechai Hod said:

We intended to force the Libyan plane down and investigate whether the pilot was mistaken in taking the course from . . . Suez to the north-east. However, the pilot ignored instructions and

turned straight westwards to the Canal, even after the Phantoms
fired warning shots.[13]

In fact, the ICAO investigation report concluded that the plane
made its turn at 1203 hours and was heading 'home' not only
before shots were fired, but before any signals of any kind,
hand, wing or otherwise, were made; before in fact the IAF
section leader brought his planes alongside 5A-DAH's
cockpit.[14]

The direction of the plane's flight at the point of attack is
important for other reasons. In the hours just after the event,
Israeli officials explained the need for drastic action to 'force
the plane to land' in terms of fears that the plane might have
been a hijacked civilian airliner, loaded with explosives and
heading for an Israeli city or military installation.[15] It was said
that weeks previously, Israeli intelligence had received information that such an attempt might be made. Obviously, if the
plane was headed directly for Cairo and was, as the ICAO
investigation established, only two to three flying minutes from
the Suez Canal and Egypt at the time of the final, fatal attack, it
was not shot down because of fears it was going to bomb Tel
Aviv.

One of the reasons why the Israeli pilots were said to have
suspected that the Libyan Airlines 727 was possibly a decoy
plane on a 'terrorist' or military mission, was their report that
the curtains were drawn on the plane. In the 22 February press
conference attended by Defence Minister Moshe Dayan and
Air Force Commander Mordechai Hod, the two F-4 pilots flatly
stated that curtains covered the passenger cabin windows.[16]
Passengers Elsterie and Khaufa, however, in separate statements to the ICAO investigation team, stated that the curtains
were open and the faces of terrified passengers were pressed to
the windows.[17] Cabin attendant Jean-Pierre Burdiat was asked
about this by the French Bureau Enquêtes-Accidents before his
death:

Question: Were some curtains drawn in the cabin during the
interception?
Reply: No, I was told [by the Israelis] to say that the curtains
were lowered, but this was not true.[18]

73

The Israeli pilots had a problem, of course. They could not credibly claim on the one hand that they had been close enough to the airliner to make hand signals that were understood, and at the same time maintain that they could not see civilian passengers through the windows. So the curtains had to be drawn. Another explanation may be that they simply did not want to remember those faces.

If the Israeli pilots knew that the plane (a) had passed over Bir Gifgafa air base and done no damage, (b) was headed toward Egypt, and indeed, was nearly in Egyptian airspace, and (c) was clearly a civilian airliner filled with civilian passengers, why then did they shoot? The reason may lie in the word 'Springflower'. In the days and weeks after the downing, no Israeli military officials said so directly, but they may have thought at the time the attack was approved that 5A-DAH had taken photographs of the Bir Gifgafa base.

Why would they suspect that? Because virtually all El Al civilian airliners *were* equipped with high-resolution cameras, and did regularly conduct espionage by overflying and photographing sensitive military areas on their scheduled flights. Beginning in the late 1960s, the US Central Intelligence Agency gave El Al planes this capability in a programme known by the code-name 'Operation Springflower'. El Al Boeings coming off the assembly lines in Seattle were flown to Houston, Texas, where E Systems Inc, under a contract funded by the CIA, fitted the planes with the finest high-resolution cameras available.[19]

Article 4 of the Convention on International Civil Aviation, known as the 'Chicago Convention', states:

> Each contracting state agrees not to use civil aviation for any purpose inconsistent with the aims of this Convention.

Both Israel and the United States were signatories to the Chicago Convention in the late 1960s.

No camera was found by the Israelis in the wreckage of 5A-DAH. While they searched for it, however, IDF soldiers looted the personal belongings of the passengers. Four of the soldiers were subsequently court-martialled for this.[20]

Airliner 5A-DAH was equipped with both HF and VHF radios. On the day after the attack, the Israeli Defence Forces issued a formal statement in which it was claimed that 'efforts were made to establish radio contact with the plane but the pilot did not respond'.[21] The previous day, the Israeli Minister without Portfolio had said that 'repeated efforts to contact the airliner had been made over a fifteen-minute period'.[22] Israeli Air Force Commander Mordechai Hod, when interviewed by the ICAO investigation team, claimed that 'an attempt was made through a distant VHF station in Israel to contact the aircraft on 129.4 mcs'.[23]

None of these statements holds water. Cairo International Airport's air traffic control frequencies were published and were well known, certainly to Israeli military intelligence. Libyan Arab Airlines Flight 114 was scheduled. Cairo International was the likeliest major airport in the vicinity to which a Libyan Arab Airlines plane would be going or from which it would be coming. The Israelis admitted to the ICAO investigating team that they were monitoring the plane's progress while it was still in what they knew to be Cairo International's air-traffic control zone.[24] In all probability, Bir Gifgafa air base and/or other nearby IDF facilities were monitoring Cairo air control at the time of the incident, but even if they were not, it would have been very easy during the crucial fifteen minutes of the interception for the IDF to contact the airport to ask if they were in contact with a 'lost' Libyan Arab Airlines plane.

The answer, of course, would have been yes. But the attempt was never made. There is no evidence from air control or cockpit recordings that any effort was made by Israel to contact either the airport or the plane. The 'Libyan airline incident', as it has come to be called, was quite literally a case of 'shooting first and asking questions later'.

While the Israeli Air Force, by its own account, had fifteen minutes in which to determine the identity and 'mission' of 5A-DAH, Captain Bourges in the airliner's cockpit had considerably less time in which to gauge the intentions of his assailants. From the transcripts of cockpit and air control recordings, it can be determined that Bourges had exactly three minutes, forty-five seconds from the moment when the Israeli section leader first hand-signalled 'instructions' to the pilot, to the moment when the fatal shots were fired.[25] Bourges, who at the time of the signalling thought that the planes off his wings were Egyptian MiGs, had even less time to react after the first warning shots were fired – exactly one minute and fifty-seven seconds – at a time when he must have been wondering why 'friendly' aircraft were firing warning shots, and he still was not certain of his location – and had, only fifteen seconds before the fatal shots, locked on to Cairo Airport ILS (instrument landing system).[26]

And when the Israeli fighters shot, they shot to kill. At a press conference on 22 February, IAF Commander Mordechai Hod said that the decision to 'intercept' the plane was taken 'at the highest military command levels according to standard procedure in emergencies'.[27] Specifically, the decision was made by IDF Chief of Staff David Elazar, who was reached by Hod by telephone during the incident. According to Hod,

> the plane was hit to damage its wings so that it could not fly much longer. It was then only that the Libyan Boeing 727 tried a forced landing, but failed.[28]

At the press conference and later, in statements to the ICAO investigating team, Hod and the F-4 pilots insisted that the F-4s fired only at the 'starboard upper wingroot area', and that machine guns, not rockets, were used.[29] There is some dispute about the use of rockets in the ICAO report: both co-pilot Younis and cabin attendant Burdiat insisted that rockets were used.[30]

It is likely that Hod and the F-4 pilots were truthful about the rockets, however, for the weapon that *was* used could easily have been mistaken for a rocket at its 'business end'. What the Israelis did fire at the wingroot area, *and the passenger cabin and engines* of 5A-DAH, was the M-61 Vulcan 20mm rotary cannon, or gatling gun. This US-made weapon fires 3,000 to 6,000 rounds per minute, at the option of the pilot, and can be very effective against tanks and other armoured vehicles. In the event, the aluminium skin of the Boeing 727 was shredded like tinfoil. Moreover, the F-4's guns that day were armed with incendiary tracer rounds, which is why the inside walls of the passenger cabin began to burn immediately.

Every fighter pilot – certainly every fighter pilot in the IAF – knows that the wingroot area of a Boeing 727 houses the fuel tanks. After the first burst from the Vulcan, the F-4 pilots saw smoke and flame, and the plane began to descend rapidly. During the descent, the F-4s returned yet again to fire into the passenger cabin.[31] The Israeli pilots, acting under instruction from the IDF Chief of Staff, were not trying to force the plane to land. They were trying to make it explode in mid-air – which, according to the ICAO report, is probably what happened, just prior to ground impact.[32]

Captain Bourges was ridiculed by the Israeli pilots at the 22 February press conference for having botched his attempt at a 'forced landing'. In fact, with two engines gone, impaired flight controls and a burning fuel tank and fuselage, 5A-DAH had about as much a chance for a 'forced landing' as a piano thrown from a third-storey window.[33]

The ICAO investigation report was made available to the *New York Times* by 'diplomatic sources' on 6 June, 1973, and the *Times* published its assessment the following day:

> The report largely verified Israel's description of many of the circumstances leading up to the crash.[34]

With the help of the *New York Times*, the Government of Israel had finally got the story 'right'.

In memoriam, William Borysoglebski

One aspect of the downing of 5A-DAH that the *New York Times* (and other US news media) just did not have the space or the time to cover, was the fact that there was an American aboard the plane. He was William Borysoglebski, a businessman and Polish immigrant from Chicago. The *Times* devoted a total of one column inch to this story: half on 24 February, announcing his death, and half on 28 February, informing that the body was being shipped home.[35]

It is tempting to contrast this with the coverage of the *Achille Lauro* hijacking in October 1985, and the murder of Leon Klinghoffer by Palestinian terrorists. The *New York Times* carried several dozen articles on Klinghoffer over late 1985 and early 1986, and mention of him was made in dozens more. Many hundreds of column inches of 'news-space' examined not only the circumstances of his death and his burial, but the details of his life, his political philosophy, and the details of his wife's life and her political philosophy.

William Borysoglebski had a wife as well, and probably had a political philosophy, But Americans were spared, or deprived of, the details, and not only by the *Times*. *Time Magazine* and *Newsweek* did not even mention the fact that there was an American citizen who died in the flames of Flight 114. Even the *Chicago Tribune*, Borysoglebski's 'home town' newspaper, had only one small article on the man's death and, in fairness, a small obituary. It is hard not to conclude that Borysoglebski, unlike Klinghoffer, had been killed by the wrong people.

Henryka, William Borysoglebski's wife, was not however ignored. Several days after the downing of 5A-DAH, Shaul Ramati, the Consul General of Israel in Chicago, visited her in her small apartment on West Lunt Avenue, to offer the sincere condolences of the state of Israel on the event of her husband's death. Compensation would be paid, he assured her. Soon, he would deliver a cheque for $30,000. All he asked was that she sign a small paper absolving Israel of all responsibility, and waiving future claims.[36]

Poisonous mushrooms

Some in Israel, to their credit, did not think it would be so easy. The responsibility was there. On 1 March Foreign Minister Abba Eban addressed a group of college students. He warned that 'mishaps caused by our style have multiplied as of late'. He cited, among other things, false claims in Israeli newspaper editorials that the world press had blamed Israel for the downing of 5A-DAH, but had not condemned the killing of Israeli athletes at the Munich Olympics, and what he termed the 'scurrilous, unfounded' charges (about Captain Bourges) made by the government, which 'denigrated the honour of a dead pilot'.

The events, said Eban, represented 'outbursts of an evil spirit' in the country. He called for a searching look at Israel's 'collective self', and a greater adherence to traditional Jewish values, such as 'the love of freedom, tolerance, equality and human brotherhood'.

The Israeli daily newspaper *Haaretz* referred to this evil spirit as 'poisonous mushrooms' and noted that 'an atmosphere of arrogance and boasting descended upon us. We are scoffing at the world.' *Davar*, another major Israeli newspaper, was also critical of the government's decision to down the airliner, though on a far less philosophical level. *Davar* wondered whether using the F-4 Phantoms to shoot down a civilian airliner might make President Richard Nixon less inclined to approve future sales of the aircraft.[37]

Such worries were misplaced, however. Nixon, who had expressed his 'dismay' to the Libyan President at the downing of the plane by whomever – he did not say in his message – obviously did not believe that the incident was relevant to policy. On 13 March, barely three weeks after the destruction of 5A-DAH, the Nixon Administration approved the sale of an additional $220 million in F-4 Phantom and A-4 Skyhawk aircraft to Israel.

As far as the US Government was concerned, in fact, the incident was insignificant in terms of international civil aviation. In late February, the US delegate to the ICAO, Betty C. Dillon, voted only 'reluctantly' (her words) for a resolution proposing an investigation by the organization of the circumstances surrounding the downing of 5A-DAH, because the resolution contained in its preface the words 'condemning the Israeli action'. Ms Dillon had proposed, earlier in the meeting, an amendment that would have removed from the resolution any reference to the state of Israel.[38]

It was only when the Soviet Union downed a Korean airliner,

ten years later in 1983, that the US Government became concerned about the sanctity of civil aviation. After that incident, President Ronald Reagan loudly condemned what he described as a 'terrorist act', and later added:

> This murder of innocent civilians is a serious international issue between the Soviet Union and civilized people everywhere who cherish individual rights and who value human life . . . they speak endlessly about their love of brotherhood, disarmament and peace. But they reserve the right to disregard aviation safety and to sacrifice human lives.[40]

Secretary of State George Shultz added:

> We can see no explanation whatever for shooting down an unarmed commercial airliner, no matter whether it's in your airspace or not.[41]

Unfortunately, no American Abba Eban came forward in 1983 to point out the naked hypocrisy, the poisonous mushrooms in Washington.

SIX

The Yom Kippur War:
and the War it Almost Was, 1973

The unpleasant taste of the Libyan airliner affair faded quickly in Israel, and as always in the Middle East, there were other events to take its place. In April 1973, in an operation code-named 'Spring of Youth', two teams of Israeli commandos entered Beirut at night by sea, and executed gang-land style several PLO officials and their families. A number of the commandos were wounded in the process, and there was bad publicity about the deaths of civilians caught in the cross-fire, but in Israel, so soon after the murder of Israeli athletes at Munich, the operation was greeted as a spectacular success.

In August two IAF fighters forced down a Middle East Airlines plane on a scheduled flight from Beirut to Baghdad. Eighty-one passengers were removed at gunpoint and questioned for several hours. Israeli intelligence had apparently thought that Dr George Habash, head of the Popular Front for the Liberation of Palestine (PFLP), was aboard. He wasn't. For Israel, there was more bad publicity and a loud accusation from the US State Department that the action had been 'a clear violation of international law'.

The government in Jerusalem/Tel Aviv was not impressed, however. Said Defence Minister Dayan at a news conference the day after the event, 'We had reliable information that certain leaders of [the PFLP] should have been on that plane.'[1] In the weeks to come, there would be more reliable intelligence like that, and it would cost Israel dearly.

In the meantime, however, the spring and summer of 1973 were a mini-era of good feeling in Israel. The Bar-Lev line was quiet; the Syrian military was in disarray; the Soviets had been ejected from Egypt. Rumours filtered out of Egypt of a collapse

81

of the air-defence network and poor morale in the army. In Jerusalem, Moshe Dayan told a convention of paratroopers that Israel was 'on the threshold of the crowning era of the return to Zion'. It was heady stuff. A few days later in a dramatic speech atop Masada mountain, he attributed these propitious times to two factors: 'the superiority of our forces over our enemies', and 'the jurisdiction of the Israeli Government from the Jordan to the Suez'.[2]

There were, however, clouds on that part of the horizon which faced Cairo. A week or so before the Beirut raid, Egyptian President Anwar Sadat had warned a *Newsweek* reporter that Israel's occupation and settlement of Arab lands, and America's unreserved military and diplomatic support for Israel, were pushing Egypt toward a 'military solution', at least in the Sinai. Egypt could not defeat Israel in a war, said Sadat, but that did not mean that a limited military blow could not and would not be struck.[3]

Slowly, the signs accumulated. A few days after the *Newsweek* interview, Iraq delivered a squadron of Hunter fighter planes to Egypt. A week later, Libya provided a squadron of Mirage aircraft. From Russia came arms deliveries which reflected a new (or perhaps resumed) supply relationship fraught with danger for Israel. MiG 23 fighters began to arrive in May, as well as Scud surface-to-surface missiles, armoured personnel carriers, Sagger anti-tank guided weapons, and SAM-6 anti-aircraft missiles. The Soviets even agreed to send back to Egypt the MiG 25 high-altitude reconnaissance aircraft which had been pulled out in July 1972.[4]

The rumour was that Egyptian forces would attempt to cross the Canal in mid-May. Taking no chances, the IDF declared a state of alert code-named 'Blue-White', on the southern front. Through the late spring and early summer of 1973, the possibility of a surprise Egyptian attack continued to preoccupy the IDF High Command, engendering seemingly endless discussions and operational planning sessions. The repeated mobilization crises were costly for the Israeli economy in terms of lost working days, as reserves were alternately activated and deactivated. This predicament was resolved, finally, when the

Nixon Administration agreed to share regularly with Israel high-altitude, high-resolution photographs, showing the exact disposition of Egyptian armed forces. At the United Nations Security Council, Israeli Ambassador Abba Eban proudly displayed these same photographs as evidence of Egypt's threatening moves. They were, he said, obtained by the Israeli Air Force.[5]

Throughout this period, however, Israeli military intelligence issued report after report denigrating the ability of the Egyptian Army to do anything significant in secret, much less undertake a full-scale invasion. It was also thought unlikely that Syria and Egypt could co-ordinate an invasion. Given the sorry state of the Syrian armed services, said Modiin (IDF Intelligence Branch), Syria would be likely to do no more than open fire in a symbolic show of sympathy if Egypt were to attempt a military operation in Sinai.[6] On 30 July Dayan gave an interview to *Time Magazine* in which he predicted that no war would break out for ten years. In mid-August condition 'Blue-White', the military alert, was cancelled. In September the chief of the IDF Southern Command, General Ariel Sharon, retired to enter public life. One of his last official acts was to propose that the Bar Lev line be dismantled.

In Syria, the late summer and early autumn saw the installation of an advanced integrated anti-aircraft missile system which included the SAM-6, a missile that Israeli planes had never faced. In the early, devastating hours of the Six Day War, Syria had not had a single anti-aircraft missile deployed. Now that lacuna had been corrected.

In a remote corner of upper Egypt a secret training exercise was being conducted, involving co-ordinated boat and bridge crossings of a fake canal constructed for the exercise. On 20 September the Egyptian Army began night-time deployments of artillery along the canal. Under cover of darkness, bridging sections and ferry components were moved to final concentration points. And on 27 September the Egyptian High Command announced its twenty-third mobilization of the Army in nine months.[7]

The IDF yawned. It was a game they had grown tired off.

Later, IDF Chief of Staff David Elazar would tell a commission investigating the disaster of the surprise attack that Israeli military intelligence had received four hundred messages signalling the impending war. Some he had ignored. Others were never even passed to him.[8]

A day of atonement

6 October 1973: 2 p.m. Even the Israeli sentries in the sheltered revetments atop their strongpoints along the Bar Lev line might not have noticed the black dots on the horizon, or the fact that the dots were growing larger. The white heat rising from the sand would have made the dots dance as they came on. And then, the dots exploded into form and sound as two hundred Egyptian fighter bombers streaked over the Suez Canal at low altitude. The planes were gone in an instant, headed for Israeli airfields and armour bases deep in the Sinai.

But the Israeli soldiers, regulars, many of whom were veterans of previous wars, would have guessed what was going to happen next. Across the Canal, the artillery boomed. Suddenly the sand and concrete on and around their bunkers came alive. There was noise and concussion and fire everywhere. Jagged pieces of metal whistled through the dust and smoke. The Bar Lev line had become hell in a very fortified place. From most of the strongpoints, the Israeli soldiers could not see the Canal itself, because it was hidden behind a huge, sixty-feet-high wall of sand pushed up to the eastern side of the Canal by their own bulldozers, as protection against what was about to take place.

On the Egyptian side, the waiting in the afternoon heat had been hard. The tension would not have been relieved by the slow, deliberate movements of units assuming their positions. For the first time in twenty-five years, Arab armies were preparing to invade Israeli-held territory. The War of Attrition had brought some of the confidence back in small commando actions, missile engagements, the defence of Suez City and the like. But this was a full-scale invasion, against a powerful, vengeful enemy.

The roar of the planes was the signal. Two thousand artillery pieces had been emplaced and sighted. Now, as the fighters disappeared over the Canal, the high-trajectory guns, howitzers and heavy mortars opened up on the Israelis, arching their shells over the sand barrier on the eastern side. The initial Egyptian fire plan was to hit the crew-served weapons atop the strongpoints, and the minefields and barbed wire around their perimeters.

As the barrage began, Egyptian engineer reconnaissance teams paddled across the Canal in small rubber boats to check the water for signs of oil:

> The secret weapon of the Bar Lev line was a device to transform the Canal into a moat of fire. In the early hours [of the previous day] Eyptian commandos had slipped across the water and sabotaged it.
>
> The device was simple. Beneath main Bar Lev strongpoints was a series of underground storage tanks, pipes interconnecting them and finally leading to wide nozzles down by the water's edge. A switch in each strongpoint started pumps to spray the oil over the Canal in a thin film – which a thermite bomb would then ignite. The blaze would have incinerated any Egyptian assault force . . . each Bar Lev strongpoint could pump 200 tons of oil.[9]

What the commandos had done the previous night was to encase the end of each of the oil pipes in concrete.[10] Now, as the artillery began to boom, the engineers checked to see that the concrete had held. It had.

Other small boats, carrying commandos, fairly raced across the Canal. Heavily laden with RPG-7s (rocket-propelled grenades) and Sagger anti-tank missiles with their guidance controls carried in suitcases, the commandos laboured up the sand ridge on the eastern side, and then ran to the sand ramps which the Israelis had constructed as tank platforms, in some cases arriving at the ramps just seconds ahead of the Israeli tanks.

Behind the commandos, the main assault began – four thousand men in 720 rubber dinghies came across in the first wave. A second wave came forty-five minutes later. Eight waves crossed in just over two hours. The battle was joined. At this point, engineers began assembling ferries and light and heavy bridges to get the heavy stuff across – armoured personnel carriers, tanks and mobile anti-aircraft guns and missiles to protect the bridgehead from the expected onslaught of the Israeli Air Force.

Several Western journalists were present for the crossing, and their single most vivid impression was of the order and discipline of the undertaking. Arnaud de Borchgrave wrote:

> There was none of the usual chaos I had come to expect of troop movements in covering 11 other wars. After a 2-hour trip from Cairo, 6 fellow journalists and I made our way north along the palm fringed Suez Canal. Suddenly, our Soviet-made jeeps veered sharp right through a hole in the embankment. We found ourselves bumper to bumper with hundreds of other military vehicles, all waiting to cross the Canal via pontoon bridges. But there was no confusion, no disorder . . . Soon after we had made our Canal crossing, Israeli artillery fire began to explode around us. At the first sound of the telltale whistle, a fraction of a second before impact, my companions and I ducked and ran for cover. But we soon realized that the Egyptian Army was going about the business of war practically oblivious to the shells kicking up clouds of sand nearby . . . During 4 hours in the Sinai, I didn't see a single casualty or even an ambulance.[11]

Waiting for the Egyptian Army on the eastern bank was a line of some thirty-five hardened fortifications, spaced between two and five miles apart. Behind the Israeli strongpoints was a series of fortified tank emplacements, beyond the effective range of Egyptian artillery. And behind the tank emplacements were battalion-strength concentrations of Israeli armour.

The deployment of the Israeli forces was designed so that, in the event of a main-force crossing of the Canal and direct assaults on the strongpoints, a company of tanks would be able to intervene within twenty to thirty minutes, a battalion within sixty to ninety minutes and a concentrated brigade within three to three and a half hours. The theory was that even in the 'worst case', a successfully initiated surprise attack, these forces would delay the invasion until the mobilized IDF reserves could cross the Sinai and deliver a killing blow. On 6 October the 'worst case' had materialized. As one Israeli military historian summarized, 'the surprise was total, and the ratio of forces was appalling'.[12]

To the north of Israel in the Golan Heights, the Syrian front had exploded at almost the same moment that Egyptian planes shot across the Canal. It was a co-ordinated attack, a two-front war, and from the outset the Israeli High Command was faced with decisions about the apportionment of air force sorties and reserve forces to be sent to each of the fronts. In the Golan, an infantry division and six reinforced Syrian tank battalions had penetrated the 1967 cease-fire lines at two points. Although the small IDF strongpoint on Mount Hermon fell almost immediately, the Syrian advance appeared to bog down in the late afternoon and, initially at least, did not seem to pose as great a threat as did Egyptian forces in the Sinai. IDF Chief of Staff Elazar would later observe 'It was 2 or 3 in the morning before we began to realize how serious the situation was, after a few more waves of assault during the latter half of the night.'[13]

One of the most disturbing aspects of the Egyptian assault to the IDF command was the boldness of it. The two hundred plus planes that began the war attacked targets deep in the Sinai, causing serious damage at Refidim, Ofira and Um Hashiba air bases. At the onset of dusk, helicopters dropped four battalions of commandos behind Israeli lines to attack radar and communications installations, and to set ambushes for Israeli units rushing to the front. By morning the Egyptians had put the astounding total of 90,000 men, 850 tanks and 11,000 vehicles across the Canal, mostly under the cover of darkness.[14]

In the first hours after the crossing, the phased Israeli response failed to go as planned. Small units of Egyptian infantry, carrying the tube-like RPG-7s and the Sagger missiles with their strange-looking suitcase guidance system, had more often than not beaten Israeli armour in the race to the tank firing platforms between the Canal and the Bar Lev fortifications. As IDF tanks came forward, they began to take heavy losses from these units, and in particular from the wire-guided Sagger missiles, effective at upwards of 2,000 metres. An

American military historian has summarized this phase of the fighting:

> The IDF tanks recoiled. The Arabs advanced into the desert and set up anti-tank defences in depth. Israeli tanks attacked for two days, not continuously or even at the same time, but by companies and erratically. When they did attack, they charged wild-eyed and full of elan, but they were clobbered by the Saggers at long range and ambushed by RPG-7 teams firing volleys of cheap ballistic – not controlled in flight – missiles . . . the Israelis were using tactics reminiscent of horse cavalry and were being destroyed by well dug-in and consolidated anti-tank weapons teams.[15]

Confusion, doubt, panic

At IDF Command Headquarters on the night of 6 October, Elazar began to realize that the information he was receiving from the field at both fronts was contradictory and unreliable. All he knew for sure was that the situation looked worse in the south. Minister of Defence Dayan remained optimistic through the early hours of fighting, but by late evening the confusing reports began to sow doubt in his mind as well, and (according to Elazar) he was talking of a retreat by all IDF forces to a line well back from the Canal.

Early in the morning of 7 October the situation worsened. Syrian tanks were spotted some three miles south of the Israeli Northern Command divisional headquarters, and Elazar had to consider the possibility that a large part of his forces in the Golan had been flanked and surrounded. Urgent calls came from General Schmuel Gonen, commander of Israeli forces in the Sinai, requesting air support to deal with the flood of Egyptian soldiers which he now knew was crossing in the darkness.

Elazar was determined to evacuate the strongpoints in the southern sector of the Golan. One of them, like the IDF positions on Mount Hermon in the north, was cut off and under siege. Defence Minister Dayan decided to fly north to judge for himself how critical the situation was. All involved knew that there was a good deal less room for error in the Golan than in the Sinai: as of that morning, some of the fighting was occurring within three miles of the Israeli border.

It was in the Golan in the very early hours of 7 October that Dayan began to show signs of cracking under the pressure and the pessimism. At one point he spoke of ordering the bombing of Syrian forces advancing on Ein Gev on the Sea of Galilee, even though the Syrians were in close proximity to IDF troops. Then, he ordered General Iska Shadmi to drive to the Jordan Valley to prepare the bridges for demolition. Elazar eventually countermanded this directive, but the senior officers of the Northern Command were left with the clear impression that Dayan's intent was to abandon the Golan altogether.[16]

Later that morning, IDF Command Headquarters learned that *all* the strongpoints of the Bar Lev line had been surrounded. From the Golan, Dayan flew south to visit the senior officers of the Southern Command, where he ordered another retreat, to the Artillery Road some six to eight miles east of the Canal, or in the event that line could not be held, all the way to the passes deep in the Sinai.[17]

By the afternoon of 7 October, virtually all the IDF Command Headquarters staff began to share the Defence Minister's bleak assessment of the situation. Twenty-four hours after the fighting began, the Egyptians had destroyed 90 per cent of all IDF tanks in the Sinai.[18] Barely thirty Israeli tanks stood between the Negev border and the forces Egypt had already put across the Canal, which now totalled 100,000 men, 1,020 tanks and 13,500 vehicles.[19] Dayan later wrote in his memoirs: 'I could recall no moment in the past when I had felt such anxiety . . . Israel was in danger.'[20]

Returning from the fronts, Dayan was overheard by his staff to say 'We have lost the Third Commonwealth', a Biblical reference to the destruction of the state of Israel, and the statement spread like wild-fire through the highest levels of the Israeli Government and Army. At 2.30 p.m. Dayan chaired a conference of senior officers at the Command Headquarters, and at 4 p.m. he met with Prime Minister Golda Meir and several of her cabinet ministers. Afterwards, Dayan closed the

Prime Minister's door, and privately again forecast to her the end of the State of Israel unless something drastic was done. He tendered his resignation as a way of assuming his portion of responsibility for the state of affairs.

Israeli journalists and historians who have subsequently written about the first days of the war have frequently referred to Moshe Dayan's and Golda Meir's state of mind at the time in very guarded terms. Menachem Meir, in his biography of his mother, wrote that 'something inside Dayan ... seemed to have snapped'.[21] Robert Slater, in a biography of Mrs Meir, has written that the Prime Minister ... 'was shocked to see an immobilized, pessimistic and despairing Dayan facing her', and quotes Lou Kaddar, one of her aides, to the effect that Dayan had spoken to the Prime Minister in their closed-door sessions about conditions for surrender, and that she had considered suicide rather than contemplate such a thing.[22] Hanoch Bartov, describing Dayan's speech to the IDF Command staff on 7 October, wrote of 'the emotional upheaval that gripped the staff as they witnessed the collapse of an entire world view and with it the image of a leader who had embodied it with such charismatic power'.[23] Mrs Meir herself, in her autobiography, wrote of having nearly 'gone to pieces' after hearing Dayan out.[24]

Jericho!

In America, the Washington Special Action Group on the Middle East Crisis (WSAG), chaired by Secretary of State Henry Kissinger, had several contacts with Dayan on 7 and 8 October which caused genuine concern about his mental state. Sam Hoskinson, who represented the CIA on WSAG, has spoken of Dayan's evident panic: 'He went batshit.'[25] William Quandt, a senior NSC staffer who also attended WSAG meetings, confirms that Dayan's condition was a matter of deep concern to the Group in the early stages of the war.[26]

It was in this context that US intelligence, through electronic communications intercepts, learned that one 'defensive' measure being prepared by the Israeli Government, in the event that Egyptian forces broke through the passes in the Sinai in the dark days of 7 and 8 October, was the arming of Jericho missiles. William Quandt:

> There was some evidence that the Jerichos were being readied, but I don't know what they had on the ends of them, if anything. But you can begin to infer that if you're going to contemplate the use of a relatively inaccurate surface-to-surface missile, it's not for very precise targeting on a place like Golan, or places where you might have your own population. The only sense it makes is as a threat against Egypt proper or possibly for some use in Sinai around the passes.[27]

In fact US military intelligence, or that part of it directly concerned with nuclear proliferation, had known for years that the missile was being developed as a nuclear weapons delivery system. In 1965 the air attaché at the US Embassy in Tel Aviv had reported that a 'usually reliable' senior IDF source had revealed that an early version of the Jericho was then being tested on the Isle of Levant off the southern coast of France. The source indicated that when the test series was completed (in co-operation with the French Government), the missile would have 'the right kind of warhead'.[28]

In succeeding years, this missile became a primary collection target of US intelligence operations in Israel. Photographs were obtained, and at least one test firing of the weapon was monitored via satellite, but US intelligence was not certain how many of the weapons had been produced and stockpiled, or where they were stored. About one year prior to the Yom Kippur War, a military attaché at the US Embassy in Tel Aviv 'got close to' the Jericho, and was declared *persona non grata* by the Israeli Government. By 1973 the US Government has 'confirmed but not proven' intelligence on the performance characteristics of the missile and its nuclear warhead. Enough information had been obtained, however, for the Jericho to be featured in the 'Grey Book', a constantly updated compendium of current nuclear weapons capabilities maintained by a nuclear proliferation sub-group of the US Intelligence Board.[29]

The communications intercept revealing the arming and

preparation for firing of the Jerichos in Israel was made on Sunday afternoon, 7 October. By Sunday evening, Washington, DC time, this information was causing great concern in the higher echelons of the Nixon Administration. Nuclear weapons intelligence is closely held, however, and according to Quandt, the matter was never formally discussed by WSAG, though the word spread very quickly at the White House and NSC.[30]

Quite apart from what was already known in Washington about the panic that had gripped the Israeli leadership in the hours after the attack, the Jericho information was disturbing because of the sheer logic of the situation. If 100,000 Egyptian soldiers were indeed to breach the passes and traverse the desolate Sinai on their way to the Israeli border, the use of a tactical nuclear weapon against massed infantry and armour in or just east of the passes would make terrifying sense, the more so because it would send a sober message to Syrian troops who might be tempted (and seemed at the time able) to head down off the Golan Heights and into northern Galilee. While the weapon could not have been used directly on the Golan without endangering Israeli soldiers and civilians, the populations of Damascus and Cairo would have clearly understood the message of its explosion in the wastes of Sinai.

In the early morning hours of 8 October the IDF counter-attacked on both fronts. In the north, exhausted Israeli soldiers who had been fighting for close to forty-eight hours against enormous numerical odds were asked to push the Syrians back to the 'Purple Line', where the fighting had begun on 6 October. But two Syrian brigades who were no doubt just as exhausted refused to get the message, and continued to press the attack. By now, it was obvious to all that this war was not going to be concluded in six relatively easy days, as had been the case in 1967. Moreover, the IAF had, as of the afternoon of 8 October, effectively lost over seventy planes. If airpower was to play the decisive role in 1973 that it had in 1967, the turning point in this war would have to come soon.

In the south, on 8 October the IDF's situation deteriorated badly. General Ariel Sharon, depending upon which version of the events one chooses to believe, either sent his division out on a useless mission in conscious violation of his orders, or he misunderstood what was expected of him and his division and, virtually out of communication with the other divisions in the south (Adan's and Mandler's), wandered aimlessly in the central Canal zone. Adan's and Mandler's units, with insufficient artillery and no air support at all, were badly mauled by attacking Egyptian forces. By 5 p.m. Adan was undergoing what he later described as 'the worst crisis I had experienced in four wars'.[31] By sundown, his three brigades were in full retreat.

Again, as on 6 and 7 October, IDF units in the south had fought, as Bartov has described it, 'independently and in a fragmented manner'.[32] And again, armoured units had made repeated charges on dispersed infantry, and had been slaughtered by Saggers and RPG-7s. By the evening of 8 October, with Egyptian troops continuing to stream across the Canal at three or four points, Chief of Staff Elazar's main hope was that the enemy would attempt to consolidate their gains by digging in, rather than push on to the passes.

Early on the morning of 9 October at IDF Command Headquarters, Dayan addressed the general staff, proposing that civilians – the elderly, the infirm and youth below draft age – be issued anti-tank weapons to defend the heartland of Israel. He again spoke of a retreat to the passes in central Sinai, then stood and walked out of the briefing room, leaving those present 'stupefied'.[33]

It is possible that we will never know exactly how the Jericho crisis was defused. In the event, the Egyptians *did* dig in on 9 and 10 October, giving IDF reserves time to cross the Sinai and reach the southern front. Perhaps more important, the IAF managed to knock out the last of the Syrian air defence missiles and the Soviets, whether purposely or through bad planning, had a gap in the pipeline and were unable to replace them. The result was that Israeli fighter bombers made quick work, on 9 and 10 October, of Syrian armour and massed infantry.

It was the turning point of the war in the north, but just as important, it freed Israeli planes to provide air support in the south. Beginning on the afternoon and evening of 9 October, then, Israel had a powerful conventional response to any major Egyptian move toward the Sinai passes and the Negev beyond. Just how important air power was, was demonstrated on the evening of 10 October, when Israeli planes caught the Egyptian 1st Infantry Brigade in open country outside the missile umbrella as it headed down the Suez Gulf coast after defeating an Israeli unit at Ayoun Musa. The brigade lost 90 per cent of its men and equipment. El Shazly would later observe that this engagement 'disagreeably confirmed ... the underlying vulnerability of our position'.[34]

Direct pressure to de-activate the Jerichos may also have been brought upon Mrs Meir and Dayan by Henry Kissinger. During the early days of the war, Kissinger saw the Israeli Ambassador to Washington, Simcha Dimitz, several times a day, and had even installed a direct phone line between his office and the Israeli Embassy. The American Government, unlike the Israelis, was clearly focused upon the likely Soviet response to such a threat and in any event, according to William Quandt, Washington did not believe that the circumstances were present in which Israel's vital security interests were threatened. Egypt appeared to have limited objectives in the Canal crossing, were already digging in, and finally, did not have the tactical mobility to push across the barren Sinai in the face of overwhelming Israeli air superiority.

The other airlift

If Henry Kissinger did attempt to apply pressure on Israel, his influence with Meir and Dayan in those first days of the war was certainly enhanced by the fact that, literally within hours of the outbreak of the fighting, extraordinary measures were being taken by the US Defence Department to get critical weapons to the battlefield, in response to urgent requests from a discouraged, confused and frightened Israeli leadership.

This was the 'other' airlift, and should not be confused with the overt operations of the US Military Airlift Command between 13 October and 22 November 1973. In the latter case,

$2.2 billion of weapons were shipped in the largest airlift operation in military history.[35] But virtually none of the material which came in this airlift reached the battlefield in time to be deployed in the critical phases of fighting on either the northern *or* southern fronts.

The public airlift may not have had a direct impact on the fighting, except for the boost in morale it provided to the IDF in the first few days after 13 October, at a time when the Israelis were still dealing with the shock of the crossing and what had followed. But it was an impressive show. The State Department's Middle East Task Force carefully kept, at Henry Kissinger's personal insistence, daily comparative tonnage figures for the Soviet and American airlifts through the course of the war. Assigned to the operation were 22,909 US military and 4,164 civilian personnel: 276 C-141 Starlifter aircraft were used, as well as 77 giant C-5A Galaxies. The latter carried M-60 tanks (100,000 pounds each) as well as CH-53 'Jolly Green Giant' helicopters (23,000 pounds), 175 mm cannons (50,000 pounds) and 155 m howitzers (49,000 pounds). All together, 22,497 tons were airlifted in less than six weeks.[36]

By 2 November the US Military Airlift Command had equalled the Soviet airlift tonnage, and by 22 November the Soviet effort had been doubled. This in spite of the fact that the US flew 566 missions to the Soviet's 900, and had been obliged to cover 6,450 miles as against a Soviet supply line of 1,700 miles. It was an impressive show. If nothing else, the operation must have filled Arab and Soviet radar screens. One rather silly DIA report exulted:

> There have been many examples of the international significance of military airlift since World War II. The Berlin Airlift saved a city; in South Vietnam there were many examples where timely airlift of men and supplies turned the tide and now, in the Middle East it saved Israel and supports the cease-fire.[37]

In fact, less than 39 per cent of the material transported in the 'official' airlift arrived in the Middle East before the second, permanent cease-fire was effected on 24 October.[38] And of that 39 per cent, as previously indicated, virtually none made it to the battlefield before the fighting stopped.

There was, however, another airlift, much smaller than that just described but having a far greater impact on the war. It was conducted without formal authorization from the President and Congress, and may have involved violations of the agreements between the US and its NATO allies, and was at last partly responsible for the Arab oil embargo declared on 20 October.[39]

At 4 p.m. on 6 October, Washington time, some nine hours after the fighting started, Israel Defence Attaché Mordechai Gur came to the Pentagon to see General George S. Brown, Chief of Staff of the Air Force, and General Creighton Abrams, Chief of Staff of the Army. He brought an unofficial list of the urgent equipment needs of the IDF. Included were dozens of advanced weapons the export of which was proscribed for reasons of national security by the Arms Export Control Act (AECA): airborne warning and control systems (AWACs), the most advanced 'L' version of the AIM 9 air-to-air missile, and cluster bomb units (CBUs), among many, many others.[40]

Gur was convincing. After a discussion of the early, disastrous stages of the fighting, General Abrams turned to General Brown and said 'George, they will crucify our asses, but we've got to do it anyhow.' Whereupon their aides were instructed to start breaking out weapons for immediate shipment from those stocks which were immediately available: weapons of active duty, front-line units in the US and Europe. Within hours of the meeting, Abrams travelled to Europe, where he stripped weapons from US Seventh Army units and arranged for both air and sea (via Bremerhaven) shipment of the items. This was done without the required consultation with the Government of West Germany, and later became the subject of bitter complaints from the FRG.

The front-line units were stripped in the interest of time: their weapons were easily policed up, whereas locating and breaking out weapons from depots would have been a far more complicated process. In America air shipments from Oceana Naval Air Station in Virginia began less than twelve hours after Gur's meeting with Brown and Abrams. The weapons in this case were taken from stocks maintained at Langley, Virginia.

To be sure, the IDF did not get the *exact* weapons requested

... at least not always. The Oceana flights, for example, sent AIM 9-J missiles, not the AIM 9-L version of the weapon requested by Gur.[41] The first plane to leave Oceana was an El Al 747 cargo jet which took off at 2 a.m. on Sunday morning, 7 October.

Early shipments out of Oceana contained, in addition to the AIM 9 missiles, artillery and tank ammunition (particularly 105 Heat rounds) and cluster bomb units (CBUs). The latter were clearly proscribed for export. Early European shipments included the AIM 9-Js, mortars and 155 m howitzer ammunition, 105 m tank rounds and communications equipment. Also sent were Tow anti-tank guided weapons (ATGWs) and Redeye anti-aircraft missiles, which were also proscribed for export at the time.

The arms shipped in the early, covert airlift arrived in time to be utilized in the extensive fighting that developed during the critical week of 10–17 October on the southern front, when the tide of battle was gradually, finally turned in Israel's favour. The weapons were rushed to the front, however, at considerable cost to US relations with the Arab world.

Beginning on 10 October, US planes flew the weapons directly into El Arish in occupied Sinai, cutting the supply line in distance and time. Egyptian air defence radar tracked the planes into their territory. Strangely the Egyptian Government, which had known for several days of the covert airlift itself, and had taken that blow with equanimity, was enraged at the fact of the direct shipments to the battlefield. The flights were a violation of Egyptian territorial integrity, and appeared to the Egyptians to be a more direct form of US intervention in the conflict.[42] James E. Akins, who at about this time left the Near East-South Asia section at the State Department to become US Ambassador to Saudi Arabia, maintains that it was the direct flights into El Arish which finally tipped the balance among Arab leaders in favour of the oil embargo.[43]

On 12 October, five days after the 'other' airlift began, a Pentagon spokesman acknowledged that a 'minor effort' was under way to provide Israel with a 'few cargoes' of ammunition and Sidewinder and Sparrow missiles. The shipments were said to be advance deliveries on orders already placed before the fighting had begun.[44] There is minimizing and there is lying. This particular bit of 'public information' was considerably closer to the latter.

Another one of those bitter, ironic postscripts

On 14 October the Egyptian High Command, under pressure from President Sadat and his Minister of Defence General Ahmed Ismail Ali, brought the Egyptian Army out from under the missile umbrella, and began an ill-fated drive toward the Sinai passes. 'The outcome', as General El Shazly later wrote, 'was predictable.'[45] Israeli air power and re-supplied armour cut the Second and Third Armies to pieces, though not without taking further heavy losses themselves. With an Israeli bridge-head established on the western side of the Canal, and the Egyptian Third Army surrounded, a first cease-fire was concluded on 22 October and a second and final one on 24 October. The Yom Kippur War was concluded. Israel again had the Sinai and the Arabs again had their self-respect.

The early aid provided by the US to Israel on the initiative of Generals Abrams and Brown had, as previously indicated, been important in the critical, middle stages of the war. Furthermore, by proceeding on their own to break out and prepare arms for shipment, Abrams and Brown prevented enormous further delays in the official airlift when President Nixon did finally, unequivocally approve it on 13 October, after a solid week of in-fighting on the matter between two members of his cabinet.[46] When the authorization was finally given, the critical stuff was selected and ready to go.

Finally, the 'other' airlift provided tangible evidence of US solidarity with Israel and commitment to its security at a time when that country's leadership was desperately pessimistic about the course of the fighting and considering the use of nuclear weapons to stave off 'the end of the Third Commonwealth'. We may not soon know what role the timely US aid played in the decision *not* to use the Jericho missiles. Understandably, neither Mrs Meir nor General Dayan has touched upon the nuclear aspects of the Yom Kippur War in their meetings and public statements since the event, and both are now dead. Israeli military censorship is not likely to allow their aides to address this matter soon, even if any are so inclined.

In August 1974, less than a year after the war, General Creighton W. Abrams died of cancer at the age of fifty-nine. General George S. Brown was appointed Chairman of the Joint Chiefs of Staff and lived five years after the war, dying also of cancer in 1978. They were five years of controversy, however, because of a series of statements General Brown made about the role of Jews in American politics, and about US–Israeli relations. During this time General Brown became a target of frequent attacks by leaders of American Jewish organizations. On 6 December 1978, the day after his death, the *New York Times* ran an obituary of General Brown, recounting in some detail the controversy and the statements, made at Duke University in one instance, to a French journalist in another, etc.

The obituary neglected to mention, however, the role that General Brown had played in preventing the fall of the Third Commonwealth.

SEVEN

Middle East Watershed – Egypt's Unilateral Disarmament, 1973–9

During its first quarter century, 1948–73, Israel defeated its neighbours in three wars and scored a creditable draw in the fourth, the War of Attrition. None of these victories reassured Israel's leaders or its staunch supporters in the United States and Western Europe who said, at least, that they feared the Jewish homeland was about to be driven into the sea.

In fact, through all but the last few months of this period, Israel maintained a decisive military edge over the other countries of the region. The Arabs, individually and collectively, simply lacked the essential elements of an advanced regional military power, namely modern military hardware, a technological base including trained manpower, and a great power willing to provide all of these unreservedly and on soft financial terms.

Even before the foundation of the modern state of Israel, Jewish Palestinians were able effectively to draw upon the (private) financial and manpower resources of the international Jewish community. Advanced nuclear energy research, carried out by scientists trained in Europe and America, was being conducted at the Weizmann Institute in Tel Aviv even before the birth of the state of Israel. In the mid-1950s France became Israel's security partner and armourer, and sold Israel state-of-the-art fighters and bombers, as well as the most advanced nuclear reactor in the Middle East. French planes and pilots even flew air cover for Israel in the Suez War in 1956.

By contrast, Syria, Egypt and Iraq received from the Soviet Union only dated planes, tanks and other weapons, albeit in large numbers. As the wars of 1956 and 1967 showed, the Arab equipment and training were substantially inferior to those of the IDF. Moreover, the Arab armies receiving this material were trained and ultimately moulded by a Soviet military doctrine which was essentially defensive in nature. Finally, the Soviets drew a strict line against assisting the Arabs with any non-conventional weapons programmes, whether chemical-biological, radiological or nuclear – a line that neither France nor America was willing to draw where Israel was concerned.

In 1965–7 America replaced France as Israel's armourer, and shortly thereafter shipped to the region the most advanced and complex weapons system ever seen there – the nuclear-capable F-4 Phantom fighter bomber. As we have seen, the Soviets finally responded, bringing into the region for the first time advanced air defence rockets and fighter-interceptors, together with sufficient technicians and pilots to both train Egyptian cadres and man the systems until the Egyptians could handle the weapons in actual engagements. The result was that in 1970–3 Egypt developed a considerable defensive capability *vis-à-vis* Israel, in that the missile umbrella erected around the Suez Canal could and did make further attacks on Egyptian soil very expensive indeed for the Israeli Air Force.

In the first few days of the October 1973 war, the Egyptian Army even demonstrated a modest offensive capability, successfully attacking Israeli front-line fortified positions under that missile umbrella. None of the military professionals involved – the Soviets, the US Defence Department, the IDF and the Arabs – failed to appreciate the significance of 'Operation Badr'. Nor did the American airlift and the eventual outcome of the 1973 war blunt this appreciation. The strategic balance in the Middle East in 1970–3 had begun to shift slightly but perceptibly toward the Arabs.

And then, a stunning thing occurred. Between 1973 and 1979, the year in which the peace treaty was signed with Israel, Egypt became the first nation in modern history to disarm unilaterally while in a formal state of war with a powerful neighbour. What makes this even more remarkable is that in this same period, Israel dramatically increased its military power. The Center for Strategic Studies at Tel Aviv University has summarized the principal characteristics of

Israel's build-up before and just after Camp David (1973–80) as follows.

(a) A significant increase in ground forces order of battle by the addition of three armoured mechanized divisions.
(b) A marked quantitative and qualitative increase in combat material, tanks (mostly of high quality), armoured personnel carriers and artillery – to complement the increased order of battle; and increase of 1,300 tanks and 600 artillery pieces (including mortars).
(c) The establishment of an anti-tank missile network force of various models. The number of anti-tank missile launchers increased from 50 in 1973 to approximately 500 in 1980.
(d) Improvement in air defence by the addition of five surface-to-air missile batteries (of the Hawk and improved-Hawk varieties).
(e) Continuation of the build-up in airpower (including latest model F-15 aircraft).[1]

For whatever reason, the Center for Strategic Studies at Tel Aviv University failed to include in this summary the dramatic strides made in acquiring and testing major offensive strategic weapons, including nuclear warheads jointly tested with South Africa in 1977–9 and nuclear-capable F-15 aircraft and Lance missile systems to deliver them, obtained from the United States.

In the same document, the Center for Strategic Studies summarized what it termed the Egyptian 'build-up' during 1973–80 as 'a modest increase in the ground forces order of battle . . . an increase in the number of anti-tank missile launchers . . . [and] a reduction of air force strength'.[2]

A more impartial source examining the same subject sees no Egyptian 'build-up' at all, modest or otherwise. John Keegan, writing in 1979 in *World Armies*, noted that in the six years since the 1973 war Egypt had not even replaced the tanks lost in that war. In fact, Keegan said, 'scarcely anything new had been bought for the army since 1973 except anti-tank guided weapons'. The Egyptian Navy and Air Force had done nothing more than replace or recondition some of the old Russian equipment in this period, and the Air Force, according to Keegan, had severely reduced the numbers of its operational (i.e. battle-ready) aircraft as well as the average monthly flying hours of its pilots.[3]

The statistics for arms imports for Egypt and Israel in the post-war period, 1974–9, tell a similar dramatic story.[4] Egypt, whose arms imports had exceeded those of Israel by more than two to one in the four years prior to the war, suddenly decreased the level in 1974. From 1974 to 1979 Egypt imported only $1.73 billion in arms, less than one-third of the amount of Israeli arms imports in the same period ($5.2 billion). The table below shows the relative expenditures year by year.[5]

Arms Imports in Current Millions of US Dollars		
Year	Egypt	Israel
1970	650	230
1971	350	260
1972	550	300
1973	850	230
Totals 1970–73	2,400	1,020
1974	230	950
1975	350	725
1976	150	975
1977	270	1,100
1978	360	925
1979	370	525
Totals 1974–79	1,730	5,200

Similar conclusions may be drawn when one looks at development in the composition and equipment of the opposing forces. Between 1973 and 1979, Egypt's active army manpower increased by 4.6 per cent, from 260,000 to 272,000. But in the same period Israel's total mobilizable army manpower (i.e. including the reservists, who had fought creditably in every previous Middle East war) rose from 275,000 to 375,000, an increase of 36.3 per cent. Egyptian operational combat aircraft in this period dropped from 768 to 563, while Israel's increased from 488 to 720. Egyptian medium-tank strength in the period dropped from 1,880 to 1,680, while Israel's rose from 1,700 to 3,000. Even more dramatic was Israel's rate of acquisition of armoured personnel carriers during the period. From 1973 to 1979 Egypt increased its APCs from 2,076 to 3,080, while Israel more than doubled its strength, from 3,450 to 8,000, greatly enhancing the IDF's mobility and deep-strike invasion capability.

To be sure, substantial strength increases in the armed forces of the other Arab 'confrontation' states are not included in these totals. Jordan and Syria, for example, more than doubled their medium-tank strength during this period. Without question, part of the motivation for Israel's build-up derived from the new arms flowing into these other countries. The point here, however, is that Egypt was fast losing ground to both Israel and the other Arab states, and its influence diminished accordingly.

By late 1976 Egypt's traditional role as the Arab military counterweight to Israel had been emasculated; the army was reduced by attrition to 25–30 per cent of the military capability it had had prior to the October war, and Israel was militarily astride the Middle East more surely and completely than it had been since the 1948 war.

The question one might ask is 'Why did Sadat do it?' Why would a country emerging from the extended frustration of the Jarring negotiations (1968–71) and the equally sterile Kissinger/Rogers diplomatic initiatives (1969–73), a country which had finally, after twenty-five years of trying, developed the trained manpower and the industrial and technological base to begin to deal with its enemies, voluntarily lay down its arms and opt for negotiations?

Mark Heller of the Jaffee Center for Strategic Studies at Tel Aviv University has given the conventional, if somewhat unsatisfying, explanation.

During the October 1973 war, the [Egyptian] army reached its peak in size and strength. However, the policy adopted by President Sadat after 1973, political negotiations to resolve the conflict with Israel and a shift toward a pro-American orientation, together with the economic burden of the post-war period, caused

Egypt to fall behind Israel and other Arab states in the Middle
East arms race.[6]

Without question, Egypt's defence expenditures had reached
intolerable levels in the early 1970s – approximately 35 to 40 per
cent of the total national budget. That is close to the level of
defence 'burden' which nearly ruined the Israel economy in the
early 1980s. But Egypt then, like Israel in Lebanon, had bene-
factors able and willing to absorb that burden.

The Soviet Union was still an option for Egypt after the 1973
war. The flow of arms from that source had continued through
the war, in spite of the humiliation of Sadat's edicts in July
1972. Indeed, it was not until much later that Egypt burned the
last of its bridges, ejecting the remaining advisers and closing
Soviet port facilities in 1974 and abrogating the Soviet–
Egyptian Friendship Treaty in 1976.

Nor were the doors to the oil-rich Arab Gulf states closed
until Anwar Sadat went to Jerusalem in 1977 on the first leg of
his personal peace process. He still had in his pocket Arab
offers to underwrite the Egyptian economy, and any future war
effort, to the extent of $2.5 billion a year. In the years immedi-
ately following the 1973 war, the phenomenal rise in oil prices
drove Arab oil wealth to its apex, relative to other regional
economies. The Arabs could have re-armed Egypt in style,
purchasing heavily from both European and Eastern Bloc arms
markets.

True, Egypt faced political, economic *and* social problems
that had reached crisis proportions by 1977. Nevertheless,
Sadat would not have been the first Third World leader to have
staved off internal dissent by moving his country toward (yet
another) war, had he chosen to do so.

In the end, it may have been promises of arms from another
source – America – that led Sadat down the garden path of
disarmament by attrition. According to Major General
Muhammad Abdel Ghany el-Gamasy, who was Egyptian
Minister of Defence during the period of the disarming, Anwar
Sadat relied heavily on promises of future purchases of advanced American arms, promises that came personally from US

Secretary of State (and National Security Adviser) Henry Kissinger.[7]

The first face-to-face discussions on the subject occurred during the early stages of the Kilometre 101 negotiations in November 1973, on the separation of forces following the Yom Kippur War, and then soon afterwards during the 'Egyptian–Israeli shuttle' negotiations in January 1974. In April and May 1975 Kissinger brought to Egypt tangible, if token, evidence of the willingness of America to sell Egypt arms once a peace treaty with Israel had been signed: he arranged for the diversion to Egypt of six C-130 transport planes destined for Libya. Sadat was impressed, apparently, for this was about the time that Egypt ceased purchasing Soviet arms.

General Gamasy and Egyptian Foreign Minister Ismail Fahmy were cut out of these 'back channel' discussions between Sadat and Kissinger, and were only informed of the results later.[8] Interestingly enough, neither Sadat nor Kissinger mentions the discussions on future Egyptian arms purchases in their respective memoirs.[9] General Gamasy is still working on *his* book.

Long before Carter, Sadat and Begin gathered to talk peace at Camp David in September 1978, Israel began to take into account the new military map of the Middle East, in determining its policies toward the other countries of the region. With Egypt gradually neutering itself through attrition in its armed forces, it was only human nature for Israel to begin to take a far more active, assertive role throughout the Middle East.

In August 1975, for example, Israel agreed to return to Egypt the Abu Rudeis oilfields in the Sinai as part of the force disengagement process begun almost two years earlier, with the participation of Henry Kissinger. At almost the same time, however, Israel began negotiating oil exploration agreements for other sites in the occupied Sinai, with a Texas oil drilling concern. The deal caused a furore in the Israeli Knesset because three American Jewish millionaires were granted minority interests in the venture.[10] Drilling of exploration wells near El Tur, on the Gulf of Suez coast, began in November 1975.

Presumably, the concession included offshore rights in the Gulf as well.

The Government of Egypt, however, with the support of the US State Department, claimed for itself the right to explore for oil in these same waters off El Tur, and signed a concession agreement with Amoco, an American company, to begin development. This might have appeared to Amoco and to the US and Egyptian governments to be a legal issue, but it wasn't. When Amoco sent a vessel into the area to begin work, Israeli gunboats turned it away and fired on the markers and structures used in prospecting.[11]

It was not a legal issue because Israel had the military means at hand quickly to resolve the dispute in its favour. America did not have the political will to respond to Israeli force with force of its own and Egypt simply did not have the planes, ships and rockets with which to respond. Ambassadors were called in, protest notes were sent, and so on. After all that was finished, Amoco quietly ceased exploration. In the spring of 1977, the Israelis began drilling in earnest off El Tur, while the State Department 'reiterated its contention that the drilling was illegal' and added sternly that the Israeli action was 'not helpful to efforts to get peace negotiations under way'.[12]

Egypt's decision to remove itself from the Middle East military equation meant that every other Arab country stood alone where Israel was concerned. Not surprisingly, the IDF began to pay some aggressive visits to other parts of the region, including some countries which had had relatively peaceful relations with Israel for decades. In 1975 Israel began repeatedly violating Saudi Arabian airspace, overflying Red Sea ports and even northern Saudi air bases. In 1977 two Israeli F-4s even touched down at Tabuk air base, dropping empty fuel tanks as they did.[13] It was a campaign of humiliation against America's oldest and perhaps closest security partner in the Arab Middle East. At first, US officials protested to the Israelis, but when that had no effect, as the overflights continued into the early 1980s the Reagan Administration finally (in 1982) agreed to an established frequency of overflights.[14] Some security partner!

It was also in 1975 that Israel first began direct meddling in

Lebanese internal affairs, at the beginning of that country's civil war. Regular contacts were established with the Christian Phalange, and in the following year Israeli arms began flowing to the Phalange, including anti-tank rockets and tanks, as well as hand-carried weapons. In March 1978 Israel took 25,000 troops into Lebanon to occupy temporarily the area south of the Litani. Syrian troops already in Lebanon as part of an Arab League peacekeeping force invited by the Lebanese Government, were in no position to resist the Israeli invasion. In previous Middle East wars, Syria had counted on Egypt's opening a 'southern front'. But now in 1978, with Egypt disarmed, Syria had virtually no military option *vis-à-vis* Israel.

When Anwar Sadat dramatically announced in November 1977 his willingness to go to Jerusalem, Menachem Begin responded quickly with an invitation to the Egyptian leader to address the Knesset. The presumption was, as President Jimmy Carter has written in his memoirs, that after this symbolic gesture the major disputants in the Middle East conflict would move toward a multinational peace conference in Geneva.[15] It was a time of particular vulnerability for Sadat, however, as most Arab governments and indeed many Egyptians, viewed Sadat's peace initiative as a sell-out to their long-time common enemy. Israeli leaders did not seem, at least in Carter's view, to understand the fragility of the peace prospects. After a particularly acrimonious meeting between Begin and Sadat in Ismailia in December 1977, Carter summarized the situation as he understood it:

> The Israelis were not honouring the commitment Dayan had given me about their settlement policy, but were building up those enclaves in the occupied territories as rapidly as possible. Whenever we seemed to be having some success with the Arabs, Begin would proclaim the establishment of another group of settlements, or make other provocative statements. This behaviour was not only very irritating, but it seriously endangered the prospects for peace and Sadat's status both in Egypt and within the Arab world. The repeated Israeli invasions or bombings of Lebanon also precipitated crises; a stream of fairly harsh messages was going back and forth between me in Washington and Begin in Jerusalem.[16]

After a good deal of pushing and hauling by Jimmy Carter, however, the three leaders finally gathered at Camp David,

Maryland in September 1978. No one was sure at the time
whether this was a meeting to negotiate peace, or merely a
meeting to agree to continue to meet.

Unfortunately Anwar Sadat came with his pockets empty.
His armed forces were weakened and, naturally, demoralized.
His popularity was at a low ebb, as the food riots in Cairo in
January 1977 had demonstrated. His relationships with other
Arab governments, so important to the Egyptian economy, had
deteriorated steadily through the successive force disengage-
ment agreements, and the trip to Jerusalem.

One person who was fully aware of Sadat's position was
Menachem Begin. Three respected Israeli journalists have described Begin's veiw of Sadat's peace 'initiative' as follows:

> Begin was not unmindful of Sadat's courage in proposing the visit
> to Jerusalem, but he also regarded Sadat's move as an act of
> weakness, even desperation. The Egyptian president would not
> have taken this risk, Begin thought, if he had had any choice.[17]

In effect, Sadat had already surrendered the single most important bargaining chip in his possession – Egypt's central role in
the Arab–Israeli military balance. All Sadat could offer to trade
was a peace treaty with Israel which would be little more than a
formalized recognition of what was already fact: Israel's total
military domination of the region.

Curiously enough, there is scant reference to this basic context to the Camp David meetings, by some of the key participants who have written of the event subsequently. One searches
in vain in the exhaustive account of the Camp David process in
Jimmy Carter's memoirs, *Keeping Faith*, for any mention of
Egypt's disarming and Sadat's position as a military mendicant.
Anwar Sadat himself nowhere acknowledges the military factor
in his autobiography, *In Search of Identity*. Even William
Quandt, American Middle East and national security expert
and Camp David participant, makes no reference to this subject
in his more recent, authoritative account, *Camp David:
Peacemaking and Politics*.[18]

It would appear that after Camp David, a consonance of
interest existed to depict the accords as a fair bargain, freely

struck. Nothing could be further from the truth.

True, Egypt emerged from the meetings (and subsequent treaty-signing in March 1979) with a promise that the Sinai would be returned. But it also emerged totally dependent upon the US for its economic and military needs, and therefore frozen in a position of inferiority *vis-à-vis* Israel. Relations with both the Arab world and the Soviet Bloc lay in total shambles.

Israel seemingly left Camp David with little more than a 'scrap of paper': the Egyptian–Israeli Peace Treaty. It is not until one observes Israeli Government behaviour since Camp David, that one comes to understand what the piece of paper meant . . . in terms of Jewish settlements in the West Bank, the annexation of the Golan, the stagnation of the peace process on the Palestinian issue and a series of military adventures which become a major focus of the second half of this book.

The disarming of Egypt was, in terms of its effect on the Middle East conflict, more important than the 1973 war, and arguably was even more important than the 1967 war, which gave Israel the occupied territories. The Camp David Accords merely confirmed Egypt's status as a huge eunuch in the Arab world. Egypt's disarmament, simply put, made Jerusalem the administrative capital of the Middle East, controlling the military and security policies, and in most respects, the foreign policies of the other countries of the region. Prior to 1973–8, tensions ebbed and flowed in the region and occasionally flared into violence, as the superpowers manoeuvred and threatened in the background. The possibility of a negotiated resolution of the roots of the conflict was constantly, hopefully hovering in the area, as Western intermediaries moved from capital to capital.

After the disarming of Egypt, and most particularly after Camp David there was, as Menachem Begin constantly publicly reminded us, nothing left to negotiate. Henceforth, disputes between Israel and its neighbours would be fairly and equitably, and certainly swiftly, adjudicated by the Israeli Air Force.

EIGHT

Pariahs with Bombs: the South Atlantic Nuclear Test, 1979

It was Friday evening, 21 September, and the bars along Highway A1A in Cocoa Beach, Florida were buzzing with business. Just to the north, night-duty NASA staff at Cape Canaveral were preparing for the first shuttle launch, then planned for the following summer. To the south of Cocoa, at Patrick Air Force Base, the work hadn't stopped either, for this is headquarters for the US Air Force's Nuclear Detection Agency.

It was not going to be a routine evening at Patrick. Shortly before 9 p.m. a uniformed technician saw a stylus on one of his monitors draw two big blips. The machine, called a 'downlink console', was registering coded electronic signals from one of the Vela series of satellites – America's primary means of detecting nuclear explosions around the globe. Built by TRW Corporation, twelve Velas had been launched in 1963–70, into near-circular orbits at altitudes of 60–70,000 miles. From this height, each satellite's double sensors viewed nearly half the earth's surface.

The watch officer was called over as computers whirred, calculating the exact place and time of the twin flashes of light which had been picked up by the satellite's two optical sensors. The signals were checked. The blips were examined. It was the characteristic signature of a nuclear blast.

The place: the Prince Edward Islands, about 1,500 miles south-east of Cape of Good Hope, South Africa, roughly halfway between South Africa and the continent of Antarctica. The time: shortly before 5 a.m. (22 September) local time at the sight of the light source. Most, if not everyone standing around the console at Cocoa Beach that evening would have been aware that nuclear tests are usually conducted just before dawn,

III

to allow both a visual check of radiation yields in the dark, and then measurement of radiation debris and blast effects as soon as light permits.

It was enough. US Air Force Intelligence Chief Major General George Keegan later explained what would then have happened, in the normal course of events:

> We'd have gotten an indication I'd say within two to three minutes, delivered to our headquarters at Colorado Springs, to the Joint Chiefs of Staff command post in the Pentagon, and that information would have been in the hands of the national defence leadership within five minutes, and were it a nuclear event of serious implications, within the President's hand a very few short minutes after that time.[1]

The Carter Administration certainly would have considered an explosion near South Africa 'a nuclear event of serious implications', as that country had a widely known nuclear weapons programme in a very pregnant stage of development, and yet South Africa had signed the Nuclear Test Ban Treaty in 1963. During the night, Secretary of Defence Harold Brown and National Security Adviser Zbigniew Brzezinski conferred with President Carter at the White House. And the next morning, Sunday morning in Washington, a crisis committee of ten to twelve people was assembled to deal with the matter. Gerald Funk, who was at the time the senior Africa specialist on the National Security Council staff, remembers a phone call from his boss early that morning:

> I was told by Zbig to get my toucus into work, that we had a little bit of a problem. As I recall, we first convened a meeting in the Situation Room of the White House. [Presidential Science Adviser] Frank Press was there and in charge. The first reports, as we met that day and in the days immediately following . . . my assumption was that there had been in fact a legitimate sighting. In other words that satellite had never failed to react positively, and had never given a false signal.[2]

The 'problem' referred to by Mr Brzezinski could have been any or all of the political issues which would be raised by a nuclear explosion in this part of the South Atlantic. If a test had indeed been conducted, the most likely candidate – geographically at least – would have been South Africa, possessor of the Prince Edward Islands. South Africa had signed the Nuclear Test Ban Treaty, and its possession of a bomb would weaken both this and the Nuclear Non-proliferation Treaty of 1968, in the eyes of Third World governments around the globe. More directly, a South African bomb would raise questions about US overt 'official' assistance to the South African nuclear energy programme, and covert assistance to that country's nuclear weapons programme, about which there had been revelations in a US federal district court the previous year.

To complicate matters, some in the White House Situation Room knowledgeable about the close South African–Israeli co-operation in military matters speculated from the beginning that Israel might have been involved in the nuclear test, if that is what it was. If proven true, the 'Symington Amendment' would by law necessitate the termination of US economic and military aid to Israel just as the 1980 presidential election campaign was warming up.[3] Politically then, the situation was a nightmare. What the White House crisis managers did not anticipate, however, was difficulty in verifying the Vela sighting itself.

Normally, the next step in determining whether a test has in fact been conducted involves the sending of US Air Force high-altitude reconnaissance aircraft to the test site, or to a point downwind (i.e. east) of the test site, to collect air samples which are measured for radiation. In this instance the remote location of the satellite sighting complicated the process, resulting in delays before the 'sweeps' could be made. When they were made a few days later, however, no significant non-natural radiation was found.[4]

The White House crisis group, composed of mid-level White House, Defence and State Department, National Security Council and CIA staffers, continued to meet in the succeeding days, and continued to hope for a 'smoking gun' in the form of radiation samples. That would at least permit the group to turn with confidence to an assessment of the political problems posed by the nuclear event which all involved were fairly certain had occurred. But the samples never came.

As the days wore on, the group met less and less frequently. The meetings were moved out of the White House basement and over to the West Executive Office Building, and they became more formal in tone. When no unusual levels of radiation were found, several of the members of this informal group began to pin their hopes on human and/or electronic intelligence. If there had been a test at sea as the Vela satellite had indicated, there had surely been sea (and perhaps land) monitoring operations, unusual ship movements, secretive radio communications, etc. CIA and DIA operatives in South Africa were alerted. Sooner or later, someone would talk about it. But the intelligence never came.

Now in addition to the political problems alluded to above, the Carter Administration faced a situation in which questions were sure to be raised about America's nuclear test verification capabilities as a whole. If a nuclear explosion had *not* occurred, and the Vela satellite had given a false reading, the primary means of verifying nuclear tests worldwide might have to be rethought, revamped. It was, several in the White House quickly decided, a matter on which outside scientific advice and assistance was urgently required.

A very blue ribbon panel

In mid-October Dr Jack Ruina, a professor of electrical engineering at MIT and a former Defence Department scientist with top secret security clearances, received a phone call from his old friend, Presidential Science Adviser Frank Press, asking that he come to Washington on a 'highly classified matter'. The Vela sighting had not at this point become a matter of public knowledge, and was a closely held secret in the Carter Administration – only two or three staff members of the National Security Council were aware of the event.

Ruina was asked to chair an *ad hoc* panel of distinguished American scientists who would review and evaluate the satellite and other technical sensing data to assist the administration in determining whether a 'nuclear event' had in fact occurred. The panel would comprise a geologist, physicists, electrical engineers and nuclear scientists, and would include several individuals who had specific experience with satellite sensing systems.[5] The White House Office of Science and Technology Policy (OSTP), of which Frank Press was director, would act as the secretariat for the panel, marshalling documentation, obtaining testimony and arranging presentations from experts inside and outside the government. The senior OSTP staff member in day-to-day charge would be John Marcum.

Nuclear explosions, involving even small, low-yield weapons, are very notable events, and can be detected in a variety of ways. The 'signals' emitted during a nuclear blast include intense light flashes, radioactive debris, radar waves, atmospheric pressure waves, sound waves (both hydro-acoustical and seismic) and electro-magnetic disturbances. The membership of the White House panel was selected to include individuals with expertise related to all these phenomena. Moreover, most of the distinguished scientists involved were senior administrators who understood the capabilities and failings of complex technical systems such as those, scattered around the globe, which are used to detect nuclear explosions and to differentiate between these and other unusual physical phenomena.

When a nuclear test is conducted, whether clandestinely or not, there are of course other tell-tale 'signals' of the event: communications during the planning phase, movements of technical personnel in preparation for the exercise, ship movements if the test is to be conducted over water, and tactical synchronization of communications during the actual monitoring of the blast itself, to name but a few. Human and electronic intelligence on these matters is usually collected, to supplement or verify the technical evidence of the physical effects of a nuclear explosion.

The *ad hoc* White House panel was, according to its own unclassified final report, given three tasks:

1. review all available data from both classified and unclassified sources that could help corroborate that the Vela signal originated from a nuclear explosion and suggest any additional sources of data that might be helpful in this regard;

2. evaluate the possibility that the signal in question was a 'false alarm' resulting from technical malfunction such as interference from other electrical components on the Vela platform; and

3. investigate the possibility that the signal recorded by our Vela satellite was of natural origin, possibly resulting from the coincidence of two or more natural phenomena and attempt to establish quantitative limits on the probability of such an occurrence.[6]

Presidential Science Adviser Frank Press and panel chairman Jack Ruina made the final selection of the members of the group, which was without question one of the most distinguished assemblages of scientists ever to gather at the White House. Several were Nobel Laureates, including University of California's Luis Alvarez, who has since become prominently associated with an international effort to explain the possible role of interstellar movements and meteor impacts in the sudden disappearance of dinosaurs and other earth life forms. Most panel members, in particular panel chairman Ruina, Stanford's Wolfgang Panofsky and IBM's Richard Garwin, had been previously involved in Defence Department–related government inquiries.

Nevertheless, some of the government officials who attended those early meetings in the White House Situation Room noted that the panel, despite its broad charter to review 'all available data from both classified and unclassified sources', was composed uniquely of scientists. There were no intelligence analysts – no intelligence professionals at all, in fact.

Initially it made no difference, for despite the expectations of those government officials who continued to meet at the OSTP offices, no intelligence turned up to verify what virtually every person involved, including the members of the newly appointed panel, continued to assume was a 'routine' satellite test sighting. A press statement about the sighting, drafted at that Sunday morning meeting, the morning after the sighting, was simply not released. As the weeks passed, there was still no radioactive debris, no news of intelligence, and no public announcement of the sighting.

On Thursday evening, 25 October, the matter finally became

public knowledge, as reporter John Scali broke the story on the ABC evening news. That same evening the State Department, alerted about the Scali story, issued this statement:

> The United States Government has an indication suggesting the possibility that a low-yield nuclear explosion occurred on September 22 in an area of the Indian ocean and South Atlantic including portions of the Antarctic continent, and the southern part of Africa. No corroborating evidence has been received to date. We are continuing to assess whether such an event took place.[7]

It was the same press statement drafted in the White House basement on the morning after the sighting.

Several months passed before there was a public indication as to who had conducted the test. In February 1980 CBS news carried a report by Dan Raviv, its Tel Aviv correspondent, alleging that the Prince Edward explosion was in fact an Israeli device detonated in a joint Israeli–South African test exercise. The following month Israeli military censors banned publication of a book by two well-known Israeli journalists, Eli Teicher and Ami Dor-On. Working from information provided by Israeli sources, the authors detailed Israeli-South African co-operation on nuclear weapons development. The book's title: *None Will Survive Us: The Story of the Israeli A-Bomb*.

The search for technical evidence

As indicated previously, the usual initial and primary means of nuclear test verification by the US Government involves measurement of radiation in air and (when possible) water samples near the suspected explosion site. The unclassified panel report, issued in July 1980, notes that

> Vigorous attempts to locate debris were made. Background radiation is generally low in the Southern Hemisphere. All [US] collections were negative, some of them indicating unusually low levels of background radiation.[8]

These statements are correct. The report fails to mention, however, the delay of approximately three weeks in efforts by the US Air Force to collect air samples, due in part to the remoteness of the area of the sighting.[9] Similarly, after drawing attention to the generally low level of background radiation in the 'Southern Hemisphere', the report fails to add that natural radiation levels in the area immediately adjacent to the position of the Vela sighting – near the Prince Edward Islands – are, as previously indicated, the highest in the world, due to a unique thinning of the earth's atmosphere covering this area.

In mid-November, before the White House panel met, scientists at New Zealand's Institute of Nuclear Science thought they detected unusually high radiation levels in rainwater samples collected 'downwind' from the position of the Vela sighting. Within hours, however, these findings were contradicted by New Zealand's other monitoring facility, the National Radiation Laboratory.[10] The dispute was soon resolved in favour of the radiation laboratory, and the panel report would appear to be justified in its conclusion that 'A tentative positive result in New Zealand was subsequently shown to be erroneous.'[11]

At the panel's first formal meeting in late November 1979, a strong presentation was made by technicians of the US Air Force Technical Applications Center (AFTAC) who reported finding 'acoustic evidence [at the appropriate time] from listening posts in widely separated parts of the world that seems to confirm an explosion'.[12] The panel was not impressed. Under rigorous questioning, the Air Force presenters admitted that some sensors that should have picked up acoustic signals at the same time, including the sensing site (Australia) which was closest to the Prince Edward Islands, had detected nothing.

Certain government officials who attended this meeting were impressed with the AFTAC presentation, and argued passionately that a nuclear event had occurred.[13] The panel's scientists however, noting the contradictory evidence and doubting that a low-level nuclear explosion would have been acoustically detectable at any of the sites in question, concluded in their report that the acoustic data they had received was 'unrelated' to the event represented in the Vela satellite's 22 September sighting.

The panel reacted similarly to data presented by two scientists based upon observations made at the Arecibo radio observatory in Puerto Rico. A 'travelling ionospheric disturbance', known in the field as a 'TID', had been detected travelling south to north at about the time of the Vela satellite sighting. The White House panel noted that a storm system had existed south of Puerto Rico at the time in question, and also that the very sensitive equipment used at Arecibo to measure the TID had only been operative for 120 hours of observation, 'providing a very weak data base' against which to judge this particular signal.[14] The panel concluded that, like the acoustic signals, the TID data was most probably unrelated to the 22 September 'event'.

The US Air Force early-warning radar net also picked up some sort of signal on 22 September, though it was sufficiently ambiguous that (presumably natural) causes other than a nuclear event might have been the source.[15] The panel did not consider this data important enough to mention in the unclassified report.

Somewhat more persuasive was hydro-acoustic evidence presented by the Naval Research Laboratory (NRL), if only because the White House Office of Science and Technology Policy (OSTP) had specifically requested NRL to do an independent search worldwide for 'geophysical data that might bear upon' the event detected by Vela, in support of the deliberations of the panel. NRL Director Alan Berman gave this charge high priority, and assigned seventy-five staff members to the exercise full-time. The result was a 300-page study sent to the White House in final form on 30 June 1980, but whose data in preliminary form was debated at length by the panel in each of its last two meetings.

NRL concluded, on the basis of a preponderance of the (physical) evidence, that a small nuclear device had indeed been exploded near the Prince Edward Islands on 22 September. Two hydro-acoustic pulses were detected, according to NRL, at the right time and coming from the right direction. The initial, weaker pulse had been transmitted directly into the South Atlantic but its force, for sensors in the North Atlantic, had been absorbed by the southern portion of the African continent. The second, stronger pulse was caused when the hydro-acoustic wave generated by the explosion was reflected horizontally off the continental shelf of Antarctica, and straight up the Atlantic Ocean south to north. Travelling further, this second wave took longer to reach the sensors.

The panel found flaws with both signals: the first being so weak as barely to register above background 'noise', and the second having travelled such a distance that it was not synchronous with the Vela sighting, and left doubt regarding the exact position of the source. NRL Director Berman argued forcefully for mathematical computations that placed the source of the second pulse precisely where Vela had sighted its flash, but the panel was again, unconvinced.

The last formal panel meeting in April was devoted largely to a review of the draft NRL study, including a coincidence which Berman found 'indicative, if not conclusive'.[16] NRL calculated the exact moment that the sunrise would have occurred at the high point of the landforms on (the main) Prince Edward Island on 22 September, and discovered that the Vela sighting had occurred at ten minutes before sunrise, *precisely*, measured to the millisecond. The significance here is that nuclear tests are frequently conducted just before dawn to allow both visual measurements of radiation in the dark, and then immediate observation of blast effects and collection of radioactive debris in conditions of light. For purposes of synchronization of the ships, planes, people, etc, participating in the monitoring exercise, a blast at exactly ten minutes before sunrise . . .

Berman observes that 'the computation is sufficiently complicated that it would be an amusing coincidence if that were entirely accidental'.[17] The panel, however, was neither amused nor convinced. One member, Ricardo Giaconni, later noted that orderly scientific inquiry requires that you decide beforehand what subsets of data you are going to use – 'you can't go randomly looking for evidence'.[18]

In the end, the evidence which the panel considered most significant in determining whether or not a nuclear event had occurred was the light flash signatures recorded by the Vela satellite itself. In one important respect, the 22 September signal was different from previous Vela sightings. The particular satellite which recorded the 22 September event had made forty-one previous sightings of nuclear events, and in each case corroborative data of one kind or another had proven the satellite correct. It was largely on this basis that the crisis team which had originally gathered at the White House on the 'morning after', and indeed the panel itself when it first met two months later, assumed that a nuclear event had indeed occurred, and that the technical verification from other sensing systems would eventually materialize.

The Vela series of sensing satellites carried two 'bhangmeters' each – these are the devices that, as the panel report states, 'observe incident light and trigger a recording apparatus when light intensity changes rapidly'. Experience with the optical sensors over time had shown, prior to September 1979, that the double-pulse signature of a nuclear explosion was unlike anything else in nature. The Los Alamos Scientific Laboratory (LASL) issued a paper in November 1979, in which it explained why the Vela satellites are so hard to fool. After describing and illustrating a typical nuclear event signature, the LASL paper explains:

> The majority of the total energy radiated by the fireball comes from the second peak [of light], which is not very different in its instantaneous brightness, relative to the first peak, but it lasts about 100 times longer . . . The two-peaked character of the light pulse, together with the very large energy radiated during the second maximum, make it unmistakable that this light signature originated in a nuclear explosion . . . Pulsed light sources do occur in nature, or can be built, that match either [the] power level [of a nuclear explosion] or the pulse duration. However, no other source is known that matches both.[19]

The problem with Vela's 22 September signatures, the panel discovered, was that the two 'bhangmeters' on board had, in this particular sighting, given readings of different relative intensity, as compared to the readings of previous sightings. The optical sensors in the 'bhangmeters' are set at different intensities, and thus give two different amplitude readings, but they should give the same relative readings from sighting to sighting, even if the size of the detected explosions varies. If, for example, the values for the two readings in one explosion are 2:1, then they should be 2:1 in the next explosion.

The panel studied twelve of this satellite's previous forty-one sightings, and discovered that the ratio of the readings on the two optical sensors had been the same in all twelve previous explosions, but on 22 September the second hump in the double pulse on one of the optical sensors caused it to 'fall distinctly outside the nuclear band'. The panel report explained:

> Qualitatively, this means that during the second hump, the ratio of the bhangmeter signals is significantly different from what would be expected from a nuclear explosion near the surface of the earth. Such anomalous behaviour was never observed in bhangmeter recordings in previous nuclear explosions. Thus, although the September 22 event displays many of the characteristics of nuclear signals, it departs in an essential feature.[20]

The panel could only account for this discrepancy in the satellite's behaviour by assuming a light source (or sources) near the satellite. After examining various alternative light sources, the panel concluded that some 'zoo event' like 'sunlight reflected from particles ejected from collision of meteroids upon impact with the spacecraft', was a possible alternative explanation for the 22 September signatures.[21] 'But,' the panel report added, 'we do not maintain that this particular explanation is necessarily correct.'[22]

In sum the White House panel concluded that the 22 September Vela sighting

> contains sufficient internal inconsistency to cast serious doubt whether that signal originated from a nuclear explosion or in fact from any light source not in the proximity of the Vela satellite.[23]

The unclassified version of the panel's report did not estimate probabilities, and merely ended with the statement that the 22 September signal 'was probably not from a nuclear explosion'. Panel chairman Jack Ruina has since estimated the odds against a nuclear event in the South Atlantic on that date at 'five or six to one'. When pressed on the firmness of the panel's conclusions, however, he adds:

> I hope you know what the report said. The report said we don't know what the situation was, that the data was ambiguous.[24]

On one point Ruina is adamant, and that is that the panel's conclusions were unanimous. Nine of the country's most distinguished scientists met periodically over eight months, reviewed certain evidence about the '22 September event', and came to the same conclusions about their review. Interviews in 1987 with a majority of the panel members, and the OSTP, NSC, CIA, State and Defence Department staff who were involved in the work of the panel, bore Ruina out on this point. There had been no serious dissent among the panel members.

Other experts, other conclusions

At the time that the White House panel released its unclassified report, 15 July 1980, the Office of Science and Technology Policy (OSTP) had already taken delivery of the final, 300-page report of the Naval Research Laboratory (NRL). As indicated above OSTP, as the panel's secretariat, had itself commissioned NRL to 'do independent analyses of this data'. What could not have been anticipated, however, when NRL was given this assignment in the weeks after the Vela sighting, was that NRL 'independent analyses' would eventually contradict those of the panel itself.

The White House panel's report was drafted in February and March 1980, and approved in final form at the panel's formal meeting in April. It was at that last meeting, however, that the panel was confronted with NRL director Berman's tentative conclusion that a preponderance of the evidence pointed to a 'nuclear event'. At the time, NRL considered the hydro-acoustical data to be the strongest single piece of confirming evidence. The final NRL study was submitted to OSTP (and the panel) on 30 June 1980, two weeks before release of the White House panel's report.

Rather than reconsider and/or redraft its report to resolve these differences, the White House panel decided to treat the NRL study as a 'very preliminary analysis', and 'too incomplete to apply to the event'.[25] To this day, Alan Berman says he does not understand why the panel chose to mischaracterize the NRL study as 'preliminary'. Berman had previously been closely associated with both Jack Ruina and Frank Press and considered both to be personal friends. Concluded *Science Magazine*:

> Berman's split with the Administration is notable because he is one of the few dissenters to speak publicly. Others may have been dazzled by the stellar cast of the White House panel, which was loaded with Nobel laureates, or silenced by a healthy respect for security regulations.[26]

The 'others' referred to here included elements in the American scientific community who found the panel's equivocation difficult to understand. Scientists at the Department of Energy, specifically at Los Alamos and at Sandia Laboratories, were repeatedly quoted in the press as supporting this or that piece of evidence for a nuclear event on 22 September.[27] The Los Alamos Scientific Laboratory took this process of leaking a step further in November 1979, when it published an LASL 'Mini-Review', cited earlier, entitled *Light Flash Produced by an Atmospheric Nuclear Explosion*. The article did not address the 22 September event specifically, but its timing and its strong argument for the absolute uniqueness of the optical sensing signature of a nuclear explosion constituted a strong if cautious statement of the existence of at least a 'dissenting view' within the American scientific community.

In sum, the White House panel scientists may indeed have been unanimous in their conclusions, but they certainly did not, in their analyses of the technical data, speak for all the specialists and scientists who were at the time professionally involved in nuclear test detection.

If American scientists were divided on the matter of the source of the Vela sighting, the US intelligence community was not. At the end of January 1980 the Central Intelligence

Agency informed a subcommittee of the House of Representatives that the South African Navy had been conducting exercises in the exact area of the Vela sighting, and under extraordinary security precautions. The CIA indicated to the Congressmen that, based upon collateral intelligence, the 'exercises' appeared to be typical nuclear test monitoring procedures.[28] In that same month, Pentagon 'sources' were quoted in the *Washington Post* as being 'statistically certain' that the 22 September event was in fact a nuclear explosion.

In June 1980, just before the final NRL report was submitted, the White House learned that the Defence Intelligence Agency, in its own study of the evidence surrounding the Vela sighting, had formally concluded that a nuclear weapon had indeed been detonated between South Africa and Antarctica on 22 September. The DIA study was due for release on 15 July. White House panel chairman Jack Ruina has since described the DIA study as being on a 'college freshman level . . . maybe college senior' from a technical standpoint.[29] But at the same time there was sufficient concern about DIA's conclusions that OSTP and the panel rushed to release an unclassified version of their report on . . . 15 July 1980.

The CIA followed its January 1980 testimony to Congress with a written report of its own, submitted to the National Security Council in June. The CIA study indicated that a tactical nuclear device of 2–3 kilotons had been detonated at the place and time of the Vela sighting, at an altitude of 8,000 metres, in a test exercise that probably involved the armed forces of both South Africa and Israel.[30]

What the White House panel wasn't told

On the face of it, the situation was absurd. A panel of eminent scientists, with positions of importance in the American scientific community . . . honourable men with international reputations to maintain, spend eight months reviewing 'all available data from both classified and unclassified sources', and decide that the Vela sighting was 'probably' not of nuclear origin. In a similar time frame, the US intelligence community reviews what is presumably the same classified and unclassified data, and, with their own reputations on the line, issue reports directly contradicting the White House panel.

The resolution to this conundrum lies in that assumption that the scientists and the intelligence analysts were looking at the same information. They weren't.

On 31 March 1980, senior OSTP official John Marcum appeared in London on the BBC programme, *Panorama*. Marcum, it will be recalled, was acting as the staff director for the panel, arranging for testimony and documentation and generally managing its day-to-day affairs. The unclassified and classified versions of the 'Report of the *Ad Hoc* Panel' had not yet been finalized, but were in nearly complete draft form at the time of the BBC programme, and the panel's broad conclusions had already been widely reported in the American media.

At the beginning of the programme, Marcum was asked by his BBC host, Tom Mangold, to explain the White House panel's charter. He responded:

> We asked [the panel] to review all evidence bearing on this event and in particular to try to determine . . . whether there was any corroborative data that would confirm that the event had in fact been caused by a nuclear explosion, to identify for us any new types of information that we might have overlooked that might bear on this event. Secondly, we wanted them to review the satellite system and to evaluate whether there was any possibility of a technical malfunction that might have caused this signal. And finally to evaluate the possibility that some natural phenomenon could have generated the signal and led to a false alarm in the sensors.[31]

Marcum's description of the panel's charter is quite consistent with the panel report's account of the ground that had been covered during its existence. Indeed the report in its preamble ('background') unequivocally states that both technical data *and* human and electronic intelligence had been reviewed, that is, 'all available data that might tend to corroborate whether that signal was generated by a nuclear explosion', and 'analyses made by government agencies that bore on the question of whether the 22 September signal was of nuclear origin'. A sub-group of the panel, said the report, 'was briefed on available intelligence that related to the 22 September event'.[32]

Later in the BBC programme, however, host Mangold asked Marcum a direct question:

> Has the committee taken into account the fact that there was a secret South African naval exercise taking place in that region at that time?

Without realizing it, perhaps, Mangold had stumbled upon the key to how a group of internationally renowned scientists had been assembled at the behest of President Jimmy Carter, and induced to engage in a long, sterile, totally unrealistic exercise. In effect, the panel had been mightily debating how many angels were on the head of the nuclear detection pin.

To Mangold's question about the South African naval exercise, Marcum responded:

> Well, the committee that we convened in order to give us outside scientific advice on this issue was charged with the responsibility for a technical analysis of the three factors that I mentioned earlier and so they had not specifically reviewed political military intelligence bearing on that.[33]

Marcum's response was in fact a rare moment of candour – a slip of the tongue – about a very sensitive matter: what the panel was *not* told.[34]

In the days immediately following the Vela sighting, the searches for both radioactive debris and collateral intelligence (communications intercepts, high-altitude photographs, information from US defence attachés and agents in place in Israel and South Africa, etc) were carried out simultaneously. Neither was particularly successful, at first. The remote location in open ocean and the presence in the Vela sighting area of heavy storms might have accounted for the absence of radioactive debris, as the rain would 'clean' the air downwind of the explosion, particularly if it had been a small one. These collection efforts, it will be recalled, were delayed for several weeks. In any event, radioactive debris simply didn't turn up. But the conduct of an atmospheric nuclear test exercise over water involves a great deal of logistics and the communications that go with it: base to ship, ship to ship, ship to plane, and so on. Jerry Funk was probably not the only one of the White House crisis meeting participants who was waiting confidently, expectantly for the confirming communications intercepts and/or human intelligence.

The intelligence was slow in coming, but it eventually came. Within a very few days of the Vela sighting, both DIA and CIA knew that the South African Defence Attaché in Washington had requested detailed information about US and international nuclear test detection systems, from the National Technical Information Center in Washington. The logical conclusion was that the South African defence forces may have timed and located the tests accordingly, that is, to avoid detection. Both agencies knew also, at this stage, that the South African Navy had been very active – conducting some kind of exercise – in the zone of the Vela sighting on the morning of 22 September. As the days passed, however, it became very clear that, as with the aerial sweep for radiation debris, the conclusive communications intercept, the 'smoking gun', was just not turning up. No South African seaman/technician was overheard in Afrikaans, on the right ship, at the right time, saying 'ten . . . nine . . . eight . . . seven . . .' etc.

It was at this point, when the US intelligence community had begun to take what one senior official described as an 'agnostic' position on the Vela sighting, that a report came in from the US Defence Attaché in Pretoria. The South African naval ships that had been placed in the vicinity of the Prince Edward Islands on 22 September had indeed been appropriately sized and staffed to observe, if not conduct, nuclear test exercises.[35]

A few days later, on 24 October, John Scali, an ABC-TV news commentator, overheard a conversation at the Desirée night-club at the Four Seasons Hotel in Washington. And the following day, 25 October, he broke the story of the Vela sighting on ABC evening news. When the story went public, a tremendous amount of pressure suddenly developed upon the South African Government to develop a cover story for the sighting. The one chosen on 27 October, two days after Scali's story, was a statement by South African Vice Admiral J. C. Walters that an explosion on board a Soviet nuclear submarine had been the likely cause of the Vela sighting.[36]

The flurry of discussions of this and other possible cover stories, discussions involving Israeli officials as well as South African, was picked up by the US National Security Agency (NSA), which was ready and waiting this time. This created a wave of what people in the communications intelligence field call 'noise . . . signals . . . activity', a wave which crested two to three days after the Scali report. By this time, the South African Government had its cover explanation down pat, but the US intelligence community also had strong evidence of the involvement of both South Africa and Israel in a nuclear test exercise on 22 September 1979.

By mid-November, at the time of the first formal meeting of the White House *ad hoc* panel, the intelligence picture was clear. It was never a 'smoking gun', as the hypothetical recording of a South African Navy test countdown would have been, but it was 'highly indicative', and certainly important enough to have been brought to the attention of the full panel at this first meeting. And it wasn't brought to the panel's attention. Moreover, in subsequent months, as the panel continued to meet, and well before the final panel report was issued in July 1980, the CIA in particular continued to receive confirming intelligence 'seeping out' from inside senior government circles in South Africa and Israel. This information also never reached the White House panel.[37]

It was at the panel's second meeting, held in California presumably out of consideration for the four panel members from the West Coast, that a sub-group of the panel was supposedly briefed on intelligence information related to the 22 September event. Panel chairman Jack Ruina, as well as Richard Garwin and Wolfgang Panofsky were among those scientists included in the briefing, which was provided by 'somebody from the intelligence community' whose identity and agency the panel chairman and others involved fail to recall.[38] The subject of 'ship movements' was among the intelligence matters discussed in the briefing, but those involved are certain that no information was imparted which bore materially on the issue of whether or not the 22 September event had or had not been a nuclear test.[39]

On one level, denying the panel the 'clear picture' which the intelligence community (and the CIA in particular) had by mid-November 1979 is understandable. No single panel member, including Ruina, had specific authorization or 'need to know' the complete story of the test-monitoring exercise and the communication intercepts. On the other hand, the lack of this access made the panel's work a technical charade, most particularly in light of the repeated claim in the final report that the *ad hoc* panel had reviewed 'all available data' that might bear upon whether the Vela signal was generated by a nuclear explosion. This simply was not true. Moreover, according to then Director of Central Intelligence, Admiral Stansfield Turner, no request for this information was ever made to the CIA from anyone connected to the White House panel. And without that intelligence, Turner has described the panel's conclusions as 'absurd'.[40]

Conclusion

Why, one wonders, wasn't the intelligence in summary or excised form provided to the panel by President Carter himself, through his National Security Adviser Zbigniew Brzezinski, or through Presidential Science Adviser Frank Press, or someone else with both 'need to know' *and* direct involvement with the panel? Failing that, it is difficult to understand why, once the intelligence picture became clear, the scope of the panel's work was not recast along more modest lines viz, determining whether a known, single, low-level nuclear test in a remote site could or could not be confirmed if not 'verified' by the purely technical means then available?

The answer to both questions may be that either of these actions could have constituted a tacit official acknowledgement that a nuclear event had in fact occurred, and would have led directly to an active public search for the country or countries responsible. For a variety of reasons, the Carter Administration might have been uncomfortable with such an acknowledgment:

1. The United States, under the Atoms for Peace programme, had trained the majority of South Africa's nuclear experts. Much of the fuel for South Africa's nuclear programme had, through the years, been provided by United States companies with the approval of the US Government. Electronic components and ventilation and cooling systems from America had been sold to South Africa for its research reactor at Valindaba. Both US and Israeli scientists assisted at Valindaba after 1977 in developing laser enrichment techniques for uranium. On 28 October 1979, shortly after the Vela sighting had become public knowledge, Congressman Donald J. Pease had written to the White House Committee of Foreign Affairs asking for an investigation of a possible link between the 22 September event and a federal grand jury investigation then ongoing in Vermont, into the illegal shipment from the US to South Africa of a tactical nuclear delivery system, viz extended range 155mm artillery guns and shells. In sum, a nuclear explosion involving South Africa, with or without Israel, would have raised very, very unpleasant questions for the Carter Administration.

2. The Foreign Assistance Act of 1961, as amended in 1977 (the 'Symington Amendment'), would have required President Carter to cut off foreign economic and military assistance to any country manufacturing, transferring, receiving or detonating a nuclear explosive device. The countries involved in the exercise were South Africa and Israel. In 1980, a presidential election year, Jimmy Carter could probably have afforded to antagonize his pro-South Africa constituency, but would we have wanted to anger Democratic – and Republican – supporters of Israel?

3. Another politically troublesome aspect of the 22 September event was reflected in a headline over an article in the *New York Times* on the day following the official US acknowledgement of the Vela sighting. 'Vague US Statement Casts Doubt on Ability to Monitor Nuclear Blasts', said the *Times*.[41] The problem involved official US positions with respect to verification of the Nuclear Test Ban Treaty (NTBT). If (a) there had indeed been an explosion, and (b) the physical evidence for the explosion was ambiguous (as already appeared to be the case one month after the Vela sighting), then (c) the Carter Administration was going to have great

difficulty convincing the American people that the NTBT was indeed verifiable.

The administration had other potential problems in the event of a confirmed sighting. Black African governments, and Arab governments, finally confronted not only with a South African/Israeli bomb, but a sophisticated, miniaturized device which had been successfully tested, could be expected to move heaven and earth to obtain their own equivalent, countervailing nuclear weapons. And the US Government, whatever its policy on nuclear non-proliferation, would have been forced to admit the compelling logic of such acquisitions made, of course, in the name of those countries' essential national security interests.

In sum, the Carter Administration could simply not confirm that a nuclear explosion had occurred off the coast of South Africa on 22 September 1979. Those who had 'need to know' on the Vela intelligence *and* who were in a position to ensure that this information was shared with the *ad hoc* White House panel comprise, as indicated previously, a fairly short list – Carter, Turner, Brzezinski (and his deputy, David Aaron) and Press. The deception buck would appear to stop here. Brzezinski's intelligence aide, Robert Gates,[42] and Press's OSTP aide, John Marcum, were certainly aware of the 'full picture' as well, but would not have been in a position to have pushed on their own for a full briefing of the panel.

The Carter Administration may have had what seemed at the time good and sufficient reasons for fudging the detection of a nuclear test off the coast of South Africa in September 1979, by ignoring the intelligence 'take' on the event, in the context of the ongoing *ad hoc* panel's inquiry. In doing so, however, the Carter White House was undermining the US's long-standing policies on nuclear non-proliferation. The result, as Admiral Turner has indicated, was absurd: four different US Government 'reports' on the event with four different conclusions. In the end the process only served to cast doubt on US nuclear test detection capabilities.

Far more important however, the Carter White House, in taking a position which served very short-term political interests in the affair, mortgaged the security and stability of future generations of Africans, Middle Easterners and the rest of us. Two pariah states had now tested a credible, usable tactical nuclear device.

A personal afterword

In early 1987, while writing this chapter, I contacted a nuclear scientist with whom I'd been associated in a policy study project years before, to obtain help in understanding some of the basic technical aspects of nuclear weapons design and testing. Theodore Taylor, a renowned physicist, had designed weapons for the US Government, taught, administered and consulted, and had written several books on nuclear proliferation and nuclear terrorism.

In September 1986 the London *Sunday Times* Insight team had flown to Washington to ask Taylor's help in verifying more than sixty photographs of the Dimona research reactor in Israel, together with detailed descriptions, which Israeli nuclear technician Mordechai Vanunu had brought out of Israel. Vanunu had alleged that at least a hundred nuclear weapons had been manufactured at Dimona, including hydrogen bombs. It was the *Sunday Times* account of Taylor's conclusions, read as part of my research, which reminded me of our past association on a publication project for the Council on Foreign Relations in New York.

In the course of our discussion of very basic technical matters related to the Vela satellite sighting, Dr Taylor asked me if I had read the accounts of Mordechai Vanunu's defection from Israel, abduction by Israeli authorities, and subsequent return to that country for trial. He described at some length the Vanunu photos and testimony. The Government of Norway was sufficiently concerned about the details in the London *Sunday Times* articles that it has indicated an intent to invoke inspection rights for 20 tons of heavy water sold to Israel in 1959. Israel has rejected the Norwegian request.[43] It is with this shipment of heavy water, according to international experts on the subject, that Israel may first have begun the secret production of weapons-grade plutonium at Dimona. In fact, by 1966–7, experts at the International Atomic Energy Agency in Vienna believed that Dimona had at that time been producing plutonium for weapons production for several years.[44]

Midway through my discussions with Dr Taylor, a thought occurred to me. 'Was there, in the Vanunu photographs and materials, evidence that the Israeli weapons programme had previously been tested?' I asked.

'Oh yes, unequivocally,' he said. Israel was already engaging in the highly sophisticated process of 'boosting' the yields of its weapons. More important, it was doing this on a production basis. Dr Taylor explained that the Dimona reactor core was being used to make tritium and deuterium from Lithium 6, and that these two precious materials were then being infused into weapons cores in order to accelerate the fission process and thus boost the energy release, that is, the yield of the weapon. In other words, Israel was producing small but powerful thermonuclear weapons in a programme at a very advanced stage.

What was significant about this particular process, said Taylor, was that boosting introduces uncertainties in weapons production, and really can't be done without testing. The slightest miscalculation in the infusion and deuterium can result in a waste of weapons-grade materials that are precious to any production programme. Moreover, you have to test the specific piece of hardware. The process is not one that can be undertaken from borrowed or stolen charts and diagrams. And yet Israel, at Dimona was (is) mass-producing 'boosted' thermonuclear weapons. Israel, concluded Dr Taylor, has tested a miniaturized nuclear device. Somewhere.

NINE

Operation Babylon: the Baghdad Reactor Raid, 1981

Sixteen heavily loaded Israeli Air Force planes lifted off from Etzion airbase in occupied eastern Sinai on Sunday afternoon, 7 June, 1981. Eight of the planes were F-16 Fighting Falcons, each carrying two 2,000-pound laser-guided bombs. They were to do the damage. Eight F-15 Eagles, bristling with Sidewinder and Sparrow air-to-air missiles, were to fly air cover. The latter also carried the latest ECM (electronic counter-measure) pods and extra fuel tanks.

Flying at low altitude and in tight formation, the planes crossed the Gulf of Aqabah and headed into the airspace of Saudi Arabia. There, they met IAF Boeing 707 tanker aircraft equipped with boom refuellers, and took on the fuel needed for the long flight on to Baghdad.

At about this time, Saudi technicians picked up the tight formation of planes on their radars near Tabuk air base. Consulting with their American colleagues, the Saudis decided that the large blip on their screens must be a Boeing 747.[1] It was, after all positioned in an airway designated for scheduled civilian airliners.

The fighter bombers entered Iraqi airspace flying at about 600 knots, just above the hillocks and palm trees. Not far from Baghdad, in a suburb, the huge dome of the nuclear reactor at Tuwaitha loomed. It was now 6.25 p.m. local time.

The F-16s increased their altitude, dived on the target and dropped their bombs swiftly from several hundred feet, and then pulled into a steep climb to avoid SAMs (surface-to-air missiles) and anti-aircraft guns. The F-15s circled above, ready, should there be opposition from aircraft. But there was none; and there were no missiles or anti-aircraft fire either. It was a piece of cake. An hour later, during the Italian National Day celebration at the embassy by the Tigris River, there was a fifteen-minute display of anti-aircraft fire at no apparent targets, but it was too late.[2] The reactor, core and all, was virtually destroyed. One French technician and several Iraqis were dead.

One of the F-15s lingered to take photographs, but soon joined the others who formed a tight formation, climbed high, and shot back westward toward Israel at nearly Mach 2. As the planes passed over Jordan, military radars recognized enemy 'signatures' and launched a Hawk air defence missile. The F-15s easily scrambled the projectile's target acquisition system, however, and it fell harmlessly to the ground. All sixteen planes returned safely to bases in Israel. Other Jordanian attempts to fire their (American) Hawk missiles failed because of equipment malfunction.

For a full twenty-four hours after the attack, there was silence. Neither Iraq nor Israel made any announcement, and there was only confusion in Baghdad. The American 'Interests Section' (the US and Iraq did not have full diplomatic relations at the time) reported back to Washington on Monday, the following day, that

> Street rumours attribute the air-raid alert, which was followed an hour later by anti-aircraft machine-gun fire, variously to the Iranians, the Israelis, the Shia Dawa party, or Iraqi imagination.[3]

US representatives in Baghdad did not expect the confusion to last for long, however, and warned that the Iraqi leadership would be likely to place 'a good part of the responsibility for the raid on the US, whatever we say', because of (a) Israel's use of advanced US air-to-ground weapons, (b) consistent US support for Israel, and (c) a deep suspicion that the US either stimulated the attack or acquiesced in it. The warning concluded:

> It is important from the point of view of our security here as well as for Americans elsewhere in the area that ... the US Government do everything possible to disassociate ourselves from the Israeli action.[4]

Several hours after these messages were sent, the Government of Iraq did finally react, and with predictable outrage. But interestingly, no mention at all was made of the United States. An official radio broadcast of Iraq's Revolutionary Command Council announced that the raid was carried out by 'Zionist enemy planes', and linked the attack to the ongoing Iran-Iraq war. Israel, said the broadcast, was supplying Iran with 'military equipment and spare parts' and had now taken a direct role in the war by attacking a facility which Iran had (ineffectively) hit in an air raid on Baghdad nine months previously. In what may have been a veiled reference to Israel's nuclear weapons programme, the statement claimed that Israel's primary reason for the attack was to maintain 'the technical and scientific gap between it and the Arab nation'.[5]

The second attack: a propaganda raid

At about the same time as the Iraqi broadcast, late afternoon on 8 June, Prime Minister Begin's office in Jerusalem issued a written statement putting forth the Israeli Government's explanation for the raid:

> The Israeli Air Force yesterday attacked and destroyed the Osirak nuclear reactor which is near Baghdad. All our planes returned home safely.[6]
> The Government finds itself obligated to explain to enlighten public opinion why it decided on this special operation.
> For a long time, we have followed with grave concern the construction of the Osirak nuclear reactor. Sources of unquestioned reliability told us that it was intended, despite statements to the contrary, for the production of atomic bombs.
> The goal for these bombs was Israel. This was explicitly stated by the Iraqi ruler. After the Iranians slightly damaged the reactor [Iraqi President] Sadam Hussein remarked that it was pointless for the Iranians to attack the reactor because it was being built against Israel alone.
> The atomic bombs that this reactor would have been capable of producing, with enriched uranium or plutonium, were of the type dropped on Hiroshima. In this way, a danger to Israel's existence was being produced.
> Highly reliable sources gave us two dates for the completion of the reactor and its operation: the first the beginning of July 1981, the second the beginning of September this year.

Within a short time, the Iraqi reactor would have been in operation and hot. In such conditions, no Israeli government could have decided to blow it up. This would have caused a huge wave of radioactivity over the city of Baghdad and its innocent citizens would have been harmed.

We were, therefore, forced to defend ourselves against the construction of an atomic bomb in Iraq which itself would not have hesitated to use it against Israel and its population centres.

Therefore, the Israeli Government decided to act without further delay to ensure the safety of our people.

The planning was precise. The operation was set for Sunday on an assumption that the 100 to 150 foreign experts who were active on the reactor would not be there on the Christian day of rest. This assumption proved correct. No foreign expert was hurt.

Two European governments were helping the Iraqi dictator in return for oil to manufacture nuclear weapons. Once again we call on them to desist from this terrible and inhuman act.

On no account shall we permit an enemy to develop weapons of mass destruction against the people of Israel.[7]

On the following day, 9 June, Prime Minister Begin expanded on the statement at a news conference in Jerusalem. He was particularly adamant on the subject of the evidence for an Iraqi nuclear weapons programme, and that government's intended use for the bomb, had it been allowed to develop it. To prove his point, Begin quoted from the 'official' Iraqi newspaper, *Al-Thawra*, for 4 October, 1980, just days after Iranian F-4s had slightly damaged the Baghdad reactor:

The Iranian people should not fear the Iraqi nuclear reactor, which is not intended to be used against Iran, but against the Zionist enemy.[8]

As for the timing of the raid, Begin repeated the claim that as the reactor was going to 'go critical' in July, the Israeli Government was forced to abandon diplomatic efforts to stop the programme, and bomb the reactor in June, to avoid civilian radiation casualties which would have occurred if the same attack were mounted a month later. Said Begin to the international press at the conference:

It is our ethics, and always has been: fight the good fight, but armed men against armed men. Never use arms against innocent and unarmed civilians.[9]

Curiously, on the same day as the press conference in Jerusalem, Senator Alan Cranston of California submitted a guest editorial to the *New York Times* containing the same quotation.[10] It may not, as we shall see, have been a coincidence.

Two days later, on 12 June, Begin personally defended the raid yet again, in a statement issued by the Israeli Foreign Ministry. Iraq had built a secret bomb manufacturing installation 130 feet below the reactor core, he said, with equipment and materials that had not been and could not be seen by inspectors from the International Atomic Energy Agency (IAEA). This facility had also been destroyed in the raid, he said, presumably on the basis of the post-attack photo reconnaissance.[11]

The astonishing thing about the official Israeli Government statement after the attack and about Begin's subsequent elaborations on the same theme, is that hardly a single statement made was true, and several were publicly disavowed by the Israeli Government in the following weeks. At the very least, Israel had undertaken a blatant act of war on the basis of very poor information.

'Sources of unquestioned reliability', said the Jerusalem statement, 'told us that [the reactor] was intended for the production of atomic bombs.' Indeed, testimony which was subsequently presented in hearing before the US Congress did reveal considerable circumstantial evidence that Iraq was stockpiling more uranium or ('yellowcake') than was necessary for the operation of a research reactor.[12] Those same hearings, however, also provided strong testimony and evidence that Iraq could not have produced nuclear weapons, or even have taken the preliminary steps toward doing so, without detection by both French technicians (who had total, unlimited access to the facility) and by IAEA inspectors.[13] Moreover, the great preponderance of expert testimony indicated that Iraq could not, on its own and without direct French and Italian assistance, have developed the bomb.[14]

'The goal for these bombs was Israel. This was explicitly stated by the Iraqi ruler,' said the Jerusalem statement issued just after the raid. When challenged on this later, the Israeli

Government was simply unable to produce any public threat by Iraqi President Sadam Hussein, explicit or otherwise, to use atomic weapons against Israel.

The US State Department even assisted in the search and concluded, as Assistant Secretary of State Nicholas Veliotes told the House Foreign Affairs Committee, that 'Those articles did not exist.'[15] Veliotes had received a telex the previous week from the US Interests Section in Baghdad, in which there was the following paragraph:

> We have seen reports out of Israel which have been picked up in the US press, that Sadam Hussein in the recent past made a statement to the effect that Iraqi nuclear weapons would be used against Israel. We can find no basis for these.[16]

The *Al-Thawra* quotation which Begin produced at the press conference on the day following the raid turned out to be bogus. The Israeli Government, in admitting this subsequently, said that Prime Minister Begin had been the victim of 'poor staff work'.[17]

'Within a short time the Iraqi reactor would have been in operation and hot,' said the official Jerusalem statement after the raid, and the Israeli planes could not then have attacked because 'this would have caused a huge wave of radioactivity over the city of Baghdad and its civilians would have been harmed.' Thus, the attack had to be conducted when it was conducted. Dr Herbert Kouts, chairman of the Department of Nuclear Energy at Brookhaven National Laboratory, later told the Senate Foreign Relations Committee that this was simply untrue. At the most, radioactive debris would have have been thrown only 1,000 feet, and thus would have been confined to the facility, he said.[18] Other experts, including Dr Herbert Goldstein of Columbia University, concurred, as did a report on the subject prepared for the US Congress by the Congressional Research Service (CRS).[19]

'The planning was precise,' said the Jerusalem statement, and the operation had been carried out on Sunday to avoid casualties among the '100–150 foreign experts . . . who would not be there on the Christian day of rest. This assumption proved correct,' said the statement, 'No foreign expert was hurt.' In fact most of the 170 foreign technicians were working on Sunday. They took off Friday, the Muslim 'day of rest', as did (and do) virtually all foreigners working in the Arab world. Fortunately, the Israeli planes had arrived just at the end of the working day. Nevertheless, one French technician, a M. Chausspied, was killed in the raid.[20] Alas, Begin had yet again been the victim of 'poor staff work'.

Perhaps the strangest Begin gaff – and the most revealing – occurred on the matter of the 'secret bomb installation' whose existence was revealed by the Prime Minister in the press statement issued by the Israeli Foreign Ministry on 11 June. The facility was purported to be forty metres below ground, but had nevertheless been successfully destroyed by the Israeli planes. When he was pressed on this in a subsequent news conference by sceptical members of the foreign press, Begin claimed that the bomb factory existed, but only four metres below ground.[21]

By the time Congressional hearings on the reactor raid had opened, Israeli officials in Washington were backing away from the existence of a 'bomb factory' altogether.[22] On 16 June 1981 Major General Yehoshua Sagi, head of Modiin (Israeli military intelligence) announced that there was no 'secret room'.[23] A few days later, Israel's chief of civilian intelligence (Mossad), General Yitzhak Hofi, complained to Begin's office that the Prime Minister had been jeopardizing secret intelligence sources and methods in his repeated public pronouncements about the raid.[24]

Menachem Begin was not the victim of poor staff work. He was repeatedly, publicly lying. And he may have compromised Israeli national security information in the process.

Conning the Congress

Tuesday 9 June, 1981, was bound to be a busy day for the Congressional Research Service (CRS). After a delay of twenty-four hours, the news of the Baghdad reactor raid had broken in the morning papers, and there were certainly going to be requests to several of CRS's divisions for research on nuclear weapons, the Arms Export Control Act and Israel's use of American aircraft, the adequacy of IAEA and other weapons safeguard regimes, etc. Several of the staffers came in to their offices that morning with the thought in the back of their heads that they should have called in sick. And then they received the request about the quotations.

Early in the morning there were several requests from members of Congress regarding general threats that Iraqi leaders had made against Israel, and these had been quickly located. Such threats were nothing new. Most were found in recent FBIS (Foreign Broadcast Information Service) materials. Then around mid-morning, a member of Congress called to ask that a list of quotations be verified for accuracy. It was a 'rush' request. The quotations, he said, proved that the Baghdad reactor facility was being used to produce weapons, and that these weapons were intended for use against Israel.

The list was walked over to CRS by courier. From the outset, several things about it seemed odd. For one thing, there was no heading – no indication as to who had compiled and translated the quotations, most of which purported to be taken from Arabic newspapers or broadcasts. Then there was the spelling – several well-known place names were misspelled.

Because of the urgency of the request, two CRS staffers split the list up, and went digging. But over the course of the whole day, they turned up almost nothing. Late in the afternoon, the requester was called and given the bad news. He said 'Keep looking.' In the next two to three days several other Congress members called to ask for verifications, and they produced the *same* list. By now, CRS was curious indeed. Other agencies and experts were called for help – CIA, DIA, DoD, and the State Department, along with several local Washington academics. No luck. The CRS staffers then called the Israeli Embassy and AIPAC (the American Israel Public Affairs Committee) asking them if they had generated the list, because there appeared to be errors in dates, newspaper names, translations, and the like. Both the Embassy and AIPAC said they were not the source of the list, but that CRS needn't worry because the quotations were probably correct. In the meantime, Begin again had used one of the items on the list, the *Al-Thawra* quotation, in the 11 June press conference. Israeli Ambassador to the UN, Yehuda Blum, had also referred to several of the quotations in the Security Council debate on the reactor raid.

Finally, several of the quotations were located by the Library of Congress's Near East Section, but the director there, Dr George Atiyeh, said he was not sure that the articles he'd located were what CRS was seeking. The quotations were similar to the texts, but there were differences; words had been changed, and meanings. CRS asked that the translations be sent over anyway.

Late Friday afternoon, CRS called back the State Department, AIPAC and the Israeli Embassy to say they were throwing in the towel and, in the case of the latter two offices, to alert those whom CRS now thought had originated the list of quotes that they might look foolish as a result. CRS would present what it had so far to the original requesters, telling them that a couple of the quotations were correct but taken out of context with totally different meanings. Others were articles that were never published, or speeches that were never given, at least at the time and date specified in the list.

CRS rules require that the original requesters can determine what if any distribution will be made of the research they have requested, and in the particular instance, the requesters agreed that distribution could be made, *after* they had received the materials. And indeed, by Friday afternoon, CRS received a request for copies of the research from none other than the office of Secretary of State Alexander Haig. Word had got round of the list of bogus and doctored quotations, and now the CRS research itself was a matter of concern at the State Department, and of course in Israel.

On Sunday, 14 June, a wire service story described the CRS effort, and shortly thereafter *Davar*, a major Israeli daily newspaper, used the wire service story to criticize Prime Minister Begin for, yes, poor staff work.

On Monday, 15 June, CRS published its research on the strange quotations and summarized the results to that point:

Of the eight quotations on the list, three were direct quotes from Iraqi officials, four were indirect quotes, and one appeared to be a direct quotation from a newspaper editorial. One direct quotation did not list a source and could not be found, and another indirect quote, from the Kuwaiti newspaper *al-Qabas* of November 30, 1976, cannot be verified because the newspaper issue cited is not available to us at present. Of the six remaining quotations from the list, two do not appear in the source cited. Of the four quotations from the list that do appear in the original sources cited, three appear to have been taken out of context in such a manner that the original meaning of the quotations may have been distorted. One quotation from the list is correct, although that quotation does not mention nuclear weapons.[25]

The last sentence in this summary may explain the motivation for creating the list in the first place. Iraqi leaders in general and President Sadam Hussein in particular, had simply not spoken or written for the record about an Iraqi nuclear weapons programme in terms that would justify to the world a 1,200-mile bomb attack on a suburb of Baghdad. And the circumstantial evidence, as we have seen, was very ambiguous and certainly not persuasive. Hence, the list.

Who had originated the list? Within a day or so of the bombing, David Kimche, Director General of the Israeli Foreign Ministry in Jerusalem, was circulating a written justification for the raid to which was attached a 'back-up sheet' with the list of quotations.[26] Prime Minister Begin's press conference at which he used the bogus *Al-Thawra* quotation as evidence that Iraqi President Sadam Hussein wanted to 'destroy Israel's existence' with nuclear weapons, was conducted at 1605 GMT on Tuesday 9 June. Speaking less than forty-eight hours after the raid itself, and only twenty-four hours after the raid had first been made public on Israeli national radio, Begin said:

> Some people ask: 'Where are the proofs for this thesis?' I will bring you today only one short quotation out of many: on the 4th of October in Baghdad, in the newspaper *Al-Thawra* . . .[27]

One place Begin did not get the *Al-Thawra* quotation, then, was from *Al-Thawra*. And yet, the quotation appeared simultaneously in Jerusalem and Washington on the morning of

9 June, in exactly the same form. It is hard not to conclude that the Government of Israel originated the list.

After about a week of trying to chase down the quotations, CRS staff members naturally became curious about their origin. Members of Congress who had commenced the requests for verification were asked and maintained they had received them from 'constituents'. And when some of those Congressional offices went back to their 'constituents', they began to hear that, well, some of the quotations had been received from American Jewish organizations. Some, however, said they had obtained them from the Embassy of Israel in Washington.[28] It is *very* hard not to conclude that the Government of Israel originated the list.

When was the list compiled, and transmitted to members of the United States Congress for use on the floor of the House and Senate? The list was first presented to the Congressional Research Service for 'verification' on the morning of Tuesday, 9 June, less than forty-eight hours after the raid itself occurred. And the following morning, 10 June, a guest editorial appeared in the *New York Times*, written by Senator Alan Cranston of California, in which the bogus *Al-Thawra* quotation appears, identical word for word to the first quotation on the list presented to CRS. [29] Assuming that the *New York Times* editorial section requires the text of a submitted article at least twelve hours or so before press time, Alan Cranston would have had the quotation prior to Begin's press conference and not very long at all after the raid itself.

Indeed, it is likely that the list pre-dates the raid, and was circulated to friends in the United States Congress shortly after or even before the raid, in order that these friends would be well prepared for the debate on questions that would predictably be raised about possible violations of US law, that is, those provisions of the Arms Export Control Act and the US–Israel Mutual Defence Assistance Agreement of 1952, regarding unauthorized offensive use of US weapons provided through the Foreign Military Sales Programme.

Noting the short time between the raid and the appearance of the list of quotations in Congress, together with the obscure, disparate nature of the sources (a speech by the Iraqi Ambassador to Brazil, and citations from Kuwaiti, Lebanese, Iraqi, Parisian Arab publication, etc.,) one CRS staff member came to the conclusion that 'that list was done beforehand ... they had these things ready to go'.[30]

Propaganda or not, accurate or not, the quotations served their purpose and have lived a remarkably long life. On 11 June, one day after CRS had begun raising questions about the accuracy of the list in phone contacts with CIA, DIA, State Department, etc., President Reagan enraged Arab ambassadors in a meeting at the White House by using the *Al-Thawra* quotation.[31]

On 18 June, three days after CRS had published its research report and literally minutes before Foreign Relations Committee Chairman Charles Percy included that report in the record, Senator Alan Cranston on the Senate floor used one of the quotations on the list, purportedly from the 4 October 1980 issue of *Al-Jumhuriyah*, which he described as 'an official party organ of the leading ruling party in Iraq'. Quoted Cranston:

> Who is going to benefit from destroying the Iraqi nuclear reactor? Is it Iran or the Zionist entity? This reactor does not constitute a danger to Iran. It constitutes a great danger to Israel.[32]

The CRS report pointed out that in this (list) version of the *Al-Jumhuriyah* article of 4 October, a paragraph from the original article is left out between the second and third sentences, a paragraph which purports to describe Israeli fears about the reactor. And the final sentence, 'It constitutes a great danger to Israel', is followed in the original by the sentence: 'This is what Begin has said and the leaders of the Zionist enemy also.'[33] The CRS report described this quotation as 'taken out of context in such a manner that the original meaning of the quotations may have been distorted'.[34] Indeed. The point here is that on 18 June, in the mouth of Senator Alan Cranston, that distortion was conscious and deliberate.

A full year after CRS released its research on the quotations, two American–Israeli academicians, Amos Perlmutter and Michael Handel, together with a former Israeli Air Force officer, wrote a book entitled *Two Minutes Over Baghdad: The Most Daring Military Raid Since Entebbe.* As a heading for a chapter on 'Sadam Hussein and Project Tammuz', the book uses a quotation from the Lebanese magazine *Al Usbu Al Arabi*, on 8 September, 1975. [35] As the CRS report (and numerous newspaper accounts of the CRS report) indicated, 'the quotation cited could not be found in the magazine'.[36] As so frequently happens with government disinformation projects, this rather clumsy Israeli effort eventually diminished the reputations of (presumably) innocent and naïve writers/researchers.

The hippopotamus at the cocktail party

Both the House of Representatives and the Senate conducted hearings on the Baghdad reactor raid within weeks of the event. There was a general desire on the part of members to review the circumstances and justification for the attack, and to examine the implications of the event for the future proliferation of nuclear weapons in the Middle East and elsewhere in the Third World. That, at least, was what several members said in their ringing opening statements. The 'business' of the hearings was to fulfill Congress's responsibility under section 3c of the Arms Export Control Act (AECA), and under the US–Israel Mutual Defence Assistance Agreement of 1952, to determine whether the Baghdad raid constituted an 'offensive' use of the US-originated weapons systems involved, thus necessitating a cut-off of US security assistance and sales to Israel.

Getting down to business on the first day of the hearings, 18 June, the Senate Foreign Relations Committee Chairman, Charles Percy, discussed the matter with then State Department Counsellor Robert McFarlane. Both agreed that (a) President and Congress had 'joint' responsibility under AECA to determine whether a violation had occurred that would necessitate an aid cut-off, but (b) amendments to AECA proposed in 1976 by Senators Jacob Javits and Hubert Humphrey and passed that same year relieved the President and Congress of these responsibilities (to make a determination) 'in politically difficult circumstances'.[37] Since it was commonly acknowledged between the White House and Congress that by definition anything having to do with potential Israeli violations of US law constituted 'politically difficult circumstances', all were agreed that, because of the amendments, the AECA effectively did not apply to Israel.

It was as if Tom Sawyer and Huck Finn had arrived at school one winter morning to find the woodstove had been cracked and school cancelled. The 'business' was put aside, and the remaining two and a half days of the hearings were devoted to testimony and grand speeches on Arab duplicity, getting the nuclear genie back in the bottle and the saving of the human race. The White House had, to be sure, taken the token step under AECA of delaying delivery of four F-16 aircraft (for three weeks, as it turned out). But to the general relief of all present at the hearings, there would be no need to determine whether to stop delivery of the few other items of military hardware scheduled for delivery to Israel in June to September 1981. These were, according to the State Department:

Item	Quantity
M109A1B 155 howitzers	11
Mortar carriers M125A2	28
Ambulance	84
Hawk missiles	153
175 mm rounds	65,000
Mark 84 bombs	1,000
Tow missiles	1,763
F-15 aircraft	5
M60–A3 tanks	49
M113 armoured personnel carriers	135
M88A1 recovery vehicles	25
81 mm mortar rounds	71,000
Sidewinder missiles AIM 9	300

The pipeline would continue to flow, with over $2 billion in deliveries scheduled for the succeeding twelve months.[38]

Several senators did seem determined that someone else, preferably the Reagan State Department, put their foot down to prevent further offensive use of Israel's formidable arsenal.

Of immediate concern was Israel's then current complaint that Syria had moved air defence missiles into Lebanon, potentially restricting Israel's use of air power against Palestinian strongholds in that country. This prompted an exchange with State Department Counsellor Robert McFarlane which proves that even the Middle East conflict had its light side:

The Chairman: Have we made it eminently clear to the Israelis that military action using American weapons to take out these missiles would be inconsistent with our 1952 agreement?

Mr McFarlane: I would reaffirm – and I do not intend to dissemble or obfuscate – that the Government of Israel is clearly and unequivocally aware of our view toward the very harmful effects that actions today would have before we have had an opportunity to allow diplomacy to work . . .

Senator Pell: I would just follow up that thought. Has Israel been informed that the use of American weapons against the Syrian missiles would be a violation of the agreement?

Mr McFarlane: The context of our dialogue with Israel both on the use of US-supplied equipment and on its actions in the context of the Habib mission, have been political in their orientation. I would re-emphasize, Senator Pell, that there is no question but that the Government of Israel clearly understands that actions, using our equipment or not, which disrupt the prospects for resolving this conflict would have a very harmful effect.

Senator Pell: I understand exactly what you are saying. But you still did not answer my question. Have they been informed specifically to this specific effect?

Mr McFarlane: Well, I take it from your question that you are asking whether we have implied a legal sanction or a legal judgement on such use as Israel might make of our weapons. Or am I missing your point?

Senator Pell: My point – and, I think, Senator Percy's point – is to ask whether Israel had been informed that if they used American weapons against Syria they would be in violation of the agreement? You may well not have so informed them because you may not have made up your mind that it would be in violation. But my question was: Has that viewpoint been passed to them specifically? I think the answer probably is 'No', but I just want to hear you say it.

Mr McFarlane: Has the United States informed Israel that the use of our weapons against Syria would be a violation of the agreement?

Senator Pell: Against the missiles in Lebanon, the Syrian missiles in Lebanon.

Mr McFarlane: Well, precisely in those terms, I do not recall any such notice. The intent of avoiding violence at this point is absolutely a fact.[39]

The justification for the attack on the reactor was examined at length in both the Senate and House hearings. Those members of Congress who generally supported the raid were pleased to have expert witnesses testify that Iraq was stockpiling amounts and types of nuclear materials far beyond what appeared to be necessary for a modest research programme.[40] Moreover, there did not seem to be a valid rationale for development of nuclear energy in a country so rich in fossil fuel resources. Congress members who opposed the raid, on the other hand, were pleased to see testimony by a majority of the expert witnesses, along with the State Department and the IAEA, to the effect that (a) both French and IAEA safeguards regimes would have detected a weapons programme once Iraq moved to obtain or reprocess weapons-grade nuclear materials, and (b) even if Iraq had wanted to develop 'the bomb', it did not have the expertise to do so on its own without direct French and Italian assistance.[41]

It was not until the third day of the Senate hearings, however, that former Ambassador James Akins made the rather obvious point that the Israeli raid, rather than delaying the nuclearization of the Middle East conflict, had made it inevitable – to Israel's great loss:

> this is the most dangerous and most deplorable part of the Israeli attack – I do not have any doubts any more. I think as a result of the Israeli attack, there has been a determination inside of Iraq, and the Arab world, to get their own bomb. It probably did not exist before, or at least was questionable. The Arabs have a lot of money. They have a lot of power. There are a lot of people who have access to nuclear technology who could sell it or give it to the Arabs ... We could start with Pakistan and we could go to India and we could go to China. I don't think the Soviet Union probably would do this. But other candidates might.[42]

Why would the Arabs want nuclear weapons? Why did Iraq (apparently) want them? What would ineluctably lead to the dangerous Middle East nuclear confrontation of which Ambassador Akins warned? These questions were never, in 299 pages of oral and written testimony, even addressed, because the answer was obvious: *Israel's* nuclear weapons programme. Like Robert Benchley's hippopotamus at the cocktail party, Israel's bomb stood at the back of the Foreign Relations Committee hearing room, while a dozen United States senators and half a dozen congressmen carefully said nothing about it, hoping no one would notice the thing.

Pakistan, India, China, Brazil, Libya and other recent or potential members of the nuclear club were repeatedly, sanctimoniously vilified at the hearings. France, Italy, West Germany and other 'supplier nations' of nuclear equipment and materials to developing countries were similarly treated. But Israel's bomb was hardly mentioned.[43] South Africa, presumably because of its then recently publicized nuclear test relationship with Israel, also escaped notice.

Senator Cranston set a lofty tone at the beginning of the hearings:

> Mr Chairman, the present international approach to controlling nuclear proliferation clearly is not working. The spread of the bomb presents the human race with our most fundamental challenge. The very survival of our civilization is placed at risk when the capacity to produce weapons of mass destruction is allowed to spread around the globe. We must all work together on this threat. There can be no more important task.[44]

You cannot determine this from the hearing transcripts, but at this point the huge hippo at the back of the room must have turned his ponderous head to stare at the bald, animated fellow addressing the lights and cameras.

Postscript: the United Nations Security Council resolution

On 19 June, the day after Senator Cranston delivered his stirring speech, the UN Security Council passed a resolution condemning the attack upon the reactor, and calling upon Israel to 'place its nuclear facilities under IAEA safeguards'.[45] The US voted for the resolution, which was in fact drafted with the direct participation of then US Ambassador to the UN, Jean

Kirkpatrick, working closely with Iraqi Foreign Minister Saadun Hamadi. No sanctions against Israel were mentioned in the resolution.

American diplomats in Baghdad, who had been amazed at the moderate reaction to the raid in Iraq and the lack of any recriminations against the US as Israel's prime supporter, breathed a sigh of relief after the UN resolution passed without the usual US veto, in a telex to the State Department:

> The consensus around [Baghdad] from East European and Arab as well as Western diplomatic colleagues is that we have weathered the storm well. However, the scenario has not yet played itself out. Having blocked what the Iraqis and the other Arabs see as justified sanctions against Israel, their attention will focus on our willingness to bring Israel into compliance with the Security Council resolution we negotiated. The Iraqis are realistic enough not to expect Israeli reparations. What they will watch is whether the US will exert significant pressure on Israel to place its nuclear facilities under international inspection as called for in the Security Council resolution.[46]

But in the weeks and months that followed, the US made no effort to 'bring significant pressure on Israel', to place its nuclear facilities under safeguards, let alone reduce or eliminate its weapons programme in accordance with the long-standing US policy on non-proliferation. Silence in the White House. In the Senate, silence from Senator Cranston. When your focus is the survival of civilization, it is best not to get bogged down in details. The hippopotamus, wherever he went after the hearings finished, went with a smile on his face. No one had noticed him.

TEN

Helping Lebanon Come Apart:
the Bombing Raids of 1981

On 9 June 1981, two days after the attack on the Baghdad reactor, State Department press spokesman Dean Fischer conducted his regular noon briefing for journalists.

He did not know, he said, when the Department would finish its report to Congress on the 'possible' use of American planes in the raid. He was not sure what form the report would take. He would not commit himself on whether the use of the planes, if it had occurred, constituted a violation of American law. He didn't want to get into the legal differentiation between 'offensive' and 'defensive' use of American weapons. He had nothing to say on whether the Department agreed with Israel that Iraq had been developing a nuclear weapons production facility at Tuwaitha. He had no details on the damage the Israeli planes had done, or on casualties to foreign advisers.

One of the reporters concluded quite reasonably at this point that this particular briefing was not going to be factually enlightening in terms of that day's deadline, so he asked, as he termed it, 'something of a philosophical question':

The Secretary [Alexander Haig] made a trip to the Middle East in early April trying to persuade the moderate and conservative Arab states there that the real threat to their security came from the Soviet Union, not from Israel. Is that strategy still tenable in view of this strike?

Responded Fischer: 'We would certainly like to think so.' There was general laughter in the room among the journalists, through which the questioner persisted:

The evidence [is] that Arab countries are vulnerable to strikes by the Israeli Air Force supplied with the most sophisticated American equipment, that the United States does not do anything to restrain Israel from those strikes, and that you're still trying to maintain that the security threat, the physical threat comes from Russia. Do you plan to try to revive that strategy? Do you plan to argue that this is an aberration? Do you plan to do anything to give some concrete evidence that that strategy is a sound one?

Responded Fischer, just as doggedly:

We're not going to abandon what the Secretary clearly stated were the purposes of his trip in April. Clearly, we have to deal with the situation and the facts as they exist, and there is no reason, in our judgement, to try to abandon what was stated by the Secretary as the policy of this Administration.[1]

In April 1981, the Reagan Administration was just finding its way into the Middle East conflict. During his trip, Secretary Haig may not have reached a common understanding with 'moderate' Arab governments, but there is little doubt that he reached an agreement with Menachem Begin in Israel which would have an enormous impact upon the land and people of Lebanon. Begin in fact had already publicly revealed that in his meetings with Haig, he had informed the Secretary in advance of Israel's intent to begin bombing strikes against south Lebanon.[2]

Haig had held two meetings with the Israeli Prime Minister, one of which had been a closed session in which no minutes were taken. Afterwards, the American Secretary of State had spoken to the press about 'a convergence of outlook in the area of broad, strategic threat to the Middle East region', including both traditional military threats from the Soviet Union, and 'Soviet proxy' activity of the PLO.[3] The Israelis involved had been a bit more forthcoming. In describing the meeting to colleagues later, Begin had said 'Ben Gurion used to say that if you're pursuing a policy that may lead to war, it's vital to have a great power behind you.'[4] Israeli Foreign Minister Yitzhak Shamir, who had also attended the meetings, spoke somewhat more cryptically of a 'revolutionary' new US approach to regional security issues. The meaning of both statements would soon become clear.

For the first quarter of a century or so of Israel's existence as a nation state, its interest in Lebanon was focused primarily on security issues in the Litani River region (south Lebanon) just north of the Israeli border. True, in the mid-1950s (former) Israeli Prime Minister David Ben Gurion had spoken and written frequently of the need to establish a Christian Maronite 'buffer' state on Israel's northern border. But at the time and for years later, the Jewish state had not had the resources to intervene directly in the affairs of Lebanon.

This changed during the Lebanese civil war of 1975–6 when Israel, which had emerged from the October war of 1973 as a regionally dominant military power, first established regular contacts with Phalange leader Bashir Gemayel. In 1978, after a particularly savage PLO attack (involving thirty-four civilian deaths) along the coastal road south of the Lebanon border, Israel took more than 25,000 troops – two mechanized divisions and an armoured brigade – into south Lebanon. 'Operation Litani', as the Israelis called it, resulted in the deaths of over a thousand Palestinian and Lebanese, the vast majority of whom were also civilians. Aside from bashing the PLO, the main Israeli objective in the affair was to extend the territory just north of the border which was controlled by Major Saad Haddad, the Phalangist warlord and Israeli surrogate. Bashir Gemayel was asked to help and did send a few troops south, but they deserted. It was, nevertheless, a new stage in Israeli–Phalange co-operation.

In 1979 Israeli Defence Minister Ezer Weizman announced a new 'security' policy for Lebanon: Israel would henceforth strike at will at suspected PLO facilities, and would not wait for PLO raids to occur on Israeli territory. By 1980 Israel was not only conducting regular air raids into south Lebanon, but had begun to provide millions of dollars in free arms to Gemayel's Phalange army.[5]

In early 1981 the Government of Israel pronounced its policy of 'pre-emptive' attack a success, claiming it had greatly reduced 'terrorist incidents' in Israel. Interestingly, Israel's own statistics, used in this statement, showed that only 7.7 per cent of the attacks into Israeli-held territory originated from Lebanon – the overwhelming majority, over 92 per cent, emanated from the West Bank and Gaza.[6]

At the beginning of April 1981 Bashir Gemayel decided to test his new relationship with his powerful neighbours to the south. Near the city of Zahle in the Beqaa Valley, he attacked the Syrian Army main headquarters in Lebanon, and then Syrian outposts along the important Beirut–Damascus highway.

The Syrians, whose soldiers were in Lebanon as part of the Arab deterrent forces at the invitation of the Lebanese Government, and initially at least, with the blessing of both the US and Israeli Governments, considered the Beqaa Valley essential to their national security to the same degree that Israel cherished south Lebanon, and for many of the same reasons. It was contiguous, for one thing, with their own border. Predictably, then, the Syrian Army responded, surrounding Gemayel's men and laying siege to Zahle. Just as predictably, Gemayel howled toward Jerusalem and the Israeli Air Force went into action, downing two of the Syrian troop helicopters bringing in reinforcements. President Hafiz al-Assad had at this point essentially two choices: back away from Syria's historic and traditional involvement in Lebanon and abandon border areas twelve miles from downtown Damascus, or escalate the crisis.

Not surprisingly he chose the latter. After offering to allow Gemayel's men to leave peaceably if they would abandon Zahle, Assad installed SAM-6 anti-aircraft missiles in the Beqaa, and Scud tactical ballistic missiles in the outskirts of Damascus. The former posed a threat to Israeli air dominance over central and northern Lebanon, and the latter a threat to Israel proper, at least hypothetically. In fact, Israeli fighter bombers already had US-supplied electronic countermeasure systems which could fool and foil the SAMs, and the Scuds were so inaccurate as to pose no serious threat to Israeli population centres or military installations.

Menachem Begin nevertheless loudly threatened the destruction of the Soviet missiles, and the Middle East once again faced the possibility of a war involving the major powers of the region. Realizing this, President Reagan notified those involved of his intent to send Special Ambassador Philip Habib to mediate the crisis. At the same time Soviet advisers began to arrive in Syria at an alarming rate. One Israeli history of the period has observed:

> As the sabre rattling grew louder, the siege of Zahle became secondary. Having achieved his aim of precipitating a crisis, Bashir Gemayel quietly capitulated and pulled his men out of the city.[7]

The leadership of Israel was probably not surprised that a US Secretary of State came to the region urging military action against 'Soviet proxies', and that he was followed in a matter of days by a presidential emissary urging peace. In the Rogers/ Kissinger era of the late 1960s and early 1970s, they had seen it all before. Nor were the Israelis in doubt about the effect of such policy confusion in Washington upon their own options – they could do as they pleased and justify to Congress, the US press, etc., virtually any action they deemed necessary in the circumstances. And Menachem Begin, who was at the time locked in a very tough election campaign and ached for a foreign threat to oppose 'decisively', was free to be Menachem Begin.

Shortly after Alexander Haig left Jerusalem, the *New York Times* correspondent in Jerusalem, David Shipler, wrote that

> A basic change in attitude of the United States toward Israeli military action in Lebanon appears to have given a new flexibility to Israel's Army and Air Force, which have been busy recently with air strikes and ground assaults against Palestinian guerrilla bases in Lebanese territory.[8]

In fact, the Israeli Defence Force's interest in Lebanon extended far beyond PLO guerrilla bases. Shipler was correct, however, in assessing a situation pregnant with the potential for new violence. PLO leader Yasser Arafat was also well aware of the danger, and in late April met with UN Secretary General Waldheim and agreed to refrain from attacks on Israel from Lebanese territory.

In May and June Israel conducted sporadic air raids into Lebanon punctuated, as we have seen, by the long-range 6 June 1981 attack on the nuclear reactor outside Baghdad. The PLO did not respond with attacks upon Israel. Through this period,

Ambassador Philip Habib shuttled between Jerusalem and Damascus, trying to defuse the 'missile crisis' in the Beqaa Valley. At the beginning of July Menachem Begin was re-elected Prime Minister, as crowds in Jerusalem chanted 'Begin, King of Israel'. Habib, discreetly out of the region during the Israeli elections, returned to Beirut on 9 July. And the following day, 10 July, Israel struck.

Initially the raids were confined to south Lebanon. On the morning of 10 July Israeli planes bombed roads and villages in the Habbush area north of Nabatiyah, and also the area south of Sidon on the Lebanese coast. Radio Lebanon estimated the casualties at six dead and twenty wounded.[9] The *New York Times* quoted 'reports' of three dead and fifteen wounded.[10] Following the strikes, the PLO rocketed the Israeli settlement at Qiryat Shemona.

US Ambassador Robert Dillon in Beirut seemed to sense from the outset that this was more than a random exchange of ordnance, when he reported to the State Department on 16 July:

> It is another repetition of the cycle of violence, but this time there appears to have been a clear beginning. Following Arafat's pledge to [UN Secretary General] Waldheim, the PLO refrained from launching military actions against Israel for more than two months, even though the Israelis conducted several air raids during that period. This was a shaky cease-fire, to be sure, but one that nevertheless held, from the Palestinian side.[11]

The timing of the attacks, said Ambassador Dillon, could not have been worse:

> The Israeli raids, coming while Ambassador Habib was in Lebanon and Israel, and while Department Counsellor Robert McFarlane was in Tel Aviv to discuss such matters as Israeli use of American arms, has resulted in more of an outcry against the US than is usually the case when the Israelis hit south Lebanon.[12]

Two days later, on 12 July, the Israeli Air Force bombed two more locations in Lebanon, killing five and wounding twenty-five people. Ambassador Dillon reported that (contrary to official Israeli reports) several of the casualties were civilians.[13]

'Bombing', noted Dillon, 'is not a precise science.' Even the *New York Times* had begun to doubt the official Israeli version of the raids. After quoting an Israeli Government spokesman to the effect that the second raids had hit PLO artillery positions, weapons storehouses and an ammunition dump, the *Times* noted that:

> Reporters who visited the area, in the vicinity of the town of Damur, about 10 miles south of Beirut, saw a burning refrigerator factory and other buildings.[14]

Lebanese press and popular anger began to be directed against their own government, which was meeting daily with Habib, a representative of the government which provided Israel with the planes and had, it appeared, given Israel the green light to use them against Lebanon. The US Ambassador in Beirut was called in to meet with Lebanese Prime Minister Shafiq Wazzan. Said Dillon to the State Department:

> I suspect the subject will be the Israeli air strikes and our reaction. A forthright statement by the Department's spokesman stating our opposition to the raids and deploring civilian casualties would be helpful.[15]

The State Department did issue a statement about the raids, but could not bring itself to deplore civilian casualties caused by Israeli planes.

The third Israeli strikes in four days were carried out on 14 July. Particularly hard hit was the village of Zifta, near Sidon. Each time, it seemed, the raids were becoming more costly for the people of Lebanon. Officials estimated the casualties at ten dead and thirty wounded, but the US Embassy reported unofficial figures of twenty-seven dead and sixty-eight wounded. A Syrian Mig 23 was shot down trying to defend Zifta. That night PLO guerrillas responded with an intense rocketing of Israeli settlements in the Galilee panhandle, killing three and wounding twenty-five. By now, both sides claimed to be 'responding' to the outrages committed by the other.

Lebanese Prime Minister Wazzan for the first time publicly raised the question of US responsibility for the raids, as various newspapers began to call for retaliation against the US and its 'interests' in the region. Ambassador Dillon, in reporting this, warned:

> The already widespread and growing perceptions of the US as supporting Israeli actions in south Lebanon will make it increasingly difficult for us to maintain any semblance of even-handedness here with the consequent weakening of our ability to influence events. The unusually high numbers of casualties and close sequence of the latest raids, coming during the presence in the area of the Habib mission are undoubtedly important reasons for this criticism . . .[16]

At this point Israel dramatically escalated its attacks, destroying five bridges across south Lebanon on the afternoon of 16 July. Bridges on both the Litani and Zahrani Rivers were hit, according to IDF Chief of Staff Lieutenant General Rafael Eitan, in order to slow the 'endless stream of weapons' moving to PLO guerrillas in south Lebanon.[17] Also struck in the raids were the Ayn al-Hilwah refugee camp near Sidon and the American-owned and managed Medreco oil refinery complex at Zahrani. General Eitan did not give the reasons for the selection of these targets. The *New York Times*, in its coverage of the 16 July strikes, did not mention the American refinery.

Unofficial estimates of casualties were thirty-two dead and ninety-seven wounded, fully half of which were not guerrillas or even Palestinians, but were Lebanese civilians. General Eitan informed the press that the Israeli Air Force had previously refrained from striking the bridges out of consideration for civilians. Now, the bridges would stay down. 'If others [than the PLO] suffer,' he declared, 'they should press the terrorists to stop their attacks on us.'[18] Naturally, the PLO retaliated by rocketing Israeli settlements that evening.

On the morning of 17 July, Israeli planes carried the destruction into the Fakhani district of downtown Beirut, killing over one hundred and fifty people and injuring more than six hundred. Whole apartment buildings collapsed on their inhabitants. Ambassador Dillon, who witnessed the bombing at close hand from the balcony of the house of Takieddin Solh, a former minister of the Lebanese Government, reported in some detail on this particular raid:

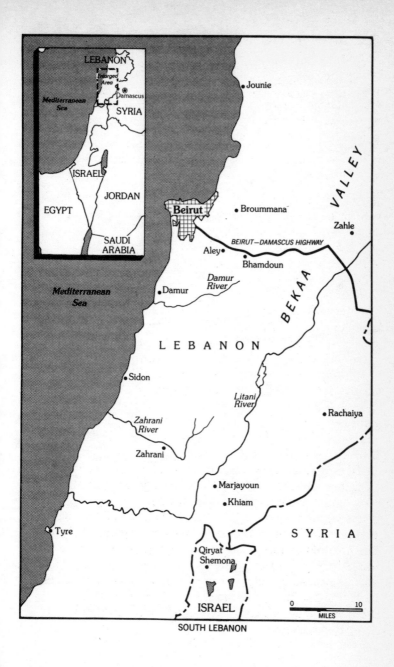

SOUTH LEBANON

the damage was massive. The Fakhani-Tariq Al-Jadidah area near the Shatila refugee camp was the hardest hit. A number of buildings were completely levelled and the devastation is reminiscent of World War II. The PLO offices that were the targets of the raids were evidently located on the lower floors of the buildings.[19]

Delayed fuse bombs were used by the Israelis, timed to go off about forty-five minutes after impact, when emergency personnel were undertaking rescue work.[20]

A statement issued by Prime Minister Begin's office after the raid stated: 'We shall give the enemy no rest until we have put an end to his bloody rampage and peace will reign between Israel and Lebanon.'[21] At least *someone* was working for peace in the midst of all this violence. Begin was at the time his own Defence Minister, but he was reportedly receiving advice on these peace efforts from his Minister of Agriculture, a former general named Ariel Sharon. Henceforth, said Begin, the IAF would strike PLO bases wherever they existed even if they were 'purposefully located in the vicinity of or within civilian concentrations'.[22] The Government of Lebanon was unable to follow Begin's logic, and on the evening of 17 July passionately charged that Israel's bombing of Beirut was a deliberate effort to torpedo 'serious peace moves' then under way, presumably alluding to Habib's shuttle diplomacy.

That same evening, the US Embassy notified Washington that it estimated casualty figures *for Beirut alone* for the Israeli air strikes in the period from 1 April to 17 July, 1981, at 438 dead and 2,479 wounded.[23]

The 'round-up' telegram from the Embassy on the events of 17 July included a paragraph indicating that the US refinery had again been struck:

> According to the Beirut-based American manager of the US-owned Medreco refinery at Zahrani, three storage tanks were hit and the refinery has been shut down. (No Americans were working at the refinery.)[24]

Even American facilities, it seemed, were receiving the attention of Israeli peacemakers. Repeatedly. Three additional bridges had been knocked out, bringing to nine the total destroyed since 10 July.

Infrastructure targets now became almost the sole focus of Israeli attacks. On 18 July, the Hamra Bridge area south of Sidon was hit, as was the Medreco refinery yet again. This time, Israeli gunboats bombarded the facility, igniting fires in storage tanks. Highways and electrical stations were also hit, as were water pumping stations and communication facilities. The US Embassy staff began to wonder at this point why an American refinery and other infrastructure targets were attracting so much Israeli attention, as these appeared to have little to do with the Palestine Liberation Organization or Israeli border security.[25]

The raids came every day now, as Israel bombed on 19, 20, 21 22 and 23 July. On 20 July, Menachem Begin informed Ambassador Habib that a cease-fire would not solve the problem of the PLO raids into northern Israel, and complained about the delay in delivery of four US F-16 aircraft, suspended after the 6 June Baghdad raid. On 22 July, the Medreco refinery was again bombed by Israeli aircraft, and was once more put out of commission, this time for what its American manager estimated would be two weeks. The resulting shortages of gasoline and oil, he told the US Embassy, would cause power shortages in Beirut and in south Lebanon.[26] Israel, using US weapons, was now waging total war on the land and people of Lebanon.

The *New York Times* did mention the Israeli attacks on the Medreco refinery in its coverage on 19 and 23 July. Neither article, however, mentioned that the refinery was US owned and operated. Not once in the *Times*'s extensive coverage of the shelling and bombing in Lebanon in July 1981 was the American ownership of the refinery revealed.

The *New York Times* did, however, at a time of mounting criticism of Israel in Europe and at the UN, begin to cover Israeli civilian casualties of PLO attacks in great detail. On 20 July, the death of a fourteen-year-old boy in a PLO shelling of the settlement of Qiryat Shemona was reported. On 21 July, it was a forty-year-old woman and a twenty-eight-year-old Israeli soldier – names were given and the manner of death was described. During the entire month of July, while hundreds of

Lebanese civilians died and thousands were wounded and dis-
figured by Israeli bombs, the *New York Times* did not identify
by name or age or circumstance a single Lebanese victim.
Lebanese victims' names, it seemed, were simply not 'news fit
to print'.

On 24 July, the US Embassy in Beirut informed the State
Department in Washington that a Lebanese Army source had
provided the US Defence Attaché with (presumably confidential) official Lebanese Government statistics on the nationality
of those killed and wounded as a result of 'Israeli/militia
actions' in the period from 10 to 22 July. Fifty-nine per cent of
those killed and 68 per cent of the wounded had been
Lebanese, while Palestinians (civilian and military) accounted
for 33 per cent of the dead and 30 per cent of the injured.
Noting that the military totals differed somewhat from those
previously reported, Ambassador Dillon commented, however,
that 'the order of magnitude is clear, as is the indication that the
Lebanese are taking most of the punishment'.[27]

The statistics reflect Israel's choice of targets during the
strange and savage July 1981 bombings of Lebanon. Factories,
bridges, electrical and water pumping substations, roads . . .
and five concentrated air attacks on an American-owned and
operated oil refinery which supplied vital gasoline and fuel to all
Lebanon. What on earth did any of this have to do with PLO
attacks on northern Galilee, even if one accepts the Israeli
contention that (contrary to US Embassy reports) the PLO
'started it all'?

The same question troubled the staff of the US Embassy in
that period. Ambassador Robert Dillon said:

> It was clear in the Embassy that the constant Israeli talk about the
> build-up of the PLO in south Lebanon, the constant talk about
> artillery, heavy weapons, etc, was greatly exaggerated . . . This
> was a period in which we had pretty fair access [in south Lebanon]
> and the idea that there was a modern PLO army being raised
> there was just . . . greatly exaggerated. I tended to see the raids as
> preparation for what followed in June of 1982.[28]

At several points during the July bombing raid, as Ambassador Philip Habib shuttled in and out of Lebanon, reports

surfaced in Washington and Beirut that his mediating role had been changed and broadened. Originally sent to the region to try to defuse the Syrian–Israeli 'missile crisis', there were persistent reports and finally State Department confirmation that Habib, and the US sought broader objectives, specifically the resolution of the Lebanese civil war, and the stabilization of the Lebanese Government.[29]

Was this what Israel sought at the time? The destruction of bridges, factories, roads, refineries, etc, would seem to indicate that it was not. If there were any PLO fighters, weapons, offices and the like at the Medreco refinery during the first Israeli attack on 16 July – and the Israeli Government never claimed that there were – surely none were there during the four subsequent attacks, which included bombing runs on the pipeline to Beirut.

In backing the Phalange forces of Bashir Gemayel with weapons and finally with tactical air support, and in directing repeated, concentrated attacks against Lebanon's infrastructure, Israel's primary goal in July 1981 was the destabilization of the Government and economy of Lebanon. In this, Israel was working directly against stated US policy.

On 20 July, 1981 the Reagan Administration finally decided openly to express some displeasure at the devastation of Lebanon from the air. Secretary of State Alexander Haig announced the President's decision to delay the shipment to Israel of an additional six F-16 fighter bombers, bringing to a total of ten the number of deliveries delayed in June and July. On 22 July Israeli Ambassador to Washington Ephraim Evron expressed his 'deep disappointment' at the decision. It was, he said, 'a decision that would destabilize the area'.[30]

A cease-fire involving the PLO, Israel and the Lebanese Government was finally concluded with the assistance of Ambassador Habib on 24 July. It would last for almost eleven months, until 30,000 IDF troops stormed across the Lebanese border in June 1982. Ambassador Dillon, asked to describe the July 1981 cease-fire, said:

> It was a good cease-fire, and it stuck. The Palestinian side so far as I know never violated it. That hardly surprises me. In situations

like this, it's rarely the weaker side that violates these things. When you suddenly hear that weak country X has violated the airspace and borders of strong neighbour Y, and has therefore forced Y to come in and beat the hell out of X, you can be a little sceptical that that was exactly how it happened. Yet we're asked to believe that over and over again.[31]

Lebanon and most of the Arab Middle East was having difficulty believing it. And that is why Alexander Haig was having so little success in convincing governments in the region that the principal threat to their national security was the Soviet Union.

ELEVEN

Semper Infidelis:
Israel and the Multinational
Peacekeeping Force in Lebanon, 1982–3

At first, no one made anything of it. The US marines involved thought of it more as a nuisance than a real danger, even when it happened for the second and the third time. But it didn't make any sense: why would Israeli planes and patrol boats want to harass the US Navy ships and marine helicopters preparing for the arrival in Beirut of the American peacekeeping contingent?

It began on 8 August, 1982, with Israeli SAAR patrol boats careening into the path of the marine amphibious landing craft ferrying men and supplies back and forth between the port of Beirut and the ships of the US amphibious task force lying offshore. Then Israeli F-16 fighters began to make dangerously close passes on the UH-I 'Huey' helicopters shuttling the planning and logistics officers to and from the port and nearby Beirut International Airport.

A mild protest was sent to the IDF through channels – 'We just asked them to knock it off,' recalls one marine officer who saw the message. Brigadier General James C. Mead, who commanded the 32nd Marine Amphibious Unit (MAU) in August 1982, remembers being 'very confused by it, as to what their intentions were'. He was sure these were not accidents, 'since there wasn't anybody else in the water at the time'.[1] Routine incident reports were sent via chain of command back to Marine Corps and JCS Headquarters in Washington.

That was pretty much the end of it, or seemed to be. In Washington the Israeli Embassy acknowledged that the incidents had occurred, but said they were due to 'unfortunate misunderstandings' caused by a lack of information from US military authorities about the helicopter flights.[2] One marine

officer attached to the JCS didn't think so, however, warning
that the incidents were just a harbinger of what was to come
when the multinational force (MNF) itself landed. 'These bas-
tards have their own agenda,' he said, 'and we're just getting in
their way.' At the time, his words were dismissed by his colleagues as a statement of opinion from someone who was
thought to be anti-Israel.[3]

On 21 August, 1982, 800 US marines arrived in Beirut as
peacekeepers. Except for marine guards at the Embassy and
individual American officers attached to United Nations
peacekeeping forces, these were the first units of US troops to
be sent to Lebanon since President Eisenhower had intervened
in an internal government crisis in 1958. In August 1982, however, the crisis into which the marines were being inserted was
anything but internal. Two and a half months previously, 30,000
Israeli soldiers had marched into south Lebanon for the stated
purpose of clearing PLO guerrillas from a 'security zone' north
of Israel's border. The Israeli cabinet named this invasion
'Peace for Galilee'.

Within a very few days, however, there developed – even in
Israel itself – a confusion about the scope and actual objectives
of the war. Prominent Israeli journalist and author, Jacobo
Timmerman, has written that one of the first signs in his country
that this war was more than a security operation, was the smell
of unburied bodies which his colleagues brought back from the
front. They didn't comment about it on radio or television, due
to IDF military censorship, but they brought that smell back,
and an understanding:

> The reporters said they could not get rid of it. And very soon at
> family reunions, at receptions, while waiting for the children to
> come out of the kindergartens, in the lines waiting their turns at
> the banks, the middle class of Israel started to discuss the smell
> . . . The reporters brought back something else. Using binoculars
> from different vantage points, they had witnessed the systematic
> destruction of three great cities: Tyre, Sidon, and what was left of
> Damur after the civil war. This, too, was a first. Israeli Air Force
> bombs, along with artillery and navy barrages, were demolishing
> cities. The reporters had never seen such a thing before, never
> believed it possible; but they soon discovered it was the normal

and natural result of a war in which you have an enormous military advantage.[4]

West Beirut in particular was singled out for the IDF's attention. A densely populated Muslim section of the city, west Beirut was bombed and shelled more or less continuously from the second day of the invasion. By 19 June, less than two weeks after the beginning of operation 'Peace for Galilee', the US Embassy estimated eighty thousand homeless people on the streets and in parks and deserted buildings in west Beirut.[5] In the confusion of total warfare, the Embassy said it was difficult at that stage to estimate accurately the dead and wounded.

Peace for Galilee, it seemed, was to mean anything but for the people of west Beirut. Napalm, phosphorous and even advanced fuel-air mixture weapons, along with cluster bombs, were being used in high- and medium-density residential sections of the city. The use of these weapons was reported extensively in the international printed and broadcast media, as was the fact that there appeared to be no discrimination among targets.[6] The target was, quite simply, west Beirut. The London *Sunday Times* reported that in the first two months of the war, the targets hit in the city included five UN buildings, 134 embassies or diplomatic residences, six hospitals and clinics, one mental institution, the Central Bank, five hotels, the Red Cross, Lebanese and foreign media outlets and innumerable private houses.[7]

In an effort to protect the civilian population of the city, the UN Security Council voted on 1 August to send observers into west Beirut. And a few days later, President Ronald Reagan and other Western leaders called for the safe and orderly removal from west Beirut of the people who were supposed to be the primary objectives of all this high-tech fury: PLO and Syrian soldiers.

A draft detailed plan for the withdrawal was negotiated by US envoy Philip Habib, between Israel and Lebanon. The US, Italy and France were committed in principle to participate in a multinational force which would oversee the affair. And the American marines (specifically the 32nd Marine Amphibious

Unit attached to the US Sixth Fleet) would fly the US flag in what everyone understood would be a very tense operation.

What none of the diplomats involved, nor the US marines, could have known was that on 8 August, the day that the harassment in the harbour had begun, Israeli Defence Minister Ariel Sharon had expressly ordered IDF units to interfere with the deployment of the MNF.[8] Those incidents were not occurring spontaneously. Philip Habib may have thought he had an agreement in principle on the MNF with Prime Minister Begin and the Israeli Foreign Ministry, but the IDF soldiers in Lebanon took their orders from Sharon. Indeed, Habib was in one of the helicopters harassed that day by the Israelis. And when Habib presented his final, detailed plan for the evacuation two days later on 10 August, Sharon rejected it, demanding that the MNF not land before the evacuation (he called it an 'expulsion') was under way, in effect insisting that Israel, not the MNF, would oversee the evacuation of the PLO.[9]

Evacuation, extermination, expiation

Under pressure from the White House, the Israeli Government did finally accept the Habib plan on 11 August, and a few days later, 800 marines of the 32nd MAU landed to assist French and Italian MNF contingents in the supervision of the evacuation. Over three weeks, around fifteen thousand PLO guerrillas and Syrian soldiers along with some civilian dependants, departed Beirut peaceably over land and sea. By and large, this first marine peacekeeping mission was carried out without major confrontations with the IDF, though Sharon did aggravate the MNF – Americans, French and Italians alike – by turning back some of the departing ferries packed with PLO fighters, and by establishing a photo-surveillance unit at the dockside.[10]

On 10 September, the 32nd MAU departed Lebanon thinking its task was completed. The PLO, or most of it, was gone from Beirut. Lebanon had a new President, Bashir Gemayel, elected on 23 August. As part of Habib's negotiations on the evacuation, Israel had agreed not to invade Muslim west

Beirut. President Reagan, calling for a 'fresh start' in the region, had on 1 September put forward a new plan for resolution of the Palestinian problem which had for eight years exacerbated Lebanon's on-again, off-again civil war. Although the 'Reagan plan' was immediately, firmly, formally rejected by Israel, the level of fighting had subsided in early September, and as the MNF departed, there was reason for optimists to hope that a withdrawal of foreign forces from Lebanon might follow. For a moment, it looked like there was light at the end of the Lebanon tunnel.

The marines were gone from Lebanon exactly nineteen days. During that period, sectarian violence once again broke out in Beirut; the IDF recommenced heavy air strikes in central and eastern Lebanon; Bashir Gemayel was assassinated; and on 15 September Ariel Sharon, in violation of the cease-fire agreement, sent the IDF into west Beirut. The battle which no one but Sharon seemed to want had begun.

On 16 September, the US and Israeli Governments publicly argued about security arrangements for civilians in west Beirut. The White House and State Department simultaneously issued a statement condemning Israel for the invasion of west Beirut, and accusing Prime Minister Begin's Government of breaking confidential agreements made 'both in Washington and in Israel'. Furthermore, said the statement, the IDF's presence in the Muslim sector of the city was 'a clear violation of the cease-fire understanding to which Israel is a party',[11] referring to the accord by which Yasser Arafat and the PLO agreed to leave Beirut, published four weeks earlier on 20 August. Privately, Reagan Administration 'sources' blamed Ariel Sharon for the latest move, apparently made 'with the approval of Prime Minister Begin'.[12]

Stung by these accusations, Jerusalem issued a statement of its own, after a four hour cabinet meeting, saying that the IDF had entered west Beirut 'to prevent the danger of violence, bloodshed and anarchy', and would not be withdrawn until the Lebanese Army was ready and able 'to ensure public order and security'.[13] The cabinet meeting and official statement coincided with the beginning of the massacres at Sabra and Chatila, carried out by Phalange militiamen in large, crowded refugee camps literally surrounded by armed Israeli soldiers. The killing took a full two days to complete, and was revealed on 18 September. Twelve hundred people had died or had 'disappeared' in the rubble and in hastily dug mass graves.

Just before and after the news of the massacre, the Israeli printed and broadcast media carried news that the IDF in Beirut had escorted the Phalangists into the camps (Radio Kol Israel, 16 September), had charged the Phalangists with the responsibility of purging the camps of terrorists (IDF Radio, 17 September), and had early reports from its own soldiers that a massacre was in progress, early enough to have prevented the event (*Haaretz*, 23 September).[14] In succeeding days, Israelis learned that the IDF had had two 'co-ordination' meetings with the Phalangist commanders, just prior to the killings; that the IDF had established a rooftop command post overlooking Sabra and Chatila during the affair, and had provided flares to light the camps during the two nights of killing, and military bulldozers with which the Phalangists had tried to hide the enormity of their deed by means of mass burials in trenches. IDF soldiers had physically prevented groups of hysterical women and children from fleeing the camps during the massacre.[15]

Israel suffered a guilt complex. There were echoes of Warsaw in west Beirut, and echoes of Lidice at Sabra and Chatila. Protesters burned tyres on the Tel Aviv-Haifa road, and demonstrated in Jerusalem and in a tourist centre near the Lebanon border. On 25 September, an anti-war, anti-massacre rally took place in Tel Aviv, involving a number of people variously estimated at 100,000 to 400,000. Jacobo Timmerman, known for his opposition to fascism and antisemitism in Argentina, wrote on 21 September 1982:

> Only the world's Jewish people, I believe can now do something for us. The Diaspora Jews who have maintained the values of our moral and cultural traditions – those values now trampled on here by intolerance and Israeli nationalism – should establish a Jewish tribunal to pass judgement on Begin, Sharon, Eitan and the entire general staff of the Israeli armed forces. This alone

could be the means of working free of the sickness that is destroying Israel, and, perhaps, of preserving Israel's future.

What is it that has turned us into such efficient criminals?[16]

An opposition Labour Party forum in Tel Aviv, in extraordinary session, called for a judicial inquiry, and for the immediate resignations of Prime Minister Begin and Defence Minister Sharon. Even a member of the ruling Likud coalition demanded the ouster of Sharon.[17] Speaking before the Knesset, Labour Party chairman Shimon Peres recalled the fate of Jews in Europe in the 1940s, and spoke of the 'moral ruins' under the rubble and bodies in the camps. Peres was careful not to assign direct responsibility for the massacres to the government, but there was responsibility nonetheless. When the decision was made to send the IDF into west Beirut, said Peres, Begin and Sharon took upon themselves 'public responsibility for what was to happen in Beirut'.[18]

Ronald Reagan agreed, or appeared to. On 18 September, the day the massacre had been revealed, he had expressed 'horror', and called for the immediate withdrawal of the IDF from west Beirut. The following day he had met with the National Security Council to discuss possible US involvement in an international peacekeeping force that would enter Beirut to prevent further killings; and the day after that, Reagan announced agreement among the US, France and Italy on the formation of a second multinational force that would enter west Beirut to assist the Government of Lebanon to restore order and sanity.

The US Government was not a disinterested observer of the events in Beirut. The agreement on evacuation of the PLO had been negotiated by US Ambassador Philip Habib, and its terms had been published. In the eyes of the world, therefore, the US had become a guarantor of the safety of civilians in besieged Beirut, and by extension, bore partial responsibility for what Sharon and his IDF commanders had consciously allowed to happen there. This was the context in which Reagan moved so swiftly to pressure Israel to withdraw from Beirut, and to form yet another MNF which would move in to protect civilian non-combatants.

Ariel Sharon's reaction was swift and bitter. In a long, rambling disjointed speech to the Israeli Knesset, made primarily to defend himself and his government against charges of responsibility for Sabra and Chatila, Sharon returned again and again to a curious theme: those who criticized his and the Israeli Government's performance in west Beirut were providing aid and comfort to 'the Americans', who wanted to take from Israel what was rightfully hers – the lands of 'Judea and Samaria'.[19]

Lieutenant General Rafael Eitan, Chief of Staff of the IDF, went even further, blaming 'American officials' in Lebanon for the massacres because, inter alia, they had early knowledge of the killings and they had prevailed upon the Lebanese Government not to send the Lebanese Army into the refugee camps after the IDF went into west Beirut. 'The Americans', said Eitan, 'had at least as much responsibility as Israel had.'[20]

Conflicting missions

During the week prior to the return of the 32nd MAU to Lebanon, Ronald Reagan and Menachem Begin argued repeatedly and publicly about the timing of the IDF withdrawal from Beirut International Airport, which was that portion of west Beirut which would be assigned to the 32nd MAU.

The placement of the individual units had been given considerable thought. French marines patrolled the streets of the northernmost section – including most of the commercial district of west Beirut, and the Sabra and Chatila camps. The Italians, who came with a large, fully equipped medical unit, were assigned the central portion of the city, including the Burjal Brajneh refugee camp. The Americans agreed to take the southernmost district, including the airport, ironically because it was thought that they were most familiar – and friendly – with the IDF, whose headquarters was yet further south in Khalde, on the coast between Beirut and Damur.

This was the physical setting in which the second marine peacekeeping mission served. The policy context was somewhat less certain. One student of the Middle East summarized the situation:

> In the confused circumstances of 1982 an American policy toward Lebanon was formulated that was predicated on the anticipated gradual consolidation of Amin [Gemayel's] Administration and the state's authority: Unlike his brother, Amin [Gemayel] was to base his government on dialogue with the Maronites' traditional partners, as well as, it was hoped, with new ones. Israel would evacuate its troops in return for an agreement, negotiated under American auspices, and the prospect of that withdrawal would be used in order to obtain a comparable (though not necessarily a simultaneous and identical) Syrian evacuation.[21]

The Lebanese Army was ill-prepared in September 1982 to restore order and to 'consolidate' the rule of Amin Gemayel's Government. Seven years of virtually constant sectarian violence involving Sunni and Shiite Muslims, Maronite and Greek Orthodox Christians, Druze and sub-groups within these categories, had culminated in the invasion and occupation by Israel. Through all this, the army had remained multi-confessional, and to a certain extent was seen as such by the people of Lebanon. It was, however, small, poorly trained and underfunded.

The initial mission of the second marine peacekeeping force, as defined by the JCS Alert Order of 23 September, was:

> To establish an environment which will permit the Lebanese Armed Forces to carry out their responsibilities in the Beirut area . . . to occupy and secure positions along designated sections of the line from south of the Beirut International Airport to a position in the vicinity of the Presidential Palace . . . [and to] be prepared to protect US forces and, on order, conduct retrograde operations as required.[22]

From the outset, the Marine Corps commanders quarrelled with their Israeli counterparts about their relative positions and roles. The Israelis wanted to occupy parts of the airport area jointly with the marines, failing to understand, or refusing to understand, that they could not be parties to the conflict and peacekeepers at the same time. Marine commanders instructed

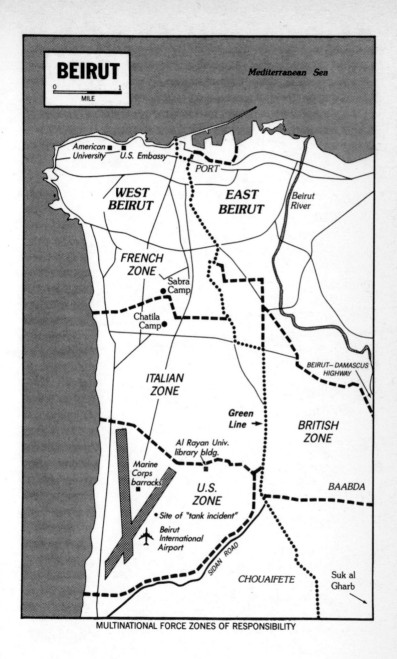

MULTINATIONAL FORCE ZONES OF RESPONSIBILITY

their troops, however, that 'The Relationship with the Israelis ends at the Lebanese border.'

The Sidon Road area, which began south of the airport and circled it on the east, contained the best natural defence positions for the marines. The IDF insisted, however, on using the road to re-supply their checkpoints to the north and east on the Beirut–Damascus highway. Consequently, the marine MNF commanders settled for inferior defensive positions nearer the airport, to avoid the appearance of protecting IDF supply routes.[23]

Corporal Reagan's accident

There was another bad omen. The day after the 32nd MAU arrived in Beirut, the first marine peacekeeper died, and three others were wounded. Corporal David Reagan was demonstrating how to disarm the unexploded ordnance that littered the Beirut International Airport grounds. Bending over, Reagan accidentally detonated a small anti-personnel bomb, sending small pellets into his groin, abdomen and thorax. Mercifully, one or more of the pellets penetrated his brain, numbing the pain elsewhere. He died at the temporary battalion aid station.

What had killed Corporal Reagan was a bomblet from an Israeli CBU-58 cluster bomb. That was one type of ordnance which Reagan should not have had to worry about. The Israel–US mutual security agreement, signed as required by the Mutual Defence Assistance Act of 1952, proscribes the use by Israel of certain weapons, without prior approval by the US Government. So lethal are these particular weapons when used in densely populated areas, that the Ford Administration required a special agreement governing the use of cluster bombs at the time they were first provided to Israel in 1976.

In March 1978 Israel had used the weapons extensively in civilian residential areas during its invasion of south Lebanon. As a result, the Carter Administration following formal, written certification to Congress that the weapons had in fact been used, took the unusual step of leaking details of a new, classified specific written agreement under which Israel solemnly promised to use cluster munitions only against fortified military targets, and only in self-defence, if attacked by more than one country.

Nevertheless, during the June 1982 invasion the Israeli Air Force had once again used the weapons widely against both military and civilian targets. Several had been dropped in refugee camps, including Sabra and Chatila. As a result, President Reagan declared on 19 July that further shipments of the weapons to Israel would cease pending a review of the manner and circumstances of their use in Lebanon.

The type of cluster bomb that killed Corporal Reagan was a particularly nasty version of the weapon which does not detonate upon impact. It is 'spin armed' by the 'magnus effect' as it falls through the air, and then detonates later when it is jarred, like the 'butterfly bombs' used by the Soviet Union in Afghanistan. The use of this generic type of weapon in proximity to civilian populations was prohibited in a protocol adopted at the United Nations Conference on Prohibitions or Restrictions of Use of Certain Conventional Weapons, in October 1980. The protocol was adopted by consensus with representatives of both Israel and the US participating.[24] Cluster munitions, with or without the deadly delayed fuses, have long been determined to be weapons which, in terms of the international law applicable to conflicts, cause 'unnecessary suffering' and have 'indiscriminate effects'.[25] Eric Hammell maintains that 'tens of thousands of unexploded US-manufactured cluster bomblets' dropped by Israeli planes littered the Beirut International Airport when Corporal Reagan picked up the one with his name on it.[26]

The *New York Times*, on 1 and 2 October, 1982, carried four articles relating to the death of Corporal Reagan and the wounding of the three other marine MNF members. None of the four articles indicated that the accident was caused by an Israeli weapon, though one article, by William Farrell, contained near the end one paragraph completely unrelated to the surrounding text:

> During the invasion the supply of cluster weapons to Israel by the United States caused controversy in Washington because of a reported agreement that Israel was to use them only if attacked.[27]

Robert Dillon, US Ambassador to Lebanon in 1982, does not think the *Times* reporters were to blame for this strategic omission:

> They certainly knew. We were clear with everybody that the man had picked up a cluster bomb . . . Israeli ordnance . . . and indeed that the use of this weapon had been in violation of a US agreement. I suspect that if the press didn't make much of that back in the States, that had something to do with the editors rather than the [reporters] who were there. They had good guys there, and all of them from time to time had trouble with their editors.[28]

In the case of the *Times*, it seems, editors in New York were yet again exercising political judgement in determining which news was 'fit to print'.

In November 1983 the US Secretary of Defence signed a memorandum of understanding with the Government of Israel, which provided, inter alia, for the resumption of the shipment to that country of US-made cluster munitions, suspended by President Reagan in July 1982. This portion of the memorandum was gratuitous, however CBS News revealed that the shipments had continued despite the President's order . . . in a programme broadcast on 29 September, 1982, the day before Corporal Reagan died.[29]

Friendly misunderstandings

The 32nd MAU was replaced in Beirut on 3 November by the 24th MAU. The next two months were spent performing routine guard duties in the airport area, conducting individual and small-unit training for the Lebanese Army, and undertaking regular patrols into east Beirut and Baabda in the Shouf mountains above the presidential palace.

The initial operational agreement allowing the IDF to re-supply along the Sidon Road which flanked the airport, was supposed to limit the Israelis to two 'small' convoys a week, but by mid-November the IDF had major convoys on the road several times each day. Inevitably, this led PLO, Shiite and Druze guerrillas operating in the area to begin mining the road and taking potshots at the convoys as they passed Baabda on the way north. Thus began what the marines came to call the 'early morning follies'.

> Every morning the Israelis would start up the road and they hit a mine or were sniped at, and they'd open up and shoot everything that moved ... 360 degrees ... and we'd gather on the roof and see this. Frequently they'd put us down in our holes shooting like that ... that's about the time we started to get angry.[30]

In time, whole towns along the Sidon Road – such as Chouaifete – were completely flattened by this hysterical IDF reaction to any kind of attack, including a single sniper round.[31] The technique, called 'reconnaissance by fire' in the Vietnam War, is the ineffective, frightened reaction of 'green', undisciplined troops in situations where discipline and leadership have broken down. The marines, who had come to Beirut with respect and admiration for the IDF, or at least for the IDF's reputation, began to have doubts. There was also the matter of security:

> The Israelis had good troops in the first push. Then they brought in reserves and those guys would leave their equipment unguarded and they'd go to sleep, and they'd come out the next morning and crank the son of a bitch up, and it'd go up on them because there was no security.[32]

On the afternoon of 5 January the inevitable happened. Two IDF tanks and an armoured personnel carrier (APC) drove through the airport fence into the marines' area of operation, and moved southward along the perimeter road. When challenged, the IDF commander Lieutenant Colonel Rafi Landsberg said that he was lost. He and his vehicles were promptly but politely escorted from the area. The zone in which this intrusion occurred was clearly marked both by painted barrels and by the fence, and the marines found it difficult to believe that Landsberg had lost his way.[33] They'd not lost *that* much respect for the IDF. Then there was the matter of his rank – what was a lieutenant colonel doing leading a small section of tanks in an active war zone? This was normally the task of a sergeant, or a lieutenant at most.

The following day, two IDF jeeps and a van approached a checkpoint in the same area, manned jointly by marines and Lebanese Army soldiers. This time the Israeli officer in charge stated that he wanted to use the perimeter road to visit the science faculty at al-Rayan University, to conduct a search. Again, the Israelis were escorted out of the airport area.

Lieutenant Colonel Landsberg was back two days later, on 8 January, this time a bit more determined. Wearing no identifiable rank insignia and leading two jeeps and an APC, Landsberg asked to see the USMC battalion commander. He was told that as per the MNF-Government of Lebanon agreement (which was well known to the Israelis) such a request should be directed through political channels – in this case the US Embassy. Landsberg returned an hour later, this time with two tanks and fifteen soldiers. The marines called up reinforcements, but the situation was defused when the Israelis departed. Both incidents involved IDF units leaving the Sidon Road to approach checkpoints in clearly marked MNF-controlled zones.[34]

The stakes were rising. In the late afternoon of 10 January a Lebanese man with an ancient shotgun entered a scrub-covered vacant lot to the east of the marine lines and began hunting pigeons. This was a not uncommon occurrence in the area. When he took his first shot, the IDF opened up on him with .50 calibre machine guns, wounding the fellow. Somehow, he made it to his car and drove off, whereupon the IDF began searching the area, and approached a USMC/Lebanese Army checkpoint, and asked to be let through, claiming that the individual had fled through MNF lines. Half an hour later an IDF unit returned to the checkpoint, deployed crew-served weapons, locked, loaded, pointed the weapons at the marines and demanded to be allowed to pass. The answer was 'no'. The Israelis left.[35]

The *New York Times* version of this event was interesting, reporting that an Israeli soldier had 'briefly' pointed his machine gun at a marine, 'apparently more as an act of bravado than as an actual threat'.[36]

One week later, on 17 January, an IDF patrol approached a

USMC/Lebanese Army checkpoint commanded by Captain Charles Johnson. Again the Israelis were refused entry, and again they departed and then returned. This time, when their path was blocked by Marine Corporal John Thibodeaux, an Israeli soldier popped the clutch on his jeep and struck Thibodeaux, nearly knocking him down. Now it was the marines who went to lock and load, threatening the Israelis, who thereupon departed.[37] One former senior marine officer recalls that, at Marine Headquarters in Washington, 'we were getting very nervous at this point, because we could smell a firefight coming'.

It was time to defuse the situation. In Beirut, IDF and US Marine Corps officers held an unusual ninety-minute meeting attended by US Middle East envoy Morris Draper. No agreement was reached on the precise boundaries of the USMNF/IDF adjacent zones of operation, although both sides agreed to try to avoid further incidents. An observer at the meeting recalled that the problems were 'resolved within a framework of irresolution'.

US multinational force personnel were not the only Americans having confrontations with Israelis in Lebanon at the time. On 25 January, Marine Major John Todd serving with the United Nations Truce Supervisory Organization (UNTSO) was singled out of a UN convoy on the Beirut–Damascus highway, and was held at gunpoint for twenty-five minutes before being released. All other vehicles were allowed to pass. Five days later, on 30 January, US Army Major Herman Kafura, also with UNTSO, was fired upon by the IDF while riding in a UN vehicle clearly marked as such, and flying the UN flag. At the time, Kafura was investigating the deaths of two civilian women killed in one of the Israeli 'reconnaissance by fire' operations. The next day, 31 January, Marine Captain Bruce Denault, attached to UNTSO, was fired upon on the Beirut–Damascus highway by an Israeli tank, using its .50 calibre gun.[38]

On 2 February, Rafi Landsberg came back. Again the scene was a multinational force USMC/Lebanese Army checkpoint near al-Rayan University Library. This incident, by far the most publicized of all to this point, involved three Israeli tanks commanded by Landsberg, and the 24th MAU's Lima Company commander, Captain Charles Johnson.

The tanks either turned off the Sidon Road and advanced toward marine MNF lines, or were accosted near the Sidon Road by Captain Johnson on foot, depending upon whether one accepts the US Defence Department or Israeli version(s) of the event. What is agreed is that Landsberg requested passage through the marine lines, and when this was refused, and two of the three tanks moved closer to the lines, Johnson mounted Landsberg's tank with pistol drawn, and ordered Landsberg to turn the procession around. Which he did. Two hours after the tanks departed, a 75 mm tank round landed fifty yards from one of the marine positions along the runway. There were no injuries. An Israeli officer called the local marine commander immediately to deny that it was an Israeli round.

The incident created a furore in both the US and Israel, involving contradictory press releases by the DoD in Washington and the IDF in Jerusalem, statements by Begin and Reagan, and at least two press conferences by none other than Lieutenant Colonel Rafi Landsberg. The fundamental Israeli position appeared to be that the incident occurred in 'Israeli territory', clearly outside the MNF's zone of responsibility. A Pentagon official, reacting to that, doubted that a marine captain would wander out from his lines, on foot, hunting for tanks with a pistol.[39]

There were other bizarre aspects of the Israeli version of the Johnson affair. In Landsberg's interview with Israel Radio and with ITIM, an Israeli news agency, he had the tanks on patrol 400 metres from the MNF line. The Israeli Embassy in Washington moved that back to 660 metres. In one interview, Landsberg said that Johnson walked to his tank, in another that Johnson advanced at a run. Landsberg, who (naturally) had a radio in his tank, claimed in his interviews to have been unable to communicate by radio with his headquarters, which was within sight of where the incident took place. Finally, Landsberg said Johnson smelled of alcohol when he mounted the tank, and that this may have affected his judgement. Johnson's colleagues (and later his family back in the States) said that

Johnson didn't drink. Ever. A Marine Corps spokesman's response to the charge of drinking on duty, was according to NBC News, unprintable.[40]

The incidents continued. On 28 February, a US officer attached to UNTSO told reporters that on several occasions in the previous days, IDF troops had threatened to kill UNTSO officers moving along the Beirut–Damascus highway. On 1 March, and again on 12 March, the IDF interfered with marine MNF routine patrols which the Israelis had previously agreed the MNF could conduct into IDF-occupied areas. In the latter instance, the Israelis repositioned a mobile checkpoint so as to intercept the marines.[41]

Some of the marines who were there recall many, many unreported instances of Israeli provocations – incidents which were not publicized at the time. Marine outposts at the Beirut International Airport, for instance, experienced frequent Israeli helicopter probes, with lights being shone on their positions, potentially exposing them to gunfire from nearby buildings and hills. When challenged on the radio, the IDF pilots would refuse to respond and identify themselves. To get rid of the helicopters, the marines would finally train floodlights and fire-control radar on them. The same pattern of 'helicopter harassment' occurred with US Navy ships at sea during the MNF's tenure in Beirut.[42]

Late on 12 March, as telexed reports of the 'patrol incidents' reached Marine Corps Headquarters in Washington, the Marine Commandant, General Robert H. Barrow, received a letter from a US Army major assigned to UNTSO in Lebanon. The letter described a 'pattern' of Israeli attacks and provocations against the UNTSO forces, including instances in which US officers had been singled out for abuse, threats, detention and/or 'near miss' shootings.

Barrow called an assistant to his office and showed him the UNTSO letter. 'Is this consistent with our experience with the Israelis?' he asked. His assistant replied that it was, and that he could produce signed affidavits showing a clear pattern of IDF provocations of the US multinational force and the US officers assigned to UNTSO. Barrow, a man who was normally slow to anger, blew up.

The Marine Commandant and his staff discussed their options. Initially, it was decided to draft a formal complaint to the United Nations Security Council, and Army and Air Force Headquarters were contacted to obtain the details of incidents involving their officers serving with UNTSO. Upon closer look, however, a formal UN complaint appeared to be a long and, most likely, sterile exercise. And in the meantime – and this was Barrow's chief concern – the lives of US servicemen serving as peacekeepers in Lebanon were at risk.

Thus, a second course of action was considered. General Barrow contacted the Chairman of the Joint Chiefs, General John Vessey, to ask that he address a letter to Defence Secretary Weinberger, drawing attention to this situation involving the US MNF and America's presumed ally, Israel. General Vessey was not sure that he wanted to take the heat on this one, given Israel's many, many strong friends in Congress. He did not want to be the 'point man', he said, but he would not oppose a letter from General Barrow to Weinberger.[43]

It was dated 14 March, 1983. 'I must formally register my deep concern', said Barrow in a letter which mentioned 'serious harassing incidents' involving both the US MNF and US officers attached to UNTSO. In an attachment entitled 'USMC–IDF Incidents' Barrow described in detail eight separate instances of what he identified as 'life-threatening situations, replete with verbal degradation of the officers, their uniform and country.' Efforts had been made to defuse these problems previously, he said, and a viable communications procedure had been established between the marines and the IDF. The problem persisted, however, and anticipating what would indeed be Israel's response to the letter, Barrow said that 'the expansion of communications links and the use of liaison officers' would not resolve the situation until 'the attitude and actions of the Israelis are altered'.

Certain portions of General Barrow's letter reflected genuine puzzlement at Israel's behaviour:

It is inconceivable to me why Americans – serving in peacekeeping roles – must be harassed, endangered by an ally . . . It is time for firm and strong action, to demonstrate to the Israelis that a role as peacekeeper does not presume weakness. If anything, the Israelis should respect our efforts in this region.

But the heart of Barrow's letter, the section which was to elicit the strongest response from the IDF, the US Congress, the *New York Times* and others, was the following sentence:

> It is evident to me, and the opinion of the US commanders afloat and ashore, that the incidents between the marines and the IDF are timed, orchestrated, and executed for obtuse Israeli political purposes.

Attached to General Barrow's letter was a copy of a classified cable from the US Defence Attaché in Beirut detailing the particular instances in which IDF provocations had involved shooting and/or verbal threats to kill US military personnel in Lebanon.

At Secretary Weinberger's urging, the State Department formally transmitted Barrow's letter to Israeli Foreign Minister Yitzhak Shamir. Administration spokesman Larry Speakes announced that the White House would conduct an inquiry into the allegations in General Barrow's letter.

In an interview with NBC Nightly News, General Barrow expanded a bit upon what had precipitated his action. The sheer number of incidents, he said,

> does raise some question as to whether at some level there hasn't been perhaps some actual contrived effort at provocation. Who can say?[44]

The same NBC news segment quoted 'top Pentagon officials' who contended that the Israelis were deliberately trying to discredit the international peacekeeping forces 'in order to bolster their argument that only some kind of Israeli military presence in that country can guarantee peace'. One month earlier, *Washington Post* reporter George C. Wilson had cited 'US military leaders' who believed that it was Israeli Defence Minister Ariel Sharon himself who was deliberately trying to discredit the MNF by ordering the confrontations.[45]

General Barrow did not mention Sharon by name in his public letter, but the implication of Barrow's description of incidents 'timed, orchestrated, and executed for obtuse Israeli political purposes' was clear. In fact, few if any Defence Department officials involved in or knowledgeable about peacekeeping in Lebanon, doubted that Sharon was the conductor of the orchestra. General James C. Mead, marine MNF commander, recalls that 'the circumstantial evidence [for Sharon's involvement] was overwhelming . . . how could Rafi Landsberg make the same mistake four times?'[46]

David Halevy was a correspondent for *Time Magazine* working in Jerusalem at the time of the incidents. He had numerous friends and contacts in the IDF, as he had previously been a brigadier general in Israeli military intelligence. Halevy recalls hearing from IDF officers serving in Lebanon that they had received orders directly from Defence Minister Sharon to provoke and harass the soldiers of the Marine Corps MNF unit.[47] American military intelligence (i.e. DIA) received confirmation of Sharon's orders shortly after they were issued, Halevy was told. If that is true, the information was not passed along to the Marine Corps, as none of the marines interviewed was aware of 'hard evidence' that Sharon was causing the trouble directly and deliberately.

A rational framework for the incidents

Why would Ariel Sharon, the Israeli Minister of Defence who had signed the November 1981 memorandum of understanding on strategic co-operation between the IDF and the US Defence Department, want aggressively to challenge American troops in their peacekeeping role in Lebanon in 1982? General Sharon is, to be sure, arguably the most quixotic leader in the Middle East, not excluding Moammar Qaddafi. Moreover, he does not always choose the most direct route to his goal, as, for example, when he tricked the Israeli cabinet, of which he was a member, into approving a major expansion of the scope of the invasion of Lebanon by presenting it as a 'flanking movement' around the Syrians.[48] Nevertheless, a number of possible motivations for the IDF-marine contretemps, motivations which are not mutually exclusive, present themselves.

From the moment of the landing of the first American MNF unit, that which came to Beirut to assist with the PLO evacuation, it was apparent that the IDF wished to co-opt the marines. Israeli forces purposely dragged out their own evacuation, giving the marines the option of delaying their landing, or jointly occupying parts of the city with the IDF, and thus appearing both to protect the Israelis, and to co-operate with them operationally on the peacekeeping mission. When the second marine MNF contingent arrived in September 1982, the Israelis proposed to occupy jointly first the airport, and then the Sidon Road district.[49]

When these efforts were resisted, for the obvious reason that they would have compromised the MNF's peacekeeping mission, the IDF began to 'demonstrate' the need for closer liaison to Israel's friends in Congress and elsewhere, by repeatedly creating dangerous confrontations. And when these incidents received the inevitable publicity in the United States, the response from Begin, Sharon, the Israeli Embassy in Washington, etc, was invariably to blame the situation on the lack of close liaison between (US) peacekeepers and (Israeli) fighters. It would have been interesting to see Israel's reaction had the US Government responded by agreeing, and then proposing similar, symmetrical liaison arrangements with the Syrian Army and the various warring Lebanese factions. One suspects that is not what the Israelis had in mind.

A second possible reason for the incidents relates to secret negotiations which Ariel Sharon was conducting with Lebanese President Amin Gemayel during November and December 1982. Sharon's objective was to demonstrate to the Israeli public that what was becoming known in Israel as 'Sharon's war' had been worth the human and financial sacrifices it entailed for the country, by obtaining tangible concessions from Gemayel in direct, secret negotiation between the occupied and the occupying power. Specifically, the draft Sharon–Gemayel agreement would have provided for an eventual Israel–Lebanon peace treaty (i.e. 'normalized' relations between the two countries) and for Lebanese Government agreement to permanent posting of Israeli troops in south Lebanon.

US Middle East mediator/envoy Philip Habib was, however, having his own secret meetings with the Lebanese, and was advising them against a quiet deal with Sharon that he, Habib, believed would destabilize the delicate Lebanese coalition government arrangement, and would create severe problems for Lebanon with its Arab neighbours. Sharon complained bitterly and publicly about American interference in his 'peace' negotiations, and may have decided to retaliate by hindering the Americans' own peace efforts, of which the MNF was one important, tangible part.[50]

Third, Sharon may simply have wanted to discredit the multinational force altogether, in terms of its ability to keep the peace in Lebanon, that is, as an alternative to the IDF which maintained peace as an occupying power. A weak Lebanese Government, physically unable to separate the various Christian and Muslim factions and to contain their fighting, would look to Israel for help, it was hoped, and would be less likely to insist upon a rigid timetable for Israeli withdrawal. A Lebanese Government which, with MNF help, could extend its dominion once again to the entire country, or most of it, would be a tougher adversary for Israel in those 'secret' negotiations.

Finally, Israel had some specific reasons, in early 1983, to delay if not forestall withdrawal from certain parts of Lebanon, and these reasons had nothing whatever to do with the PLO or the security of Israel's northern Galilee border.

On a mountain top called Jebel el Barouk, in the Shouf range east-south-east of Beirut, Israel had established an important electronic eavesdropping platform to spy on the Syrians. The mountain was almost 2,000 metres high, and barely thirty miles from Damascus. From it, the IDF could intercept communications of Syrian forces in the Beqaa Valley, and even in Damascus itself ... without the danger of exposing Israeli 'elint' spy-planes to Syrian ground-to-air missiles.[51]

And then there was Lebanon's water. In 1978 the Israeli Water Commission estimated that Israel's annual water deficit would reach 450 million cubic metres by 1985. That is slightly more than half the annual flow of the Litani, the southernmost major river in Lebanon. In the early weeks of the 1982 Israeli invasion of Lebanon, the IDF seized hydrographic charts relating to the Litani, diverted part of the river's flow into Israel by openly laying surface pipes connecting the Litani and Hasbani Rivers, and conducted seismic soundings and surveys on the Litani gorges at Deir Mimas.[52]

In early 1983 the Lebanese Government had asked for expansion of both the MNF and the United Nations Forces in Lebanon (UNIFIL) in order to speed the expansion of Lebanese Army (i.e. Government) control over all Lebanon. Extending Lebanese Government authority to southern Lebanon in early 1983 would not have facilitated Israel's various water diversion projects involving the Litani. Thus, in early 1983 the IDF harassed the MNF in Beirut and UNIFIL in south Lebanon, and the South Lebanese Army (Israel's proxy army in the south) openly attacked UNIFIL.

Underlying the specific reasons for the IDF–marine incidents was a factor, a context so obvious that few seemed to recognize it at the time: Israel's and America's interests in Lebanon were in fundamental conflict. Joseph C. Harsch, writing in February 1983 for the *Christian Science Monitor*, encapsulated the situation admirably:

> The US Marines are in Lebanon for one purpose, and the Israeli forces facing them are there for an entirely different and conflicting purpose. The US Marines are in Lebanon to try to help in bolstering the independence of the State of Lebanon and in restoring the control of the Government of Lebanon over all the territory of Lebanon. The Israeli troops are in Lebanon in an attempt to establish a permanent Israeli influence in the southern part of Lebanon. They are asking as a condition for withdrawal of their troops the right to station permanent military observer posts in southern Lebanon. They want Lebanon open to their trade and tourism. They want Lebanon to 'normalize' relations with Israel. If the Government of Lebanon were to accede to Israel's present demands, Lebanon would not be in sovereign control either over all of its territory or over its foreign policy.[53]

The Sharon factor

One of the most puzzling aspects of the incidents for many of the US marines was the obvious, genuine animosity which the individual IDF soldiers exhibited in confrontation after confrontation. General Barrow's letter referred to 'life-threatening situations, replete with verbal degradation of the officers, their uniform and country'. There was, then, an emotional as well as a rational context for the incidents, and it may have involved feelings of shame and guilt which the IDF began to experience in west Beirut in this period.

The first MNF had been formed to assist with the removal from Beirut of the PLO fighters in a situation in which Israel and the IDF refused to have any communication with the Palestine Liberation Organization, other than that which comes from the barrel of a gun. The logistics of evacuating and simultaneously disarming nearly 15,000 soldiers in a volatile situation, required the presence of a third party intermediary, in the form of neutral troops. This certainly involved no implied criticism of the humanitarian standards – the humanity, if you will – of the IDF.

The second multinational force mission was different. The day after the horrors of Sabra and Chatila were revealed, President Reagan spoke of the need to recompose the international peacekeeping forces 'to strengthen the Lebanese Government and prevent further killings of civilians in west Beirut'.[54] On that same day, the Embassy of Israel bought a full-page advertisement in major US newspapers, which ran under the heading of 'Blood Libel'. In part, it said:

> Any direct or implicit accusation that the IDF bears any blame whatsoever for this human tragedy is entirely baseless and without foundation. The Government of Israel rejects such accusations with the contempt they deserve . . . The people of Israel are proud of the IDF's ethics and respect for human life. These are the traditional Jewish values in which we have educated generations of Israeli fighters, and we will continue to do so.[55]

The sending of the second multinational force to Beirut was precisely that: an implicit accusation of the blame borne by the

IDF for the massacres, and the consequent lack of faith on the part of the international community that the IDF could or would prevent repetitions of the event. US marines and other elements of the MNF were sent to Beirut to control the 'Sharon factor' in the Israeli Army.

At the time of the marine/IDF incidents, Ariel Sharon was personally under investigation by the Kahan Commission in Israel, an investigation that would, in early February, find Sharon 'indirectly responsible' for the massacres, and would call for his dismissal or resignation. But the responsibility went far, far beyond Ariel Sharon, and the IDF in Lebanon certainly understood that. The very presence of the MNF was a palpable, aggravating reminder of that. A US marine officer who saw the IDF first-hand in Beirut, later tried to explain the strange Israeli reliance on 'reconnaissance by fire'.

> You have to understand the Israeli soldier's mind set when he faces an Arab. It's like the US cavalry officer in 1875 . . . the only good Indian is a dead Indian.

There were echoes of Warsaw in west Beirut, and there were echoes of Lidice at Sabra and Chatila.

Epilogue . . . the 'end of the world' message

In late September 1983, seven months after Captain Johnson jumped up on the Israeli tank, the United States effectively entered the Lebanon War. In July Israel had suddenly withdrawn from the Shouf Mountains and the Beirut suburbs, and had redeployed to a point south of the Awali River. The Lebanese Army had then gone into the Shouf to try to restore order and suppress the factional fighting which had worsened after the Israeli withdrawal. And the Lebanese Army was in trouble. Still poorly trained, it was under attack and was answering with wild artillery barrages. One US marine recalls:

> At Suk al Gharb they were firing 155s [millimetre howitzer shells] at a rate exceeding World War I artillery fire levels . . . I'm not talking about particularly well aimed fire; just pull the lanyard and make some noise.[56]

It wasn't working. For one thing the Lebanese Army was running out of 155 shells. The Lebanese Government, fearful that Druze militiamen would overrun the army positions and then use the heights of the Shouf to decimate the presidential palace and the airport, sent a panicky telex to the White House via Philip Habib. In effect, the message was 'Send in the marines!'

At Marine Corps Headquarters in Washington, it was quickly dubbed 'the end-of-the-world message'. Their own communications from the marine MNF contingent on the spot were less alarmist, estimating that (a) the Lebanese Army was pretty well dug in at Suk al Gharb and would probably hold its position, and (b) even if it did not hold, the hills that were being contested did not constitute unique firing points *vis-à-vis* west Beirut. In short, the marine assessment of the situation was that the end of the world was not yet nigh.

At the White House, however, the message was taken quite seriously, and through presidential aide Robert 'Bud' McFarlane, Reagan got personally involved. Via direct channels, McFarlane requested the senior marine MNF commander, who was then Colonel Timothy J. Geraghty to fire his artillery in support of the Lebanese Army in the Shouf. Geraghty refused, as this was clearly contrary to the MNF mission directive, and to the rules of engagement for the 32nd and 24th MAUs, which stipulated that 'action taken by the US forces ashore in Lebanon would be for self-defence only'.[57] McFarlane understood this very well, but in the view of more than one senior marine official at the time, he was anxious to move the US directly into the conflict. (This, of course, was what Israel had been trying to accomplish for many months, and as we shall see in the next chapter, McFarlane was peculiarly susceptible to Israeli influence.) So, 'Bud' contacted the navy, and it was at this time and in this way that the USS *New Jersey* began lobbing those huge artillery shells into the Shouf Mountains.

In September 1983 the United States began randomly killing villagers in the hills outside Beirut. Ariel Sharon had resigned, and was gone. But the Sharon factor had prevailed.

It was a month later that the marine barracks at Beirut International Airport were bombed, killing 241. Even before the bombing, however, the paper trail of policy decisions that led to America's direct involvement in the Lebanon War was being destroyed. The 'end-of-the-world message' had actually been forwarded to the White House by Bud McFarlane, who at the time had been in Lebanon. It had been sent 'NODIS', meaning 'no distribution', but in the event, copies had been made and one at least reposed in the Marine Corps Head-quarters files in Washington. Seven days after it had been sent, the sweep was conducted. Orders came from the White House through DoD. The 'end-of-the-world message' and responses to it were removed from the files and destroyed.

The direct involvement of the White House in corrupting American peacekeeping efforts in Lebanon, would remain a secret.

TWELVE

War by Proxy:
Israel and America Arm Iran, 1980–6

Historians, like explorers searching for the tiny headwaters of a great river, love to seek out and designate the obscure origins of an important policy shift. In future years, when the 'definitive' chronicles of the rise and shabby decline of the Reagan Presidency are written, some historians will no doubt agree with the Tower Commission that America's direct involvement in the business of sending arms to post-revolutionary Iran began with some confused shipping arrangements on 17 November 1985.[1]

Again, as had been the case two years earlier in Beirut, the administration was reluctantly taking part in a conflict in which Israel was already playing a partisan role against the Arab side. Again, the primary instrument for this policy shift was Reagan's National Security Adviser, Robert C. McFarlane Jr.

Israeli Defence Minister Yitzhak Rabin had telephoned McFarlane at the Reagan–Gorbachev summit meeting in Geneva to ask his help in convincing the Portuguese Government to permit transhipment of Hawk anti-aircraft missiles and spare parts by air to Iran. Three months previously, the White House had acquiesced in the shipment by Israel of American Tow missiles to liven up the Iran-Iraq war. So, Rabin's request now for direct US help with the shipping arrangements probably seemed to McFarlane to be only a small additional degree of American involvement in that war. Iran was officially branded by the US Government a 'terrorist-supporting country', however, so right away little lies were necessary.

McFarlane instructed NSC aide Lieutenant Colonel Oliver North to assist the Israelis, telling him that the President had previously approved the shipment of American arms . . . which may or may not have been true, according to testimony subsequently given to the Tower Commission and, later, to the Congresssional Iran – Contra hearings. Then, when North tried and failed to get the necessary Portuguese customs clearances for the Israeli cargo flights, McFarlane himself contacted the Portuguese Prime Minister, telling him the shipment had a 'humanitarian purpose' – which was stretching the truth to the breaking point.[2] When the Portuguese Prime Minister in his wisdom refused this request, McFarlane turned again to North, asking that he himself arrange shipment of the missiles and spares through the CIA. North finally made the arrangements, assuring the CIA that the cargo was oil drilling equipment – which was clearly false.

The operation was not a stunning success. During the Geneva summit, McFarlane had told both the President and Secretary of State George Shultz about the Israeli shipment. He explained to both men that the 'deal' involved the release of American hostages in Lebanon for the shipment of the Hawks to Iran. But when, on 25 November, the missiles finally arrived in Iran, no hostages were released. We may never know for certain exactly why they were not released, but we do have some clues. Israel was committed to deliver eighty improved Hawk missiles to Iran, and actually delivered eighteen.[3] Moreover, they were not the 'improved' version which the Iranians expected. Half of them were delivered painted with Israeli 'Star of David' markings, which angered and humiliated the Iranians. And finally, at the last moment, the Israelis doubled the price.

Not surprisingly, within hours of the delivery, the Iranian Prime Minister's office was on the phone to one of the key Israeli intermediaries, Yaacov Nimrodi in London, demanding that the missiles – and the money – be returned. Nimrodi returned the money. As for the hostages, the operation had achieved little more than the risk of their lives. One week later Robert McFarlane submitted his resignation as National Security Adviser to the President.

It was not the first time McFarlane had considered resignation. Four weeks earlier, on 8 November, Oliver North had, oddly enough, enlisted the assistance of David Kimche, Director General of the Israeli Foreign Ministry, to convince his boss not to leave US Government service.[4] That North would go to an Israeli Government official for help in influencing his boss, the National Security Adviser of the President of the United States, is a reflection of just how mixed up and confused both McFarlane and North had become on the matter of which master they were serving. It also may explain why the US/Israeli arms shipments were not terminated after the disastrous Hawk missile foul-up in November 1985. But I am getting ahead of my story.

Some senior administration officials retained their ability to distinguish between Israeli and American national interests. In June 1985, when McFarlane had sent an aide, Michael Ledeen, to Israel to discuss openings to Iran with Prime Minister Shimon Peres, in the process bypassing the State Department, Secretary of State Shultz had written to McFarlane to warn

> that Israel's agenda regarding Iran 'is not the same as ours' and that an intelligence relationship with Israel concerning Iran 'could seriously skew our own perception and analysis of the Iranian scene'. He added that we 'are interested to know what Israel thinks about Iran, but we should treat it as having a bias built in', and concluded that [Ledeen's] initiative 'contains the seeds of . . . serious error unless straightened out quickly'.[5]

A few days later, another McFarlane protégé, NSC staffer Howard Teicher, co-authored a National Security Decision Directive (NSDD) which proposed, *inter alia*, 'initiatives to include the provision of selected military equipment to increase Western leverage with Iran and minimize Soviet influence'. Shultz's reaction to that: he said the proposal was 'perverse' and 'contrary to our own interests'. Added Secretary of Defence Caspar Weinberger: 'This is almost too absurd to comment on.'[6] Perverse and absurd it may have been, but for seventeen months in 1985–6, Israeli policy on arming Khomeini's Iran became American policy.

McFarlane later testified rather disingenuously to the Senate Select Committee on Intelligence that he had been unaware of the 'bias built in' to Israeli policy, that is, the past history of covert Israeli arms shipments to Khomeini's Iran. Had he known of this, he told the Committee, 'it would have made him less responsive to later Israeli proposals to resume shipments'.[7]

The history of Israeli arms shipments to Iran could hardly have been news to McFarlane and North, much less to Middle East specialists such as Ledeen and Teicher. Moreover, had McFarlane requested information on the subject, any of several US Government agencies could have obliged. The likelihood is that McFarlane, Ledeen and others well understood that they had been co-opted to assist the US Government in a long-standing Israeli policy.

Arms and the Shah 1975–9

During the last four years of his reign, the Shah of Iran made his country the world's leading importer of arms, and around 80 per cent of his weapons were obtained in America. Iran's military expenditures in this period were $64.7 billion, 3.4 times greater than those of Iraq, which was Iran's traditional enemy in the region, and even exceeding those of her other natural rival in the Gulf, Saudi Arabia, by some $11.5 billion.[8]

And the Shah bought quality. In 1977–8 he took delivery of F-14A fighter bombers and RF-4 tactical reconnaissance aircraft, Harpoon and Phoenix air-to-ground missiles, improved Hawk anti-aircraft missiles, Spruance-class destroyers and M-60 tanks fitted with the new 105 mm gun.[9] When the Shah fled the country in January 1979, even hotter weapons were on their way to Iran, including F-16 fighters, AWACs planes and a special, land-based version of the F-18 Cobra fighter aircraft which had been developed specifically for the Iranian Air Force by the Northrop Company. Altogether, counting US construction of the huge Chah Bahar naval base complex, some $22 billion of US military hardware and training was in the pipeline at the time of the fall of the Shah![10]

Besides the heavy stuff, the US sold Iran vast amounts of police weapons and paramilitary hardware and provided training to the Iranian national police force, the SAVAK (the dreaded intelligence organization), and counter-intelligence training to the army.[11] Carter could simply no longer espouse human rights worldwide and also sell SAVAK the means and tools of torture. The national police and SAVAK training programmes were shut down in 1978, as part of President Jimmy Carter's international human rights campaign. When anti-Shah demonstrations swept Iran in late 1978, however, more American police equipment was brought in to meet the emergency.

There was another country heavily involved with the Iranian military and security forces in this period: Israel. At the headquarters building for Iranian military intelligence, recalls a former DIA official, 'we were downstairs, and the Israelis were upstairs'.[12] The Israelis, too, specialized in police and counterinsurgency training. But they also ran operations into Iraq in support of the Kurdish rebels there.

Aaron Klieman, a professor at Tel Aviv University and an expert on Israeli arms sales, has written of this period:

> The strategic interests of Washington, Tehran and Jerusalem essentially paralleled each other. The goals held in common during the decade of the seventies centred on resisting Soviet encroachment in the area, frustrating Iraqi expansionism, checking radical terrorism threatening both Israel and Iran, and on bolstering moderate Arab regimes like those in Egypt and Jordan.[13]

Whether one or another of these is a strategic interest, or a perceived strategic interest, or a purported strategic interest is perhaps arguable. Certainly it is stretching a point to speak of Israel as 'bolstering' the Egyptian and Jordanian Governments in this period. But the basic idea is well taken: while the Shah was in power, the three governments shared a common view on most regional security issues.

One 'strategic' interest unquestionably shared in Iran by Israel and America was profits on trade. Israeli exports to Iran rose markedly during the period, from $33 million in 1973–4, to $100 million in 1975–6, to $200 million in 1976–7.[14] A majority of these were military goods, particularly small arms and crew-served weapons, and the importance of this market for Israel may be seen in the fact that *total* Israeli arms exports worldwide in 1977 were only $300 million.[15] Iran was an early example, then, of 'Uzi diplomacy', a term derived from the well-known Israeli sub-machine gun. Interestingly, however, Iran was not a buyer of 'major' Israeli weapons in this period. South Africa, Argentina and El Salvador were Israel's three largest customers for planes, tanks, armoured personnel carriers and the like in 1970–9.[16] The US dominated the lucrative Iran market for these weapons. For the time being.

The US may have sold the hardware, but even before the fall of the Shah, Israel developed training and maintenance contracts with the Iranian armed forces. And it was not always forthcoming with its American allies on this business. The Defence Department was surprised to learn in 1978 from satellite photographs that Iranian F-4s were engaged in training exercises at Israeli air bases.[17]

Nor was this all that was kept from the US Government. Documents taken from the Israeli trade mission in Tehran, hastily abandoned during the chaotic first days of the revolution, revealed that the IDF and the Iranian Army were secretly collaborating on development of a surface-to-surface tactical ballistic missile (TBM) designed to carry a nuclear warhead up to 125 miles. Both countries were aware that US Defence Secretary Schlesinger had pointedly refused to sell to Iran Pershing TBMs, in conformity with America's long-standing policies against nuclear proliferation, and the obligations of both the US and Iran under the 1968 Non-proliferation Treaty.[18]

In the summer of 1977 Iranian Defence Minister Hassan Toufanian attended a test-firing of the then latest version of the Jericho, which was to have been used as a prototype for the joint Israeli-Iranian missile. The project, code-named 'Operation Flower', was one of the most important elements in a secret, $1 billion oil-for-arms agreement concluded in 1977 by Toufanian and then Israeli Defence Minister Shimon Peres.[19] The agreement did not survive the revolution, however, and Israel had to look elsewhere to meet its oil import requirements.

There may have been other elements in the covert pre-revolutionary Iran–Israel relationship. Years later, Yaacov

Nimrodi, who headed the Israeli military mission in Tehran for thirteen years and was known there as 'Mr Israel' would brag to Israeli reporter Yossi Melman in a *Davar* interview: 'When one day we shall be permitted to talk about all that we have done in Iran, you will be horrified. It is beyond your imagination.'[20] Nimrodi was not shy. To Lally Weymouth of the *Washington Post*, he would later claim that he had 'built Iranian Intelligence', that is, SAVAK.[21]

The extent of Israel's penetration of the Shah's military and security establishments is reflected in the fact that Israeli intelligence, unlike its American counterparts in Tehran, foresaw the demise of the Shah and took certain steps to reposition Israel's interests in light of this assessment, such as quiet negotiations in 1977–8 with Nigeria, Mexico and other alternative sources of oil.[22] The gentleman generally given credit for this perspicacity is Uri Lubrani, who was the chief Mossad resident in Iran at the time of the Shah's departure and Khomeini's return. Michael Ledeen, whose book (written with William Lewis) *Débâcle: The American Failure in Iran*, was strongly critical of American intelligence performance in Iran, contrasted that performance with a key report prepared by Lubrani in early 1978, predicting the Shah's demise:

> Lubrani's assessment created a mild sensation in Tel Aviv, and was challenged by many in the Foreign Office. But the Israeli Government was sufficiently concerned that it took two steps: it alerted the Jewish community in Iran that the situation looked bad (and encouraged Iranian Jews to make plans for their departure); and it transmitted the substance of Lubrani's concerns to Washington. The reply from the American Government, reflecting the view of the intelligence community, was that Lubrani's concerns were alarmist.[23]

Ledeen may have been a bit harsh on the Americans concerned, or charitable with the Israelis, as the case may be, for he neglected to mention that Mossad routinely rotated Lubrani out of Tehran in the middle of the crisis which he had predicted. Moreover, when the Shah's Government collapsed in early 1979, Israeli diplomats were trapped in Tehran and requested emergency evacuation on US aircraft after their mission was occupied by the PLO.[24]

If US and Israeli interests under the Shah were distinguished by shared perceptions but a lack of candour, they began to diverge sharply after the arrival of Ayatollah Khomeini in Tehran in February 1979. As the Shah's Government collapsed, the US Defence Department quickly sent a senior staffer from the Office of the Secretary, Erik Van Marbod, into the chaos of Tehran to find senior Iranian military officials to sign a memo terminating the foreign military sales programme in Iran.[25] This provided a legal basis for immediate cut-off of the many billions of dollars of advanced weapons that were then in the 'pipeline', heading straight to the Ayatollah's revolutionary government. There was also concern for the possible compromise of weapons systems already delivered, and at one point the DoD discussed with Anwar Sadat the possibility of Egyptian aid in the 'neutralization' of eighty Iranian Air Force F–14 Tomcat fighters, armed with state-of-the-art Phoenix missiles.[26]

US–Iranian relations disintegrated steadily through 1979. In April the credentials of the newly appointed US Ambassador were rejected, and in November five hundred 'students' stormed and occupied the US Embassy. Iran abrogated its mutual defence treaty with the US. President Carter announced the cessation of all American oil purchases from Iran and finally, on 14 November, he froze some $12 billion in Iranian assets in America. Months dragged on and the Embassy hostages were not released. Diplomatic relations were not formally broken until April 1980 but, when it was done, it was done with finality. Executive orders issued at the White House banned all exports to and imports from Iran or any contractual relations with an Iranian entity. The vast stores of military equipment in the pipeline were released for sale elsewhere. At this point, Khomeini's Iran was in a *de facto* state of war with America.

Arms during the hostage crisis 1980–1

While US interests and presence in Iran were undergoing fundamental changes, relatively little happened where Israel was concerned. Israel still agreed with Iran about Iraq. There were still Iranian Jews – mostly in Tehran – whose status remained a matter of concern to the Government of Israel. Iran continued, potentially at least, to be a nearby, convenient source of oil for Israel. Conversely Iran, particularly at a time when Iraqi relations were deteriorating, continued to be a lucrative market for arms, spare parts and training. Moreover, Iran's order of battle was standardized on the very American weapons systems that composed the arsenal of the IDF. As a market for industrial/military exports, therefore, Israel's interest in Iran actually *increased* after the fall of the Shah, and the shutting off of the US arms pipeline.

In 1980 arms exports were assuming a new importance to the Israeli economy as a whole. Israel had by that year become the world's seventh largest arms exporter, and the largest in the Third world.[27] Although official Israeli figures for 1980 are not available, Aaron Klieman quotes 'unidentified officials' to the effect that in 1981 the total value of exports of domestically produced or refurbished defence equipment was $1.2 billion. This was slightly over half the total for all industrial exports from Israel that year.[28]

In 1980, hostages or no, Iran was ready to buy, and Israel was ready to sell. Years later, former Israeli Foreign Minister Abba Eban would sadly observe about this period:

If an Iranian regime is friendly, we let them have arms to celebrate the friendship. But if it is hostile, we let them have arms to mitigate the hostility. We end up in a situation where the selling of arms is the only constant.[29]

A new impetus for Iran to seek weapons from any source available came in late September 1980, when Iraqi armed forces abruptly moved into Iran along a sixty-mile section of border the two countries share on the Shatt-al-Arab waterway. In the first few weeks of heavy fighting, which saw Iraqi forces penetrate thirty miles into Iran and overrun the important cities of Khorramshahr and Abadan, Iran suffered heavy losses in men and equipment. On 23 September the Chief of Staff of Iran's army acknowledged on Tehran Radio that Iran was having a problem with 'repairs, maintenance and spare parts'.[30] In succeeding days and weeks, news reports proliferated world-wide about Iran's frantic search for weapons and spares. Attention focused upon other countries which were major purchasers of US weapons systems. The governments of Turkey, South Korea and Japan all flatly denied that they were supplying Iran, not surprisingly, as the re-export of American weapons systems to a nation embargoed by the US would have been a violation of the US Arms Export Control Act and the bilateral mutual assistance agreements with each of these countries.[31]

On 1 October an Iranian diplomat in Brussels nevertheless confirmed that Iran was getting spare parts in the 'free market'. And a week later Iranian President Abolhassan Bani-Sadr told *Le Monde* that his country was indeed continuing to find spare parts for its American weapons through what he described as 'international dealers'.[32] Dealers, however, are merely middlemen. The question was, where were the dealers getting the stuff? Strangely, few at the time thought of the logical answer.

There were hints. On 30 September and 4 October 1980 Kuwaiti newspapers reported that Israel was using foreign planes and devious European routes to fly spare parts to Iran, all with the foreknowledge and approval of the US Government. On 2 November, the London *Observer* reported that Israel was sending F-4 Phantom spares, helicopter parts and missiles, on ships to Persian Gulf ports in Iran, including Bandar Abbas. Some shipments to Israel from America, said the *Observer*, were being diverted straight to Iran without ever touching Israeli soil.[33] Four days later, the Israeli daily newspaper *Haaretz* quoted Israeli Foreign Minister Yitzhak Shamir, saying that the Israeli Government was following the Iran–Iraq war with a 'great deal of interest', in order to be able to 'intervene if the need arises'.[34]

In early January 1981, with the American Embassy hostages still in Iranian hands, press reports surfaced in the US that Israel had been smuggling arms and spares to Iran with the knowledge and tacit approval of the Carter Administration, now in its last days before the inauguration of President Reagan. On 5 January the State Department unequivocally denied that the US had ever approved such sales by 'Israel or any other country'. Asked directly whether Israel had nevertheless provided spares to Iran, the Department spokesman said 'I have seen reports to that effect. I have nothing for you on them.'[35]

Only after they had left office were Carter and White House officials willing to acknowledge that Israel (a) had asked in September 1980 for US authorization to sell military equipment to Iran, (b) had been turned down, and (c) in October 1980 had gone ahead with the sale of tyres for F-4 Phantoms.[36] A French arms dealer who was involved in the deal would later reveal on a BBC-TV *Panorama* programme that the tyres the Israelis sent were sub-standard re-treads, so that if the sale was discovered, it could be brushed aside as trivial.[37] Because the re-treading had been done in Israel, there would also have been a legitimate question whether their re-export would have constituted a violation of US law. A civilian airport in Nimes, France which had a military base alongside, was used as the transit point. The 'switch' of the tyres from one chartered plane to another took only two hours.

Since the Carter Administration was not receptive to Israeli arms sales to Iran, 'friends of Israel' in America began to approach the Reagan team on the idea, even before it took office. In late 1980 Morris Amitay of the American Israel Public Affairs Committee (AIPAC) suggested such a sale to Reagan transition staff member Richard Allen, who was known to be an ardent admirer of the Zionist state. Nor was it the first approach Allen had received. In mid-1980 an obscure Senate Armed Services Committee staffer had offered to make contacts with the Iranians (presumably with Israeli help) and deliver the Tehran Embassy hostages triumphantly to the Reagan campaign headquarters just prior to the election. The staffer's name: Robert C. McFarlane Jr.[38]

Tango November, 1981

The F-4 tyres which composed the first shipment were from the outset considered a 'trial run'. If the covert operation went without a hitch, more would flow. A second shipment of 20 tons of spare parts, worth $600,000, was shipped almost immediately.[39] At this point the French supply line apparently collapsed, due to an unscrupulous middleman, and was replaced by a British arms dealer who established regular flights to Iran from Israel through Cyprus, using CL-44 transport aircraft belonging to the Argentinian company Transporte Aero Rioplatense.[40] These shipments involved, among other items, tank spare parts, 360 tons of ammunition for M-48 and M-60 tanks, refurbished jet engines and additional aircraft tyres.[41]

By this point, the amounts of weapons and money involved in the 'Israel connection' had doubtless begun to have an impact on the conduct of the war. Five years later, in December 1986, a dissident Iranian group would find and publish a single contract from 1981 involving arms costing $136 million.[42] The dealer involved was Yaacov Nimrodi, who had (perhaps) retired from IDF service and established himself in London, and had begun to trade on his fabled familiarity with Tehran. The dissident group, the People's Mujaheddin, claimed it had established a pattern between the arrival of shipments of Israeli arms and the timing of Iranian offensives against Iraq. The Israeli Government, which in December 1986 was reeling in the face of one 'Iran-Contra' revelation after another, denied the authenticity of the 1981 contract and any official relationship with Nimrodi.[43]

A smaller deal however – for $27.9 million – was harder to deny. It involved that leased Argentinian CL-44 plane flying to Iran out of Tel Aviv via Cyprus. Its call sign was 'Tango November'. Twelve flights were planned, but on the return (Iran-Cyprus) portion of the third flight on 18 July, 1981, in an area near the Turkish–Soviet border, the plane disappeared off the radar screens. Soon, newspapers in the Soviet Union, Cyprus, Israel, Argentina and several European countries were carrying stories based upon documentation for the plane, the lease agreement, the flight itself, and so on. Airport officials were interviewed. Finally, one of the principals in the arms delivery scheme, a Swiss citizen named Andreas Jenni, agreed to talk. The London *Sunday Times* carried the first detailed account of the aborted scheme on 26 July, 1981.

Exactly how the plane met its end may never be known. The *Sunday Times* quoted 'Western intelligence sources' to the effect that the plane was downed by a Soviet MiG 25 fighter. The Soviet news agency Tass claimed that the plane did not respond to Soviet ground air-traffic-control services, flew erratically in Soviet airspace, and finally collided with another aircraft.[44] Andreas Jenni maintained that Soviet fighters intercepted the plane in Turkish territory and forced it to fly across the border. In any event, Jenni's charter partner, Stuart McCafferty, and three Argentinian crewmen were killed. The Soviet Government took the unusual step of offering to fly the Argentinian Ambassador to the crash site. He accepted, examined the plane, and was given urns which the Soviets said contained remains of the crew. There was no evidence of a second plane.[45] Said the *New York Times:* 'Israel reacted with a less than emphatic denial, followed by silence as more details of the affair leaked out.'[46]

Arms, arms, arms 1982–4

By early 1982 Iran had begun to take the initiative in the war, regaining lost territory and actually forcing the fighting back into Iraq at several points along the border. In the Arab Middle East, Shiite Muslim fundamentalism was becoming a significant 'radicalizing' element in the political matrices of many countries. The Government of Ayatollah Khomeini was increasingly mentioned as a source of support for international terrorism in Europe and elsewhere. US relations with Iran changed little after the release of the hostages, and the arms and trade embargoes imposed by President Carter remained in effect. At the same time, the US had begun to 'tilt' toward Iraq in its view of the conflict. In March 1982 the Reagan Administration removed Iraq from the list of countries it regarded as supporting terrorism. Shortly afterwards, the Boeing and Lockheed companies were granted licences to sell airliners and transport planes, respectively, to Iraq.[47]

One would have thought that these factors, together with Israel's increasing preoccupation with Lebanon, would have conspired to cut off the flow of arms from Israel to Iran, particularly after US officials, in early 1982, bluntly told Jerusalem that continued Israeli arms sales to Iran were 'not in the American interest'.[48] Yet in early June the Joint Chiefs of Staff reported to State, CIA, etc, that they had intelligence of new shipments from Israel to Iran of 'unspecified quantities' of 105 mm tank and 155 mm howitzer ammunition, spare parts for US-manufactured F-4 Phantom aircraft, M-48 and M-60 battle tanks, and spare parts for, and complete sets of, communications equipment.[49] In 1987 Secretary of Defence Caspar Weinberger would testify before the Congressional Iran-Contra hearings that he had heard 'reports' of pre-1985 shipments of Israeli arms to Iran, but that he had seen no hard intelligence. The citation below would therefore have been helpful to him.

The flow not only continued; qualitatively it improved. In July 1983 Iranian exiles showed the *Boston Globe* invoices date-stamped 6 January 1983 for sale to Iran by an Israeli-owned company of the following:

- Sidewinder air-to-air missiles;
- radar equipment;
- 40,000 rounds of mortar ammunition;
- 400,000 rounds of machine gun ammunition;
- 1,000 field telephones; and
- 200 telephone scramblers.[50]

That same month, July, the French leftist newspaper *Libération* published what it said was new information about the Nimrodi $136 million contract, maintaining that the bulk of the military equipment involved in the sale was advanced American arms which Israel was proscribed by US law from transferring to a third country without US Government authorization. The sale, according to the paper, included Lance tactical ballistic missiles, improved Hawk anti-aircraft missiles, and Tampela and Copperhead laser-guided 155 mm artillery shells.[51]

Following the appearance of the *Libération* piece, two respected Israeli dailies, *Yediot Ahronot* and *Haaretz*, carried articles containing additional details on the Nimrodi sale, presumably based upon research done by their own reporters in Israel.[52] And just a few days later *Weltwoche*, a Swiss magazine, reported that regular shipments of 'heavy military equipment' were going into Tehran from Israel on what they described as 'US cargo planes', by which they presumably meant American-made, not US Government-owned, aircraft.[53]

The State Department's reaction to these reports was the bureaucratic version of killing – or at least doubting – the messenger bearing bad news. State asked the Paris and Berne US embassies to report on the reliability and political orientation of the European publications involved, particularly where Israel was concerned. To what must have been the great disappointment of the Department's Near Eastern Affairs Bureau, the US Embassy in Paris answered:

> *Libération* . . . has become one of France's leading and most respected newspapers. While we do not know the authors of the *Libération* piece, *Libération* editor Serge July, who would have had to pass on publication of the story, is a reputable journalist. We know of no connections between *Libération* and any of the Governments concerned.[54]

The Paris Embassy added that editor July had publicly stated his 'high regard for Israeli democracy', but that the 'general editorial line of *Libération* is pro-Palestinian'.[55]

The news was no better from Berne. The US Embassy in Switzerland reported a few days later:

> *Weltwoche* is a widely read and respected German-language news magazine with a circulation of about 150,000 throughout Switzerland. Politically, it is middle of the road, generally supportive of US policy although on occasion constructively critical of specific US positions.[56]

It is probable that the editors and reporting staff of these publications were unaware that their attitudes toward America were being officially questioned and investigated because they had reported that Israel was sending US weapons to Iran.

In January 1984 another 'respected' publication, this one American, *Defense and Foreign Affairs Daily*, reported that Israel was shipping 'proscribed' cluster munitions to Iran, and

added: 'Parts for the few viable Grumman F-14 Tomcats in the
Iranian Air Force are being delivered directly from Israel by
transport aircraft on a regular basis.'[57]

The articles and the evidence continued to pile up, almost
faster than the State Department could question the integrity of
the publications and institutions involved. In March 1984 *Stern*
magazine in Germany produced yet another article on the
Yaacov Nimrodi contract, reporting that the military equipment involved was being shipped on night flights of El Al cargo
jets which overflew Syrian territory to reach Iran.[58] (Syria was
at the time openly supporting Iran in the conflict.)

When the State Department made the usual inquiries at the
US Embassy in Bonn, the staff there, perhaps a bit piqued at
Washington's petty scepticism, included the following in its
response:

> For your information, an official of London's Institute for
> Strategic Studies in an interview broadcast on Germany's second
> television network (ZDF) March 8 also said that Israel was
> supplying arms to Iran.[59]

For good measure, the embassy added that on 17 March the
newspaper *Frankfurter Allgemeine*, which the embassy described as a 'conservative daily', had estimated that Israel had so
far delivered $500 million worth of arms to Iran, 'including
weapons of Israeli and American manufacture and weapons
captured in Lebanon'.[60] We were no longer talking about some
re-treaded spare tyres.

'Technical' considerations

The reports of Lance missiles, cluster bombs, F-14 spares,
laser-guided 155mm rounds, etc, being sent to Iran must have
caused some concern at the Pentagon, in part because it was
well known in the arms sales community that Iran's three other
main military suppliers at the time were, in order of importance, North Korea, Libya and Syria.[61] It had to be assumed that
advisers, trainers, maintenance personnel and the like from

these countries working in Iran would have direct access to whatever weapons systems Israel sent to that country. Finally, each of these countries had close military relationships with the Soviet Union. The compromise of the technology involved in these systems was therefore a strong possibility.

On occasion, the Israeli connection failed, though not for want of trying. In early 1983, for example, the Israeli Government, working through a dealer in Paris named Avi Mamou, proposed to sell the Iranians 200 M-48A-5 tanks. The tanks had been reconditioned for Taiwan at the Israeli tank factory in Tel Aviv, but the deal had fallen through. The equipment was 'available', and the M-48 was well known to the Iranian Army, as the tank had been in the Iranian arsenal for over ten years.

But these were very special M-48s. They had been retro-fitted with new, more powerful 105 mm guns, and had the latest Allison cross-drive transmissions. Their fire-control systems were the M1781C laser-guided type, with automatic compensation for different types of ammunition, accompanied by M-32E1 night vision periscopes and controlled by the M-13-A4 ballistic computer. It was not a weapon which the Pentagon would have wanted in unfriendly hands.

Fortunately, the deal fell through in December 1983. The Israelis, who had $600,000–650,000 invested in each reconditioned tank, offered them to Avi Mamou for $980,000. He in turn offered to sell them to Iran for $1,250,000 each – for a final mark-up of 100 per cent. The deal would have totalled $250 million, of which fully $100–125 million would have been profit. The Iranians, who disliked direct dealings with the Israeli Government in any event, decided to look elsewhere.[62] The US Defence Department, which had followed the deal closely, breathed a sigh of relief.

A policy of confusion

The problem was that the American position on arms to Iran, which had been so uniform and so intense under the Carter Administration in the time of the embassy hostage-taking, had begun to come unravelled under Reagan. And the unravelling process began long before Yitzhak Rabin and David Kimche convinced the White House to become directly involved.

When the *Libération* article on the Nimrodi contract appeared in July 1983, the Near Eastern Affairs Bureau at the State Department in Washington sent a telegram to US embassies in Middle Eastern and selected European countries. In an injured tone, the Department said:

> The numerous such reports over the past year create a perception that the US winks at, or actively encourages, clandestine re-supply of Iran with critically needed US origin parts and weapons.

But, the Department reassured its representatives abroad:

> Generally, we have found no substance to previous reports of such transfers, and we suspect that some such reports are entirely bogus ... Although there is no evidence to suggest any truth to it whatsoever, we are investigating this report [of the Nimrodi contract] as we have similar media and intelligence reports over the past year.[63]

It is not easy to dispell rumours in the face of a conspiracy by the London Institute for Strategic Studies, the Stockholm International Peace Research Institute (SIPRI) and the major news media of the US, Europe and Israel, but the State Department was determined to try, even if this meant ignoring intelligence reports from the Pentagon.

Not surprisingly the message, if there was one, was not getting through to the Government of Israel. In May 1984 General Ariel Sharon travelled to the US and stated publicly that Israel had been selling weapons to Iran, and had been doing so with the knowledge of the US Government. Although Sharon had previously been relieved of his post as Defence Minister for his role in permitting the Sabra and Chatila massacres, he had remained a minister without portfolio in the Likud coalition government until 1987. In response to press questions raised by Sharon's statement, a State Department spokesman said, on 16 May, 1984:

> The Government of Israel has assured us that it is not providing Iran with arms, either of US origin or Israeli manufacture. The

USG remains neutral with respect to the Iran–Iraq war and as a consequence sells arms to neither belligerent. We also do not permit the transfer of US-licensed arms to Iran by third parties.[64]

Hear no evil, see no evil, etc. It was a remarkable statement: part truth, part wishful thinking, and part outright falsehood. The spokesman went on to say that while the US Government favoured a negotiated settlement that would be fair to both sides, it was persuaded that Iran was the intransigent party, and had asked Israel and other allies to help in staunching the flow of arms to bring pressure on Iran to negotiate.

Superficially, the last sentence in the statement was true. Four months previously, after Iran-supported groups had been linked to several terrorist bombings in Lebanon, the Reagan Administration had 'formally' declared Iran to be a terrorist-supporting nation. And in March 1984 the State Department had designated Ambassador-at-Large Richard Fairbanks to co-ordinate efforts with Israel and with European arms-exporting nations, to cut off the weapons deliveries to Iran. The project was called 'Operation Staunch'.

In fact, however, the Reagan White House policy on this matter was already in a state of transition. In January 1984 – two months before Fairbanks's designation – Geoffrey Kemp, the senior NSC staff director for Near Eastern affairs, had written a memo to Robert McFarlane, the President's Adviser on National Security Affairs, to suggest a new, tougher line toward Iran, including a revival of covert operations against Khomeini's Government. According to the Tower Commission Report, Kemp told McFarlane 'that exiled Iranians, with whom he regularly communicated, hoped that, with foreign help, they might install a pro-Western government'.[65]

What 'foreign help'? The Tower Commission Report, and perhaps the Kemp memo as well, are not specific. But the phrase might have a familiar ring. Two years earlier, Yaacov Nimrodi and David Kimche, then Director General of the Israeli Ministry of Foreign Affairs, had openly advocated on BBC television that what was needed was 'foreign support', including arms, for a coup in Iran. Both Nimrodi and Kimche had thought they might know where to find the necessary hardware . . . in Israel, of course.

McFarlane apparently took a few months to digest the Kemp memo. In August however, he formally requested, in the form of a National Security Study Directive, an inter-agency review of US relations with Iran.[66] The requested study was produced two months later, in October, and it directly, though apparently inconclusively, addressed the issue of possible US arms shipments to Iran, that is, presumably to dissident groups. At this point, things began to move rather rapidly. In November a former CIA official who maintained loose contacts in the Agency, met in Europe with Iranian businessman Manucher Ghorbanifar, who suggested that the shipment of some Tow missiles to Tehran might result in the release of American hostages in Lebanon, and would (somehow) also hinder the spread of Soviet influence in Iran.[67] Ghorbanifar was probably not unaware that for the Reagan White House, these were the magic words. On 8 July 1987 Lieutenant Colonel Oliver North, McFarlane's aide at NSC, would testify to the Congressional Iran-Contra hearings that the CIA learned only after the European contact that Manucher Ghorbanifar was at the time working for Israeli intelligence.

Getting lost in Iran

Now here is where patience, deep breathing and a measured suspension of logic will be required, to understand how an official US policy of 'no arms for Iran' became an official policy of 'arms for Iran' in little more than one year. In January 1985 Israeli arms merchants Nimrodi and Adolph Schwimmer, together with Amiram Nir, who was counter-terrorism adviser to Israeli Prime Minister Peres, began a series of meetings with Ghorbanifar to discuss the means of obtaining US support for a 'dialogue with Iran'.[68] The Tower Commission was not specific on just what sort of dialogue was intended, but it is quite likely that shipments of weapons were contemplated, given the participants in the meetings. According to the Tower Commission

Report, an American businessman who attended some of the meetings later reflected that 'profit was certainly a motive'.[69]

Thereafter the Government of Israel, through Robert McFarlane, his assistant Lieutenant Colonel Oliver North, and NSC consultant Michael Ledeen, intervened repeatedly to encourage, initiate and then revive direct US shipments of arms to Iran ... or more specifically, to the Government of Ayatollah Khomeini. In May 1985 Ledeen made an apparently unofficial visit to Israel, where Prime Minister Shimon Peres specifically asked for McFarlane's (i.e. US) approval for an Israeli shipment of ammunition to Iran.[70] This was the trip which prompted Secretary Shultz's memo to McFarlane warning of the difference between Israel's and America's agendas in Iran ... though it is doubtful that even Shultz at this time understood just how committed Israel was – and had been – to the arming of Iran.

In July David Kimche, still Director General of the Israeli Ministry of Foreign Affairs, and acting on the specific orders of Prime Minister Peres, contacted McFarlane personally to broach the subject of direct US arms supplies to Iran.[71] McFarlane took this message to the President, but was later careful to state to both the Tower Commission and the Senate Select Committee on Intelligence that Kimche had not relayed a direct Iranian request for US arms.

The barrage continued. Later that same month, Prime Minister Peres himself raised the arms-for-hostages proposal with Secretary Shultz while the latter was on a trip to Australia. At the same time, Peres sent Schwimmer as an emissary to discuss the proposal yet again with McFarlane.[72] Still in July, Ledeen made another of those trips to Israel, this time to meet with Ghorbanifar, Kimche, Schwimmer and Nimrodi. At this particular meeting a direct Iranian proposal for an arms-for-hostages swap *was* discussed.[73] And in August McFarlane and Vice Admiral John Poindexter briefed the Reagan Administration, in the forum of the National Security Planning Group, on what the Senate Select Committee termed in its report 'the Kimche proposal to permit the sale of Tows to Iran through Israel'.[74] Present at the meeting were Reagan, Bush, Shultz,

Weinberger, Presidential Staff Director Donald Regan and Director of Central Intelligence William Casey. This was apparently the moment at which Reagan first formally expressed his agreement for the proposition of sending American arms to Iran.[75]

There was one more prompt made. On 22 August Kimche called McFarlane to ask whether the deal was still on, that is, whether the US still agreed to replace the Tow missiles Israel was about to send to Iran. The answer: 'Yes.' The result: Israel delivered 100 Tow missiles to Iran on 30 August, 1985. A second shipment of 408 Tows went on 13 September. It was half done. What remained was for the Israelis to convince the US Government to become *directly* involved in the supply operation.

In September and October North and Ledeen met several times with the usual cast of characters, viz, Ghorbanifar, Schwimmer, Kimche and Nimrodi, to discuss 'technical' questions related to the transfer of arms from Israel to Iran.[76] Then in early November Israeli Defence Minister Yitzhak Rabin got directly involved, checking with McFarlane to ensure that the President had indeed approved the next proposed Israeli shipment, this one of Hawk anti-aircraft missiles.[77] And on 17 November Rabin asked for US assistance (as described at the beginning of this chapter) in arranging the landing rights and customs clearances for the flights. In the end, a CIA propietary airline was used. It was done. The US was now directly, hopelessly involved in providing arms to the Ayatollah Khomeini.

In late November 1986 Israel's role in what was then being called the 'Iran affair' was briefly pushed front and centre in a press conference given by US Attorney General Edwin Meese. In his opening statement, he dropped the bombshell about the diversion of Iranian arms funds to the Contras in Central America. The arms transfers themselves however, said Meese, involved 'the United States providing arms to Israel and Israel in turn transferring the arms . . . to Iran'.[78] Meese went even further in the question period afterwards, claiming that the Israelis had made the August–September transfer of Tow missiles and the diversion of funds to the Contras, without the prior knowledge or authorization of President Reagan.

Israeli officials reacted somewhat angrily to these statements, denying outright that Israel had had any role in the diversion of funds to Central America, or that the arms sales themselves had occurred on Israel's initiative. Prime Minister Shamir's office immediately released a statement which acknowledged that Israel had 'transferred defensive arms and spare parts' from the US to Iran but only 'upon the request of the United States'.[79] Observed a *Washington Post* correspondent in Jerusalem:

> Israel has had to defend itself against charges – both from Washington and from some critics here – that it enticed White House amateurs into a high-risk, low-gain adventure in Iran based upon shaky intelligence from self-interested Iranian and Israeli arms dealers and others.[80]

Several days of angry finger-pointing between Washington and Jerusalem followed, during which Israeli Prime Minister Yitzhak Shamir denied any Israeli role in the diversion and, initially at least, denied that Israel had sold arms to Iran on its own over the previous few years. It was not, said Shamir, Israeli policy to supply arms to Iran.[81] A strange campaign of what might be called the Jerusalem version of official '*samizdat*' then ensued:

> In the last few days, Israeli officials have been quietly divulging to the Israeli press their inside account of the Iran affair – a version they say details precisely how the United States Government 'with the knowledge and approval' of President Reagan, used Israel to exchange arms for hostages with Iran.[82]

The centrepiece in this campaign was a lengthy article in the major daily, *Haaretz*, which was said to contain the 'authoritative' Israeli version of the Iran affair. The *Haaretz* story written by Yoel Marcus had McFarlane, through Michael Ledeen, initiating the contacts with Peres, enlisting Israeli assistance in a White House plan, and then repeatedly dragging Israel back into the affair. Israeli leadership, said Marcus, was unwilling to take the blame for the sale of arms to Iran. 'A reconstruction of the facts', said Marcus, 'shows that the episode is an American ballgame from beginning to end.'

Mr Marcus's description of the 'Iran affair' simply is not supported by the facts. By 1985–6 the various entities which compose the United States Government did not have a clearly defined policy framework for the Middle East conflict as a whole, much less a policy on the provision of arms to Iran. The Reagan Administration had certain individual goals for the Middle East region, restated periodically on ceremonial occasions, and the State Department had daily press briefings on the events of the previous twenty-four hours. But there was nothing one could call a coherent policy.

Yaacov Nimrodi, David Kimche, Amiram Nir and Shimon Peres understood this very well, and could hardly be faulted for moving quickly and effectively to turn America's resources to the service of the Government and the state of Israel. They would, in fact, have been derelict in their duty to their country had they *not* done so.

While the US position on Iran steadily came apart after the return of the hostages in January 1981, Israeli policy remained steady as a rock. Before and after the Shah; before, during and after the hostage crisis; before and after the shift in the strategic balance in the Iran–Iraq war . . . it was the clear position of the Government of Israel that Iran should be provided the weapons with which to destroy the Iraqi Army, or at least keep the war going in the effort.

One can argue the wisdom of this policy, to be sure, particularly after Iranian/Muslim fundamentalist political influence began to be felt in each and every Arab country surrounding Israel. And that debate is still raging in Israel itself, even as the Iran–Contra investigations proceed. But the continuity and clarity of Israeli policy in Iran since 1975 is a matter of considerable and detailed record. It was not Israel that became lost in Iran; it was America.

The Reagan Administration failed to appreciate that, as George Shultz warned Robert McFarlane at the beginning, Israel's agenda regarding Iran 'is not the same as ours'. With almost any other country, of course, such a remark would have been gratuitous. McFarlane, and others in the White House, would have assumed that any other Middle Eastern country, or even any one of America's European allies, would have had its own reasons for embroiling the US in the affair. Frequently, however, American officials find it difficult to distinguish between US and Israeli interests.

Epilogue . . . Adolph William Schwimmer

In this particular instance McFarlane might have been more careful had he known more about the recent history of Israel's arming of Iran. He could also have been instructed by the past history of the emissary sent by Israeli Prime Minister Shimon Peres in July 1985 to encourage the administration to proceed with the sale of Tow missiles.

He was Adolph William Schwimmer, and he was well known to the US intelligence community and the Justice Department. Schwimmer had fled to Tel Aviv from New York in January 1949 to avoid prosecution following his indictment in Miami, Florida, Federal District Court for conspiring to export arms to the Middle East in violation of US law.[83] Schwimmer's operation, run through Service Airways Inc, provided dozens of advanced fighter aircraft, scores of experienced American mechanics and pilots and many tons of weapons and ammunition critical to the outcome of Israel's 'War of Independence' in 1948–9

Originally, Schwimmer had wanted to centre his operation in Corsica or Sicily. Pressure from the US, French and Italian Governments, however, which were trying to staunch the flow of weapons to both sides in the war for Palestine, forced him to move Service Airways to a small, heavily guarded airfield at Zatek, about fifty to sixty miles outside Prague, Czechoslovakia.

The transport of all those weapons violated US law, and some of the weapons may have been stolen from US Navy ordnance dumps.[84] But what really worried American authorities at the time was the price that the Czech military was apparently extracting for Service Airways' use of the Zatek facility. In the spring of 1948 one of Schwimmer's C-46 transports flew into Zatek with a disassembled BT-13 trainer aircraft, which was promptly put together and turned over to the Czech Army.[85] A few months later, another Service Airways plane brought in and turned over a small, mobile early approach radar. The transfer, in this particular case, was personally observed by the US Air Attaché in Czechoslovakia.[86] US Army intelligence knew, in the latter case, that Czechoslovakia's military intelligence organization was specifically interested in obtaining information on recent developments in American radar.[87] The FBI in turn, and presumably the Pentagon as well, had reports that Soviet officers and officials occupied positions of authority at Zatek.[88]

US authorities eventually caught up with Schwimmer, and on 6 February, 1950 the Federal District Court in Los Angeles convicted him – and Service Airways Inc – of conspiracy to violate the Neutrality Act and the export control laws. Judge Pierson M. Hall stated at the termination of the trial:

> In the matter of control of its external relations the Government should and must be supreme. Persons who take the matters into their own hands start a train of circumstances which might be disastrous to the country.[89]

Thirty-seven years later, in early 1987, it would have been hard to find anyone in the Reagan White House who disagreed with that, surrounded at the time by confusion, embarrassment and hostile investigations.

THIRTEEN

Near Conclusion

The whole long summer's passed in fear
Waiting for the glint of their spears
In the wheat, the slither
Of leather on steel. The sky burns,
A copper roof, over the shrivelled corn.
Children and camels gasp in the noonday heat.
Enemies sweat in their steel, cry out at night,
And wake up trembling, wet with fright. We squat and stare
Across the nervous barbs, tied by our common dreads:
Hating the same we see, fearing the unsame,
The mask distrustful of the face:
Blind puppets twitched by a frantic nerve
Who scratch each other's eyes because we cannot see.

'Hating' by Aubrey Hodes
New Outlook Magazine, November/December, 1963

Late in the afternoon of 26 May 1987, about two hundred people gathered for a conference at the Radisson Mark Plaza Hotel in Alexandria, Virginia, a suburb of Washington. The group was composed largely of well-dressed middle-aged men, many with a military bearing. Some were in uniform. After registration, the attendees strolled among the company exhibits spread in the foyer of the hotel's lower lobby.

Tadiran Ltd informed passers-by that its remotely piloted vehicle carried 'payloads for real-time reconnaissance, targeting and range finding'. Elisra offered to protect combat ships of all types with early warning 'suites' which included 'computerized power management systems [with] chaff dispensers and high-power jammers'. The Soreq Nuclear Research Center said it was seeking research and development co-operation in, among others, the area of 'transport of radiation through turbulent atmosphere'. Telkoor was seeking partners who would co-operate in the development of 'data-links for guided weapons . . . accurate tracking and locating systems', and 'data-security and commercial encryption systems'.

Some companies specialized in relatively obscure fields such as thermal imaging and night-vision image-intensification. Others, like IMI, had a general expertise in almost anything that goes 'boom'. IMI, said its promotional material, supplies small arms, ammunition, explosives, bombs, rockets, fuses and aircraft accessories to 'more than 70 countries around the world'. Rafael Ltd told the visitors to its exhibit that the company used 'its full spectrum of technologies to solve the military's most demanding problems', including 'guided and unguided weaponry and . . . pyrotechniques'. And while some companies were starting fires, others were putting them out: Spectronix Ltd announced to the conference attendees that it was expert in 'fire and vapour explosion phenomena and suppression techniques'.[1]

During the succeeding two days, those attending the conference heard presentations from senior government and private sector officials in the respective military–industrial complexes of Israel and the United States. The general subject was military research and development co-operation between the two countries, and the specific presentation topics reflected the extent of co-operation already ongoing in mid-1987:

- electronics and radars;
- missiles and rockets;
- avionics and smart munitions;
- tomography battlefield casualties analysis;
- electro-optics; and
- the 'Strategic Defence Initiative'.

What was occurring here was a formal exchange of information between the military establishments of the largest and most advanced military power on earth on the one hand and on the other, the world's most active military power by far. Not surprisingly, the conference was sponsored by the Embassy of Israel in Washington. In his welcome to the attendees, Israeli

Defence Attaché Major General Amos Yaron said that the Government of Israel had made military research and development co-operation with the US 'one of its major goals'.[2]

To be sure, the Israeli Defence Forces (IDF) did not come empty-handed to this relationship. Said Yaron:

> We have fought six wars in the last thirty-nine years. So every operational need, every weapon system and doctrine has been derived from painfully gained combat experience. Every system has been tested in war. Lessons learned in war have been analysed and immediately implemented.[3]

Another conference speaker, Brigadier General Yosef Ben-Hanan, Commander, IDF Armour Corps, put the matter more succinctly, describing the IDF's frequent forays into neighbouring countries as 'combat laboratories'. What was being offered here, officially and on a broad scale, was an opportunity to test the most advanced US weapons systems against opposing Soviet and other Western systems in a variety of real conditions, on real roads, against real enemy emplacements, in real villages and cities, etc.

The level of US participation in the conference reflected the receptiveness of the Reagan Administration to this offered co-operation. Deputy Secretary of Defence William Taft delivered the keynote address, and the research directors of the US Army, Navy and Air Force made presentations. The US official assigned to address the troublesome issue of 'security considerations of technology transfer' in military research and development co-operation was a perfectly logical choice: Dr Stephen Bryen, Deputy Under Secretary of Defence for Trade Security Policy. Bryen had in the late 1970s been the subject of a formal Justice Department investigation for suspected violations of the Espionage Act involving . . . Israel.[4]

The May 1987 meeting was actually the third such conference since 1985, and it is now seen by the two governments as an annual event. Moreover, the meeting was merely a public manifestation of the extensive, indeed unique, co-operation which already exists between the US Defence Department and the IDF. General Uzi Eilam, Director of Defence Research and

Development for the IDF, did not exaggerate when he told the Alexandria conference attendees:

> Over the last several years the memoranda of understanding between the US and Israeli Governments have evolved from signed documents to a dynamic array of joint R and D projects, weapons evaluations, exchange of lessons learned in war, and sharing of test results of weapons systems. The activity has transformed the concept of co-operation into a fantastic process benefiting both nations.[5]

The 'signed documents' referred to by General Eilam in fact constitute an unprecedental legal framework for what one observer has described as 'strategic interdependence' between Israel and America.[6] A brief chronology of the major events might include:

1970 – The Master Defence Development Data Exchange Agreement, signed in December, which established the terms and conditions for exchange of technical data on a broad range of military subjects. Specific information exchanges are governed by Data Exchange Annexes which are added and/or updated annually, and have included *inter alia*, over time, the following:

- tank systems;
- surveillance, target acquisition and night observation;
- rocket/missile systems;
- air defence systems;
- artillery systems;
- electronic warfare;
- infantry weapons;
- tactical communications;
- wound ballistics; and
- defence against chemical agents.

1971 – The agreement for production in Israel of US-designed defence equipment, signed in November.

1973 – The Weapons Systems Evaluation Group established in November to collect, organize and distribute data concerning the interactions of 'opposing' (i.e. Soviet) and US and other Western weapons systems during the

October 1973 war in the Middle East. Both the US and Israel established data acquisition teams to carry out the study, which was completed in September 1975.

1979 – The Memorandum of Agreement on Principles Governing Mutual Co-operation in Research and Development, Scientist and Engineer Exchange, and Procurement and Logistics Support of Selected Defence Equipment, signed in March, permitted Israeli firms to bid on US defence contracts without Buy American Act restrictions, and facilitated co-operation in military research and development.

1981 – A commitment signed by Secretary of State Alexander Haig in April, establishing a Defence Trade Initiative to develop and enhance Israel's defence production and technological base.

1981 – The Memorandum of Understanding on Strategic Co-operation, signed in November, which expanded the 1979 MoA and set a target of $200 million a year for DoD purchases in Israel.[7]

1982 – The General Security of Information Agreement, signed in December, which provided for the safeguarding of all classified information exchanged between the two governments.

1983 – A second, expanded Memorandum of Understanding on Strategic Co-operation, signed in November, established terms and conditions for joint US–Israeli military planning and exercises, intelligence sharing, stockpiling of US military supplies in Israel, US use of Israeli medical facilities in time of emergency, US funding of Israeli development assistance projects in the Third World, and new, more generous terms for US economic and military assistance to Israel.

1984 – In March, the US signed a revision and expansion of the 1979 Memorandum of Agreement, governing modes of co-operation between the military–industrial complexes of the two countries as regards research and development, production, procurement and logistic support. A joint US Defence Department–Israeli Ministry of Defence Committee was established to prepare and update annexes to the agreement, as the need arises, on any of the subjects listed in the original 1979 MoA.

1984 – In May, the US National Aeronautics Space Agency (NASA) and the Israeli Space Agency (ISA) signed a collaboration agreement. The first of several joint projects commenced about one year later.

1985 – In April, the two countries signed a Free Trade Agreement (FTA), the first such pact the US has signed with any nation. The FTA removes, over time, existing barriers to Israeli access to any portion of the US market, and effectively shifts Israeli's trade orientation from Europe to the United States.[8]

1986 – A Memorandum of Understanding concerning US and Israeli government co-operation on the Strategic Defence Initiative (SDI) was signed in May. The MoU is designed to provide a basis for participation of laboratories, research establishments, companies, industries, and other entities in Israel in SDI research for the mutual benefit of the two parties.

1986 – Congress passed the Nunn and Quayle Amendments to the National Defence Authorization Act for Fiscal year 1987 in governing co-operative research and development in military fields with 'major non-NATO allies'. The Nunn Amendment allocates $40 million for this purpose, and the Quayle Amendment(s) specify Israel as qualifying for this assistance, and establish terms and conditions for joint development of an anti-tactical ballistic missile.

This list of US–Israel co-operation agreements is by no means complete, and yet even such a cursory review makes several things apparent. First, Republican administrations in America generally and the Reagan Administration in particular have tended to move quickly to expand and formalize US–Israeli military and economic co-operation. Second, over the past five years, the military–industrial complexes of the two countries have been effectively merged, and the bases have been laid for Israel's becoming the third most advanced, if not the third most powerful, military power on earth.

Finally, the relationship between Israel and the US has now indeed become unique. No other US military alliance, including those with NATO countries, is as strong or as broad based. From the standpoint of military and security matters, Israel has already become the fifty-first state, and a formal security treaty with Israel in 1987 would almost be redundant. Given the cumulative commitments of recent US presidents and the pervasive (some would say dominant) influence of Israel in Congress, both of which are reflected in the above list, it is difficult to imagine circumstances in which a concerted military attack upon Israel proper would *not* be construed as an attack upon the United States.[9]

What may not be apparent from a review of US–Israeli military co-operation agreements, however, is the fact that the Soviet Union and the Arab 'confrontation' states do not have commensurate agreements and relationships, with the result that, by and large, Arab military establishments have in the past few years rapidly lost ground to the IDF, qualitatively. With one single exception – that of Syria after the devastating Israeli air raids of June 1982 in Lebanon's Beqaa Valley – the Soviet Union has not actively sought and Arab governments have not permitted the establishment of client-state military relations such as those which existed in Egypt after the 1956 and 1967 wars. That exception, however, merits close scrutiny, as we shall see, for it may tell us a great deal about where the Middle East is now headed militarily.

Israel has frequently 'visited' other countries in the Middle East, particularly since the Camp David agreements were signed in 1979. The attack on the Osirak nuclear reactor in Baghdad in June 1981 was an impressive demonstration of deep-strike offensive military power. The range and speed and payload of the planes themselves – American F-15s and F-16s were only part of the story. Other advanced technologies, such as airborne warning and control (AWACs), electronic counter-measures (EMC), boom refuelling and smart munitions were also skilfully and effectively employed. Saudi Arabian and Jordanian air defence and intercept capabilities were challenged and easily suppressed or avoided.

In similar fashion Israel bombed villages and cities in Lebanon at will for two weeks in July 1981 without losing a single plane. And a year later the Israeli Air Force dismantled southern Syrian air defence missile emplacements and destroyed eighty-six aircraft, again without the loss of one combat aircraft. In October 1985 it was Tunisia's turn, as Israeli F-15s covered a round-trip distance of 3,000 miles to destroy PLO offices and parts of a nearby village. In May 1986 the US Air Force took a page from Israel's book, using F-111 aircraft to carry out a night attack on Libya from Upper Heyford, England.

These were not random acts, nor were they empty gestures in terms of the political *and* the military messages delivered. Iraq was taught that the Government of Israel would henceforth determine what weapons the Iraqi Ministry of Defence would or would not deploy. Lebanese leaders learned that Israel was ultimately responsible for security measures in south Lebanon. The Tunisian Government was informed which organizations would and would not be allowed by Jerusalem to be represented in Tunis. Colonel Qaddafi was reminded by Washington that Libya's right as a sovereign state to conduct its own foreign policy did not include a right to engage in the care and feeding of terrorist groups which hit Western targets.

In each of the above instances, however, there was a single, overriding military message delivered, not only to the particular country which received the unexpected visit, but to all the surrounding Arab states. The American–Israeli Air Force could at will inflict terrible damage and suffering at a time and place of its own choosing, over, around and through the air defences of any, repeat, *any* country in the Arab Middle East. The frustration caused by these repeated humiliations was no doubt exacerbated by the fact that the Arab states had continued, through the early and middle 1980s, to outspend Israel on defence generally, by a ratio of between five and seven to one, depending upon the particular year. Saudi Arabia alone outspent Israel in this period by more than two to one.

Part of the problem faced by the Arabs has to do with recent developments in military technology. Quite simply, in the 1980s offence beats defence. Flying state-of-the-art fighter bombers with advanced avionics, electronic counter-measures, chaff dispensers, smart munitions and computerized fire-control systems, the well-trained and practised Israeli pilots can finesse any air defence system they now face in the region.

The problem with the game of offence, from the Israeli standpoint, is that both sides can play it, and the Arabs have begun to understand that while they may have ineffective defences against the Israeli Air Force, they in turn can obtain and deploy weapons against which Israel has virtually no defences. The concept is not new and certainly not unique to the Middle East. It's called 'deterrence', or perhaps more accurately 'mutually assured destruction', and arguably it has kept Americans and Soviets from killing each other since the end of the Second World War.

In 1978–9, Syrian President Hafiz al-Assad adopted what Western leaders and media described as a 'rejectionist' position toward the Camp David agreements. Assad maintained that neither direct negotiations between the Arabs and Israelis nor any process mediated by the United States, Israel's armourer, would bring about a resolution of the central issues of the Middle East conflict. He made it clear that Syria would never participate in Jimmy Carter's 'framework for peace', and urged other Arab leaders to do the same.

An essential element of Assad's position was that Israel would not seriously negotiate and compromise on the critical issues of territory and refugees until the Arabs had reached military parity with Israel. To many American ears, these words in the mouth of an Arab leader sounded like a sinister threat to Israel's security. When Israel embarrassed the Syrians in Lebanon's Beqaa Valley in June 1982, therefore, many in

America rejoiced. One hundred and thirty retired US generals and admirals, for example, placed a full-page advertisement in the *New York Times* and in *USA Today*, cheering the successful air raids and air engagements as a significant victory for US weapons as against Soviet weapons, and praising Israel for its 'democratic will, national cohesion, technological capacity and military fibre'. The generals and admirals advised President Reagan to 'revitalize the strategic co-operation between the United States and Israel'.[10] As we have seen, it was advice he took to heart.

In the months following the Beqaa raids, however, Syria asked the Soviet Union to expand and modernize its air defence system. Some five thousand additional Soviet advisers arrived to deliver, install and deploy a vastly improved Syrian air defence system, and a command, control and communication (CCCI) network to direct it. For the first time since the War of Attrition in 1970, advanced Soviet weapons were being made available to an Arab army, including the first-ever deployment of SA-5 surface-to-air missiles outside the Soviet Union or the Warsaw Pact countries, and AN-26 aircraft as an airborne radio relay. Syria also received sophisticated T-72 tanks, Mig 24 attack helicopters and SU-22 and Mig 23 'Flogger D' fighter bombers with deep-strike attack potential.[11]

By far the most disturbing development, however, from an Israeli perspective was the arrival in Syria of twelve batteries of Soviet SS-21 tactical ballistic missiles (TBMs) – this is the exception to which I referred earlier. The SS-21 is quite unlike any missile – indeed, any weapon – previously seen in the Middle East. It can deliver a 2,200-pound payload over seventy-five miles with pinpoint accuracy. From Syria, the missiles can reach all northern Israel to a line just south of Tel Aviv.

In January 1986 Thomas Dine, Director of the American Israel Public Affairs Committee (AIPAC) described this new threat to Israel to a subcommittee of the Senate Armed Services Committee:

> the SS-21 has the range, accuracy and lethality to destroy hardened targets deep inside Israel ... Ballistic missiles armed with chemical warheads pose an obvious threat to Israeli population

centres, but they also could effectively suppress Israeli air bases and other military installations and significantly reduce Israel's retaliatory capabilities ... and directed against cities potentially result in 5,000 dead and wounded Israeli civilians in a future Arab-Israeli war.[12]

US Defence Department officials specifically assigned to follow the strategic balance in the Middle East believe that this is in fact a gross underestimate of the civilian casualties which would result from the use of this weapon in the manner indicated.

Since the time of Dine's testimony, Syria has deployed additional SS-21s, and has concentrated its efforts to mass produce chemical-biological agents, with two chemical warfare plants now operating to capacity.[13] The Soviet advisers who deployed the SS-21 in early 1983 and trained the Syrian missile crews in its use, have virtually all returned to Russia. The missiles are now in Syrian control. At the present time, the Syrians are negotiating with the Soviets for purchase of SS-22 and 23 missiles, with ranges up to several thousand miles.[14]

Dr Paul Katz, Director of the Rockets and Missiles Division of Rafael, Israel's Armament Development Authority, told the Alexandria R and D Co-operation Conference that Israel's modest anti-missile defence system, based upon Patriot and Hawk anti-tactical missiles (ATMs) would be quickly 'saturated', overwhelmed by large numbers of older Soviet Frog-7 and Scud-8 missiles, in any missile exchange with Syria in the near future. In fact, Katz's point was moot, as neither Israel nor the NATO countries, nor the United States for that matter, has an effective defence against the newer SS-21s, which strike their targets at speeds in excess of 2,000 miles per hour. At the distances which would obtain in an Israeli–Syrian missile exchange, the launch-to-target times would range from three to five minutes.

What Syria has here is a deterrent weapon. In the language of the Pentagon, Israel's 'threshold' *vis-à-vis* Syria is now very high, meaning that Israel would, in the opinion of US DoD officials, think very seriously before it would contemplate an attack upon Damascus, or even a repeat of the Beqaa Valley raids of June 1982. The Syrian deployment of these weapons has now reached a sufficiently advanced stage to render an Israeli pre-emptive strike against them, by aircraft, missiles or tanks, simply unthinkable. Any such attempt would risk the loss of tens of thousands, possibly even hundreds of thousands of Israeli civilians. Brigadier General Yosef Ben-Hanan, Commander of the IDF Armour Corps, advocated such a move using Israel's 'third generation' Merkava tanks, at the Alexandria conference in May 1987. Fortunately, Ben-Hanan is himself commanded by more responsible officers.

When AIPAC's Thomas Dine said in his testimony to the Senate that the Syrian missiles could be used to 'suppress Israeli air bases and other military installations', he raised an issue which bothers some senior Israeli military officials even more than does the threat which the missiles pose to Israeli cities. One of America's most experienced and decorated pilots, now a Middle East military analyst for the State Department, believes that Israel's Achilles' heel is its air bases. Without air cover, in fact without the total air superiority which Israel has enjoyed in all previous wars with the Arabs, the IDF could be fairly quickly overwhelmed by far larger Arab ground forces in any future general war. The length of time required for this would depend largely upon the degree to which the Arab armies could co-ordinate their attacks on the various fronts.

It is the accuracy and payload of the SS-21s which makes them a threat to Israeli air bases. Extraordinary efforts have obviously been made to 'harden' and disguise these bases, some of which are located virtually entirely beneath the ground. But SS-21s with high explosives and/or chemical-biological warheads might seriously damage the runways and air-control facilities enough to delay by an hour or two the launch of IAF combat aircraft.

The SS-21 attacks upon Israeli airfields would be even more devastating if carried out in conjunction with the deployment of another weapon which the Soviets have provided to the Syrians – multiple launch rocket systems (MLRS). The BM-21 122mm MLRS has been a standard fixture in Soviet-supplied armies for many years, and has been an effective, even decisive factor in several Third World conflicts, such as the Angolan civil war in the mid-1970s. Brassey's classic *Handbook on Guided Weapons* says that 'a battalion of eighteen BM-21s is able to put 30,000 lb of high explosive in a target area within twenty seconds'.[15] The latest version of the weapon fires fifteen to thirty warheads at a time, and has a cartridge reloading system. The range of the rockets is in excess of eighteen miles – well beyond the reach of tanks or most other land-based weapons which it would face. As a stand-off weapon, armed with cluster munitions or chemical–biological warheads, the MLRS could be used with terrible effect on advancing Israeli infantry units, particularly if the launchers were repositioned frequently. Israeli aircraft could of course suppress these weapons unless, that is, Syrian SS-21s had so damaged Israeli airfield runways that take-off and/or landing for refuelling were prevented.

The scenario I have just described is no longer a matter of 'if'. Syria has these weapons deployed and poised with, as previously indicated, a more advanced command, control and communications system behind them than the IDF has ever faced in battle. But this scenario does at the present time only apply to Syria. What if Egypt, Iraq and Jordan had similar capabilities?

Not surprisingly, Arab military establishments have very carefully watched the remarkable development of Syrian missile capabilities in the past few years. In the case of Jordan and Iraq, of course, part of the reason for this interest relates to the fact that they, rather than Israel, could conceivably be forced to deal with these weapons as adversaries. It is Israel and not Syria, however, which is flexing its military muscles monthly, if not weekly, in various parts of the Middle East, and has recently bombed Baghdad, Beirut and Tunis, and threatened to do the same to Amman.

Hence, there is a certain amount of risk-taking going on in several Arab countries at the present time – the risk being that while Israel may have missed its chance to take pre-emptive action against Syria, the same does not necessarily apply to other nearby countries. In particular, the 'threshold' may not be as high for Israel where Jordan, Iraq, Saudi Arabia and even Egypt, are concerned.

Jordan has already requested Frog-7 and Scud-8 missiles from the Soviets, and may have sought SS-21s. Iraq has engineers from India – which has developed a very respectable battlefield TBM capability – helping it with missiles which are currently being deployed, of course, against Iran. But even the concerted efforts of the Reagan Administration *and* the Government of Israel will not be able to keep that war going for ever and, when it is over, one or both of the adversaries will turn their attention to Jerusalem.

Saudi Arabia has so far limited its attempts to obtain TBMs to requests to the US for Lance missiles (citing the threat from Iran). The Lance was of course refused, but other non-Communist nations – notably Brazil and France – have similar systems available for sale. And the Saudis have already obtained and deployed seventy-two advanced British Tornado aircraft of which forty-eight are equipped as deep-strike fighter bombers. These planes would certainly be a factor in any future general war in the Middle East, particularly if it involved a missile exchange. As this is written, Saudi Arabia is negotiating for the purchase of additional Tornados, and other Arab Gulf states are actively considering the plane.

Even Egypt, Israel's Camp David peace partner, has been obliged to seek new offensive weapons, partly due to Libya's active military policies as well as Israel's, and perhaps also due simply to the fact that the technology is there and others in the region are obtaining it. Since 1984 Egypt has sought TBMs on the world arms market having (like Saudi Arabia) had its request for US Lance missiles rejected. Failing to find the missile it wanted from European sources, however, it settled on the Chinese. Agreement was recently reached for a joint Egyptian-Chinese conversion of the Condor, a civilian rocket originally designed as a space probe, to military purposes.

As a short-range ballistic missile (SRBM) the Condor will give Egypt a deep-strike offensive potential similar, but inferior to Syria's SS-21. But it's a beginning. Both the Reagan Administration and the Egyptian Government have endeavoured to keep the matter quiet in order to avoid upsetting Israel's friends in Congress, but agreement has been reached on the purchase from the Chinese, and the missiles will soon be deployed. Like the Syrians, the Egyptians have the technological capacity to mount chemical–biological warheads on their missiles.

So it has come to this, after forty years of failed efforts to obtain a secure homeland for Jews and a 'just and durable peace' for the other inhabitants of the Middle East. Israel has either won, or at least has not lost, all six wars in this period, and still it is not secure. Israel currently enjoys decisive qualitative advantages in every military area and total control of the Middle Eastern skies, and yet is not secure. Territorial buffer areas have been conquered and occupied, but that too did not bring security. A total monopoly on nuclear weapons has been achieved as against its Arab neighbours, and still it is not secure. By increments and over many years, Israel has finally established a unique military and security relationship with the strongest military power on earth and yet, now more than ever, the life of every inhabitant in the Jewish state is at risk. This, in a country whose cities have not seen war since 1949.

By now it should be apparent to all that no amount of land, no amount of arms will assure a safe future for Israel. Only peace will do that. Yet curiously, both the US and the Israeli Governments operate as if it is safe to wait for peace. Opportunities for peace have been almost perversely squandered in 1969 (the Rogers plan), 1973–5 (the October war cease-fire and the Sinai Accords) and in 1979 (Camp David), to name but a few. Instead, Israel and America have opted to rely on superior arms – 'the sword' – to ensure Israel's survival. And thus we will soon see the next, logical, virtually inevitable development: the acquisition by the Arabs of a countervailing nuclear 'deterrent' weapon.

In January 1952, less than four years after Israel's creation, Lebanese UN Ambassador Charles Malik tried in an article in the journal *Foreign Affairs* to analyse the Arab–Israeli conflict, long before it had become so bitter, so intractable, so seemingly hopeless. After hailing the achievement of Israel's creation, he warned that ensuring the Jewish state's continued existence would prove to be 'incomparably more exacting'. He said:

In the struggle for establishment, you treat the others as alien forces, to be crushed or pushed back or at least prevented from encroaching upon you; your relation to them is external, summary, destructive, negative; under no circumstance can you allow internal, positive intercourse with them on a basis of equality. But in the struggle for enduring existence you must come to terms with them; you must take their existence positively into account; your idea must be softened and modulated and trimmed to accommodate their idea; you must enter into interacting relationship with them, based on mutual respect and trust. Whether the leadership and the ethos of Israel are adequate to the requirements of existence, of course only the future can disclose.[16]

Six wars and over three decades later, the issue is still very much in doubt. And time is running out. One way or another, the Arab–Israeli conflict may be near conclusion.

Notes and References

Chapter 1   Introduction

1. Documents recently declassified and released from the National
   Security file at the Lyndon Baines Johnson Library provide new
   details regarding the material assistance, which amounted to $50 to
   $70 million in ammunition, spares and armoured vehicles hastily
   flown into Israel during the war. The operational assistance in the
   form of US tactical air reconnaissance flown in support of Israeli
   fighting units, is described in the predecessor to this volume: *Taking
   Sides: America's Secret Relations with a Militant Israel* (William
   Morrow, New York, and Faber and Faber, London, 1984). Since
   the publication of *Taking Sides*, the author has received two
   additional independent confirmations of the operation, which was
   mounted and managed by US Central Intelligence Agency. Both
   the additional sources are Pentagon officials; one is with DIA.

2. *The Arab–Israeli Wars*, by Chaim Herzog, Random House, New
   York, 1974, p. 209. At the time of writing, Herzog holds the largely
   ceremonial post of President of Israel.

3. Ibid.

4. 'Confidential' note to the President from Walt Rostow, dated 6
   June, 1967, National Security File, NSC History–Middle East
   Crisis, 12 May – 19 June 1967, Vol. 4, Tabs 128–50, Lyndon Baines
   Johnson Library.

5. 'Limited Official Use' Department of State Memorandum to
   Secretary of State from NEA – Lucius D. Battle, dated 18
   September, 1967, Saunders File document 3585, Lyndon Baines
   Johnson Library.

Chapter 2   A Terrible Swift Sword: the Introduction of the Phantom F-4E into the Middle East, 1968–9

1. *Aerial Warfare: An Illustrated History*, edited by Anthony Robinson, Galahad Books, New York, 1982, p. 294.

2. Donald Neff in *Warriors for Jerusalem*, Linden Press, New York, 1984, p. 204. Figures for aircraft destroyed were taken from Neff, pp. 203–4, and from *Story of My Life* by Moshe Dayan, William Morrow, New York, 1976, pp. 351–3.

3. *Strategic Survey 1968*, International Institute of Strategic Studies, London, 1969, p. 31.

4. Ze'ev Schiff in *A History of the Israeli Army (1870–1974)*, Straight Arrow Books, San Francisco, 1974, p. 198.

5. Enclosure 1 to 'Secret/Exdis' memorandum entitled 'Visit of Levi Eshkol, Prime Minister of Israel, January 7–8, 1968, Israeli Arms Request', document 23, Saunders Memos, National Security File, Lyndon Baines Johnson Library.

6. Ibid.

7. Enclosure 2 to 'Visit of Levi Eshkol', ibid. The brackets are DoD's. The A-4H is an Israeli modification of the A-4 Skyhawk.

8. Quoted in Enclosure 1, ibid.

9. 'Secret-Sensitive' Memorandum for the Record by Chairman of the Joint Chiefs of Staff, Earle G. Wheeler, dated 24 January 1968, National Security File, Country File Israel, Vol. 8, Box 141, Lyndon Baines Johnson Library. See also *Jane's All the World's Aircraft, 1967–1968*, London, 1969, p. 373.

10. Enclosure 2, op. cit. (note 7), p. 2.

11. *New York Times*, 9 January, 1968, p. 1.

12. 'Secret' State Department telegrams 2155 and 2265 of 15 and 24 January 1968, respectively, in National Security File, Country File Israel, Vol. 8, 12/67–8/68, Lyndon Baines Johnson Library.

13. 'Secret-Sensitive' Memorandum for the Record by General Earle G. Wheeler, op. cit. (note 9), states that less than three weeks after the Texas summit, Defence Secretary Robert McNamara approved the visit of a team of Israeli military technicians, headed by the Deputy Commander of the Israeli Air Force, Colonel B. Peled, to determine with USAF officials the exact configuration of the Israeli planes and plans for training.

14. Steven Spiegel in *The Other Arab–Israeli Conflict*, University of Chicago, Chicago, 1985, pp. 160 and 453.

15. *New York Times*, 16 December, 1968, p. 2.

16. Based upon interviews with US Army Colonel Thomas Pianka, who in 1968 was a Middle East specialist with the Defence Intelligence Agency and later (1969–73) became Assistant Air Attaché and then Air Attaché with the US Embassy in Tel Aviv. Colonel Pianka has detailed the opposition to the sale in an unpublished paper prepared for the American University (International Relations Department) entitled 'US Arms Supply Policy and the Arab–Israeli War of Attrition 1968–70'.

17. Based upon interviews with a foreign service officer who participated in the exercise.

18. Based upon interviews with former officials of DoD's Office of International Security Affairs (ISA).

19. *New York Times*, 14 January, 1968, IV, p. 16.

20. Ibid, 8 July, 1968, p. 10.

21. Ibid, 21 September, 1968, 32:2. Edgar O'Ballance indicates in *The Electronic War in the Middle East, 1968–1970* (Faber and Faber, London, 1974, p 39) that by April 1968 Soviet military re-supply of Egypt had 'slowed down almost to a stop'.

22. *New York Times*, 19 August, 1968, p. 33.

23. *New York Times*, 15 September, 1968, p. 1.

24. *New York Times*, 13 October, 1968, p. 1.

25. *New York Times*, 29 December, 1968, IV, p. 12.

26. Lyndon Baines Johnson in *The Vantage Point – Perspectives of the Presidency, 1963–1969*, Holt Rinehart & Winston, New York, 1971, p. 476.

27. More detailed descriptions and citations to official documentation of US intelligence on the status of the Israeli nuclear weapons programme in 1967 are contained in *Taking Sides: America's Secret Relations with a Militant Israel* by Stephen Green, William Morrow and Co., New York, 1984, chapter 7.

28. Decade of Decisions: American Policy Toward the Arab–Israeli Conflict 1967–76 by William Quandt, University of California Press, Berkeley, 1977, p. 67. See also 'Secret' memorandum to Walt W. Rostow from Harold Saunders entitled 'Rough Sketch of Package for Eshkol', in National Security File, Country File Israel,

Eshkol Visit Memos and Misc. 1/7–8/68, Lyndon Baines Johnson
Library.

29. Chapter 8 will show that Israel also has tested a nuclear device,
jointly with South Africa, in September 1979.

30. *Encyclopedia of US Air Force Aircraft and Missile Systems*,' by
Marcell Knaack, Office of Air Force History, Washington, DC,
1978, pp. 277–85.

31. Technical details on the F-4 were obtained from *Jane's All The
World's Aircraft, 1978–79*, Jane's Publishing, London, 1980,
p. 373.

32. *New York Times*, 28 December, 1968, 1:2.

33. Based upon a telephone interview with Mr Kubal in June 1985.

34. Based upon a personal interview with a former senior US Air
Force intelligence officer in March 1986. Kubal, when I asked,
responded that he had 'heard a rumour' that the planes had been
delivered 'nuclear capable'.

35. Richard Nixon was inaugurated in January 1969.

Chapter 3   Whose Desert Will Bloom? The East Ghor Canal Raids, 1968–70

1. 'Secret' Action Memorandum entitled 'Your Meeting with Israeli
Chargé on East Ghor Canal', from Talcott Seelye, NEA/ARN
section chief to Joseph Sisco, Assistant Secretary for Near Eastern
Affairs, dated 3 September, 1969, p. 2. Declassified in response to
a Freedom of Information Act request. Memo drafted by Thomas
J. Scotes.

2. Ibid, pp. 3–4.

3. 'Limited Official Use' memorandum Amman 3881, dated 15
August, 1969, declassified in response to a Freedom of
Information Act request.

4. Interview with USAID official Richard Dangler, who was chief
engineer on the East Ghor Project in 1969, in Washington, DC,
March 1986.

5. The totals are United Nations Relief and Works Agency
(UNRWA) statistics cited in Neff, op. cit. (ch. 2, note 2), pp. 320–1.

6. 'Israel's Drive for Water', by Leslie C. Schmida, *The Link*, Vol.
17, No. 4, November 1984, p. 9. Meron Benvenisti in *The West
Bank Data Project: A Survey of Israel's Policies*, (American

Enterprize Institute, Washington, 1984) indicates just how fully Israel utilizes this resource today. According to Benvenisti, 323 million cubic metres (mcm) of West Bank water are drawn off annually for use in Israel, leaving 137 mcm for use by West Bank Palestinians who compose, in 1986, well over 90 per cent of the total population of the area.

7. Green, op. cit. (ch. 2, note 27), chapter 4.

8. 'Israel and the Arab Waters', by Mahmoud Riad, paper delivered to the Joint International Symposium on the same subject, Amman, Jordan, 25 February 1984. Israel's unilateral diversion of the Jordan was, according to Joseph Sisco, one of the reasons for the US decision to fund construction of the East Ghor Canal project (telephone interview, May 1986).

9. Schmida, op. cit. (note 6), p. 7.

10. 'Unclassified' Department of State airgram number A-26 from US Embassy, Amman; subject: East Ghor Canal, dated 30 January, 1970, provided under the Freedom of Information Act.

11. Ibid, p. 2.

12. 'Secret' Memorandum for WWR (Walter Rostow) from Hal Saunders and John Foster; subject: Mid-East Terrorism; dated 11 November, 1967, in National Security File, Name File, Saunders Memos, Box No. 7, Lyndon Baines Johnson Library. Saunders's and Foster's use of the term 'terrorist' here did not reflect US Government policy at the time. Joseph Sisco insists that what Israel was experiencing in its border areas with Jordan in 1968–9 was *not* terrorism, but 'limited guerrilla activity', and at that, it occurred only 'sporadically' (telephone interview, op. cit. (note 8)).

13. Based upon a telephone interview with Ambassador Harrison Symmes in March 1986, and a personal interview with Jack O'Connell in May 1984.

14. Hanoch Bartov in *Dado: 48 Years and 20 Days*, Ma'ariv Book Guild, Tel Aviv, 1981, pp. 112–13.

15. 'Unclassified' State Department airgram A-26, op. cit. (note 10), p. 2.

16. *Arafat, Terrorist or Peacemaker?*, by Alan Hart, Sidgwick & Jackson, London, 1984, p. 258.

17. Gideon Raphael, *Destination Peace: Three Decades of Israeli Foreign Policy*, Stein and Day, New York, 1981, p. 202.

18. Ibid, p. 203.

19. Based upon interviews with a former US Government official who has personal knowledge of the matter and does not wish to be identified.

20. 'Unclassified' State Department airgram A-26, op. cit. (note 10), p. 2.

21. Interviews with Richard Dangler and Jack O'Connell, op. cit. (notes 4 and 13).

22. *New York Times*, 9 December, 1968, p. 16.

23. Quoted in Bartov's biography of General Elazar, op. cit. (note 14), p. 113.

24. Letter to the author from Arthur M. Handly, dated 22 April, 1985. Handly was USAID Director in Jordan during 1969.

25. 'Unclassified' Department of State airgram A-26, op. cit. (note 10), p. 2. All the details of the attacks on the Canal in the preceding section are taken from this January 1970 report from the American Embassy in Amman.

26. *New York Times*, 19 August, 1969, p. 6.

27. *New York Times*, 24 August, 1969, p. 19.

28. 'Unclassified' Department of State airgram A-26, op. cit. (note 10), p. 3.

29. Interview with Richard Dangler, op. cit. (note 4).

30. Telephone interview with Thomas J. Scotes in Athens, Greece, April 1986. Joseph Sisco, Scotes's former boss, agrees but adds that the two reasons are not mutually exclusive, and that the Israeli attacks probably served a 'dual purpose'. (Telephone interview, op. cit. (note 8).)

31. Richard Dangler, USAID, witnessed certain of the raids, as did Omar Abdullah Dokgan, then Jordan Valley Authority Director and later Minister of Agriculture in Jordan. He was interviewed in Amman in July 1985.

Chapter 4   The War Israel Did Not Win: the War of Attrition, 1969–70

1. Both Nasser quotations are from *The Struggle For Peace in the Middle East*, by Mahmoud Riad, Quartet Books, London, 1974, pp. 42–3.

2. *New York Times*, 16 July, 1967, p. 1.

3. The *New York Times* carried a page 1 account of the day's fighting on 15 July, 1967. In Cairo, in July 1984, I obtained further details from the eyewitness, Colonel Sami Biblawy of Egyptian military intelligence. In 1967, Colonel Biblawy had been a commando officer based in Ismailia.

4. *New York Times*, 15 July, 1967, p. 1.

5. The Egyptian High Command later claimed the ship was within Egyptian territorial waters, i.e. within twelve miles of shore. Israeli sources have claimed the ship was in international waters, variously thirteen and a half miles (see Dayan, op. cit. (ch. 2, note 2) p. 445) or fourteen and a half miles (see Herzog, op. cit. (ch. 1, note 2), p. 212) from the coast.

6. *New York Times*, 22 October, 1967, p. 5.

7. Neff, op. cit (ch. 2, note 2), p. 325; and *New York Times*, 25 October, 1967, p. 1.

8. *New York Times*, 26 October, 1967, p. 1.

9. Ibid.

10. *The Electronic War in the Middle East 1968–70*, by Edgar O'Ballance, Archon Books, London, 1974, p. 39.

11. *Story of My Life*, by Moshe Dayan, William Morrow and Co., New York, 1976, p. 447.

12. *International Red Cross Handbook*, International Committee of the Red Cross, Geneva, 1971, pp. 9–20 (Hague Convention); pp. 157–225 (Fourth Geneva Convention); and pp. 230–65 (Convention, Regulations, Protocol and Resolutions Pertaining to the Protection of Cultural Property).

13. Most serious historians of the period, including O'Ballance (op. cit. (note 10)), Walter Laqueur (*Confrontation: The Middle East and World Politics*, Quadrangle, New York, 1974, p. 4) and Lawrence Whetten (*The Canal War: Four Power Conflict in the Middle East*, MIT Press, Cambridge, 1974) put the figure at half a million. Ze'ev Schiff, in his *History of the Israeli Army* (op. cit. (ch. 2, note 4)) estimates 750,000, but much of this work appears to be hyperbole. On p. 245, for example, Schiff states that 'the Egyptians had nearly 20 times as many guns as the Israelis', and that 'the Egyptians' Russian guns fired 10 times as many shells as did Israeli artillery', statements which may charitably be described as preposterous.

14. Interview with Colonel Sami Biblawy in Cairo in July 1984. At the time of the interview, Biblawy was assigned to Egyptian military intelligence.

15. O'Ballance, op. cit. (note 10), p. 133.

16. A thorough description of the debate and those involved is contained in Herzog, op. cit. (ch. 1, note 2), pp. 214–17.

17. Herzog, ibid, pp. 216–17 and *The Crossing of the Suez* by Lieutenant General Saad el Shazly, American Mideast Research, San Francisco, 1980, pp. 8–9, Ze'ev Schiff, in *A History of the Israeli Army (1870–1974)*, op. cit. (ch. 2, note 4), p. 243, notes that 'Ironically, Soviet field manuals provided the best instructions on proper construction and reinforcement of bunkers.'

18. Herzog, ibid, pp. 223–4.

19. Ibid, p. 229.

20. *New York Times*, 10 September, 1969, p. 1.

21. These minor details are provided in O'Ballance, op. cit. (note 10), p. 88.

22. *Wall Street Journal*, 14 November, 1969, 1:1.

23. 'Decision, Process, Choice and Consequences: Israel's Deep Penetration Bombing in Egypt, 1970', by Avi Shlaim and Raymond Tanter, in *World Politics*, July 1978, Vol. 30, No. 4, pp. 486–7. Shlaim is a former Fellow at the Woodrow Wilson Institute at the Smithsonian Institution in Washington, and a respected Israeli historian. This article, which draws heavily on his extensive IDF contacts, is in my opinion the best single analysis of the issues of the War of Attrition, from an Israeli perspective.

24. 'Secret' telex 592 from US Embassy, Tel Aviv, to Secretary of State, Washington, dated 1 February, 1968.

25. 'Secret' telex 277 from US Embassy, Tel Aviv, to Secretary of State, Washington, dated 4 January, 1968.

26. Raphael, op. cit. (ch. 3, note 17), p. 207.

27. *The Struggle for Peace in the Middle East*, by Mahmoud Riad, op. cit. (note 1), p. 111.

28. *Price of Power*, by Seymour Hersh, Summit Books, New York, 1983, p. 216.

29. Raphael, op. cit. (ch. 3, note 17), pp. 209–10.

30. Ibid, p. 209.

31. Transcript from author's recorded personal interview with Mahmoud Riad in Cairo in July 1984. Riad himself proposed a means of dealing with Israel's and Egypt's concerns about secure borders. In early 1969 he travelled to Moscow to see Premier

Leonid Brezhnev, to Washington to see Secretary of State William Rogers, and then to France and Britain, to obtain support for a UN Middle East peacekeeping force which would be composed of armed troop contingents from the major powers, which would be authorized and equipped to shoot in the event of border violations from either side. Riad proposed that the force would be withdrawn only in the event of a unanimous vote of the Security Council, and might, if Israel continued to refuse to host UN peacekeeping forces, be posted entirely on the Egyptian side. The Soviets, Americans and Europeans, Riad maintains, were enthusiastic about the idea, but the Israelis refused to consider it.

32. Herzog, op. cit. (ch. 1, note 2), p. 232.

33. *New York Times*, 25 January, 1970, IV, p. 4.

34. *Haaretz*, 23 June, 1970, quoted in Shlaim and Tanter, op. cit. (note 23), p. 492.

35. *The Rabin Memoirs* by Yitzhak Rabin, Little, Brown and Co., Boston, 1979, p. 152. See also Hersh, op. cit. (note 28), p. 218.

36. Shlaim and Tanter, op. cit. (note 23), pp. 489–90.

37. 'Secret' Memorandum for the Record by JCS Chairman Earle G. Wheeler, dated 16 December, 1967, in National Security File Israel, Vol. 8, Box 141, Lyndon Baines Johnson Library.

38. Based upon a telephone interview with Mr Kubal in June 1985.

39. *Strategic Survey 1971*, International Institute for Strategic Studies, London, 1974, p. 46, quoted in Shlaim and Tanter, op. cit. (note 23), p. 496.

40. *The Arabs, Israelis and Kissinger*, by Edward F. Sheehan, Readers Digest Press, New York, 1976, p. 19. O'Ballance and Whetten both describe the deep-penetration bombing raids in some detail, and provide estimates of casualties. Henry Kissinger's memoirs (*The White House Years*, Little, Brown and Co., Boston, 1979) not surprisingly barely mention the raids, except in the context of a threatening note they generated from Soviet Premier Alexei Kosygin to President Nixon. Despite overwhelming evidence to the contrary, Kissinger could not, or would not see the raids as significant events in US–Arab or Israeli–Arab relations.

41. Interview with Colonel Thomas Pianka, op. cit. (ch. 2, note 16), see also O'Ballance, op, cit. (note 10), pp. 103–14.

42. The following account of Nasser's meetings in Moscow with Leonid Brezhnev was obtained from Mohamed Heikal, in a personal interview in Cairo on 2 November 1986.

43. Nasser knew very well that Nixon's National Security Adviser, Henry Kissinger, had used these exact words, calling for the 'expulsion' of the Soviet Union from the Middle East, in a recent press conference that had infuriated the Russians. He (Nasser) even had a transcript of Kissinger's statement in the files he'd brought to Moscow.

44. Details of the Soviet response are provided in 'Soviets Accelerating Mideast Drive', *Aviation Week and Space Technology*, 18 May, 1970, pp. 14, 15, 18.

45. 'Soviet Mediterranean Push Deepens', *Aviation Week and Space Technology*, 30 March, 1970, pp. 14, 16, 17.

46. *New York Times*, 31 January, 1970, p. 13.

47. For Dayan's statement see *Christian Science Monitor*, 23 May, 1970, quoted in Whetten, op. cit. (note 13), p. 95. Dates of arrival of Soviet pilots and of their deployment are in Shlaim and Tanter, op. cit. (note 24), p. 500 and O'Ballance, op. cit. (note 10), p. 139. Shlaim and Tanter, in turn, derive their arrival dates for pilots from the Institute for Strategic Studies in London.

48. Personal interview with a former senior US Air Force intelligence officer, op. cit. (ch. 2, note 34).

49. *Aviation Week and Space Technology*, 18 May, 1970, p. 9.

50. Whetten, op. cit. (note 13), pp. 109–10.

51. O'Ballance, op. cit. (note 10), p. 121.

52. The timing of the cease-fire, approved by Henry Kissinger, was in itself a terrible mistake. Both sides subsequently charged that their enemies had violated the agreement by improving their defensive positions, and both sides answered by saying that indeed they had done so, but between dusk and midnight, the hour at which the cease-fire took effect. The Defence Department (ISA) had warned Kissinger and the State Department to have the cease-fire take effect in broad daylight, which warning was ignored.

53. See Rabin, op. cit., p. 182. A former senior US Air Force intelligence officer who was involved in reconnaissance in the Middle East in 1970, has confirmed the story in an interview in Washington in March 1986.

54. Kissinger, op. cit. (note 40), p. 587. Kissinger, of course, makes no mention in his memoirs of the Israeli threat to shoot down US reconnaissance aircraft.

55. Interview with former senior US Air Force intelligence officer, op. cit. (note 53).

56. O'Ballance, op. cit. (note 10), p. 130.

57. El Shazly, op. cit. (note 17), p. 15.

58. Transcript of a recorded interview with Colonel Sami Biblawy, op. cit. (note 14).

Chapter 5   The Last Flight of 5A-DAH, 1973

1. At the time, the MiG was the standard fighter aircraft for the Egyptian Air Force.

2. Burdiat, the sixth attendant, would die of his injuries some weeks later.

3. 'Restricted' ICAO Working Paper No. c-WP/5764, second issue, dated 1 May, 1973.

4. Burdiat was interviewed by the Bureau Enquêtes-Accidents, Secretariat General à l'Aviation Civile, France, shortly before his death. The ICAO report appends the transcript of that interview, as well as interviews of survivors made by the ICAO investigation team members themselves.

5. *New York Times*, 22 February, 1973, p. 1. One might have expected that a colon, or at least a comma, would separate the 'deep sorrow' from the 'international procedure', but the two were inextricably, grammatically entwined.

6. The Galili, Elazar and Peres statements were quoted in *New York Times*, ibid.

7. 'Limited Official Use' State Department Telegram 211925Z, February 1973, from Secretary of State to American Embassy, Tripoli. This document was declassified by the State Department in 1985 in response to a Freedom of Information Act request. It is hard to understand how the excisions protect essential US national security interests, some twelve years after the event.

8. *New York Times*, 23 February, 1973, 13:1.

9. 'Confidential' State Department telegram 558 from US Embassy, Tel Aviv, to Secretary of State, Washington, dated 22 February, 1973.

10. 'Confidential' State Department telegram 01420, from US Embassy, Tel Aviv, to Secretary of State, Washington, dated 22 February, 1973.

11. The January 1972 version of Israel's AIP, which was in force at the

time 5A-DAH went down, is appended to the ICAO investigation report, op. cit. (note 3), as appendix J.

12. For these reasons, the ICAO investigating team's assertions in the report (p. 21) that the statements of surviving passengers and the comments of the flight crew on the transcript 'are consistent with the statement of the section leader', are astonishing and totally unwarranted by the evidence. Neither flight crew nor passengers mention wing-tipping anywhere in the transcripts/interviews.

13. 'Unclassified' State Department telegram 01469, from US Embassy, Tel Aviv, to Secretary of State, Washington, dated 23 February, 1973, p. 2.

14. ICAO investigation report, op. cit. (note 3), p. 25 and appendix A, pp. A-12 to A-15.

15. *New York Times*, 22 February, 1973, p. 12. See also *Time Magazine*, 5 March, 1973, p. 20. With a little institutional help, this canard has survived down through the years, long after the ICAO's findings were made public. In October 1983, following the Soviet downing of Korean Airlines Flight 007, the *Washington Post* carried a guest editorial by Stephen Rosenfeld comparing that incident to Israel's attack upon 5A-DAH ten years earlier. Two senior staff members of the American Jewish Congress, Phil Baum and Raphael Danziger, responded with an outraged letter (*Washington Post*, 2 November, 1983, p. 22) citing the 'bombing run' theory and Israel's supposed intelligence regarding a kamikaze plane. Certain lies, like weeds, seem to have root systems that can survive repeated applications of contrary fact.

16. *New York Times*, 23 February, 1973, 1:5.

17. ICAO investigation report, op. cit. (note 3), appendices H and I.

18. Ibid, appendix G, p. G-3. There is no comment in the report on this attempt by Israeli officials to suborn the investigation. Instead, in the usual fawning UN fashion, Israel is complimented for having 'co-operated' with the investigation.

19. Interview with a former senior Air Force intelligence officer who wishes to remain anonymous. The information about 'Springflower' has been verified by a second source who is a former official of the headquarters of the Joint Chiefs of Staff.

20. 'Limited Official Use' State Department telegram number 03325, from US Embassy, Tel Aviv, to Secretary of State, dated 27 February, 1973. See also *Between Israel and Death*, by Edward Bernard Glick, Stackpole Books, Harrisburg, Pa., 1974, pp. 43–4.

21. 'Limited Official Use' State Department telegram number 032719,

from US Embassy, Tel Aviv, to Secretary of State, dated 22 February, 1973.

22. *New York Times*, 22 February 1973.

23. ICAO investigation report, op. cit, (note 3), appendix E, p. E-3.

24. Ibid, appendix E, p. E-1.

25. See ibid, appendix A, pp. A-13 and A-17.

26. Ibid, appendix A, pp. A-15, A-16 and A-17.

27. 'Unclassified' State Department telegram Tel Aviv 01469, op. cit. (note 13), p. 2.

28. Ibid, p. 2.

29. See ICAO investigation report, op. cit. (note 3), appendix E, pp. E-2 and E-3.

30. Ibid, appendices A and G.

31. Ibid, appendix G, p. G-4.

32. Ibid, p. 27.

33. One of the more bizarre chapters of the 'Libyan airliner incident' unfolded on 25 February, 1973, when the Israeli Government announced to the world that Captain Bourges was not qualified, not legally certified to fly the Boeing 727 aircraft (*New York Times*, 25 February, 1973, 9:5). The ICAO report establishes that Bourges was properly and currently rated for the plane.

34. *New York Times*, 7 June, 1973, p. 5.

35. *New York Times*, 24 February, 1973, p. 8, and 28 February, 1973, p. 7.

36. Telephone interview with Henryka Borysoglebski, May 1986.

37. The Eban, *Haaretz* and *Davar* quotations are all contained in 'Confidential' Department of State telegram 01668, from US Embassy, Tel Aviv, to Secretary of State, Washington, dated 2 March, 1973.

38. Resolutions and Minutes, ICAO Assembly – Nineteenth Session (Extraordinary) New York, 27 February – 2 March 1973, Document 9061, pp. 46 and 56.

39. *New York Times*, 3 September, 1983, p. 4.

40. *New York Times*, 4 September, 1983, p. 16.

41. *New York Times*, 2 September, 1983, p. 5.

Chapter 6   The Yom Kippur War: and the War it Almost Was, 1973

1. *New York Times*, 12 August, 1973, p. 1.

2. *Dado: 48 Years and 20 Days*, by Hanoch Bartov, Tel Aviv, Ma'Ario Book Guild, 1981, pp. 189–90.

3. *Newsweek*, 9 April, 1973, p. 44.

4. El Shazly, op. cit. p. 198, (ch. 4, note 17).

5. Personal interview with former US Air Force intelligence official, March 1986.

6. Bartov, op. cit. (note 2), p. 197.

7. El Shazly, op. cit. (note 4), chapter 5.

8. 'Failures in National Intelligence Estimates: The case of the Yom Kippur War' *World Politics*, Vol. 28, April 1976, p. 376.

9. *The Yom Kippur War*, by the Insight team of the London *Sunday Times*, Doubleday and Co, Garden City, 1974, p. 137.

10. Interview with Egyptian commando leader Sami Biblawy, op. cit. (ch. 4, note 14).

11. Arnaud de Borchgrave in *Newsweek*, 22 October, 1973, pp. 64–5.

12. Bartov, op. cit. (note 2), pp. 209–10.

13. Ibid, p. 301.

14. El Shazly, op. cit. (note 4), p. 233.

15. 'Tanks in the Middle East', by Jac Weller, in *Military Review*, vol. 56, May 1976, p. 18.

16. Bartov, op. cit. (note 2), p. 313. The London *Sunday Times* Insight team (op. cit. (note 9)) maintains that on the early morning of 7 October, virtually nothing lay between the main Syrian armour column positioned at El Al, and the Israeli border (p. 159).

17. Dayan in his memoirs (op. cit. (ch. 2, note 2), p. 477) says that he had first reached this decision earlier, on the night of 6 October.

18. Bartov, op. cit., (note 2), p. 324.

19. El Shazly, op. cit. (note 4), p. 234. Justly proud of his army's achievement, El Shazly described this as 'the largest first day crossing in world military history'.

20. Bartov, op. cit. (note 2), p. 325.

21. *My Mother Golda Meir*, by Menachem Meir, Arbor House, New York, 1983, p. 220.

22. *New York Times*, 23 September, 1981, p. A-6.

23. Bartov, op. cit. (note 2), p. 326.

24. *My Life*, by Golda Meir, G. P. Putnam, New York, 1975, p. 429.

25. Telephone interview with Sam Hoskinson, December 1983.

26. Personal interview with William Quandt, November 1986.

27. Ibid.

28. 'Secret' Defence Department telegram 48816 to RVEAHQ/CSAF from US Embassy, Tel Aviv, dated 30 March 1965. This document is reproduced in *Taking Sides*, op. cit. (ch. 2, note 27), pp. 337–9.

29. The details in this paragraph were obtained in several personal interviews with a US Air Force intelligence source who wishes to remain anonymous, May 1983 to March 1987.

30. In April 1984 the author submitted an FOIA request to the National Security Council for documents in its possession, 'pertaining to the arming and potential use of Jericho missiles or other nuclear weapons by Israel in the October 1973 war'. In June 1985 NSC responded by letter that five documents on this subject had been located, but could not be released as they remained classified 'in the interest of national defence or foreign policy'. The letter left some doubt as to which nation's defence or foreign policy was at issue in their determination.

31. *On the Banks of the Suez*, by Avraham 'Bren' Adan, Presidio Press, San Francisco, 1980, p. 144.

32. Bartov, op. cit. (note 2), p. 317.

33. Ibid, p. 373.

34. El Shazly, op. cit. (note 4), p. 241.

35. 'Airlift Operations of the Military Airlift Command During the 1973 Middle East War', Report to the Congress by the Comptroller General of the United States, 16 April, 1975, *Digest*.

36. Ibid. Another 68,000 tons was transported by sea.

37. 'The Arab–Israeli Airlifts', by General Ira Eaker, dated 9 December, 1973; declassified by the Defence Intelligence Agency in 1984 in response to a Freedom of Information Act request. DIA did not distinguish itself generally during the October war, in terms of intelligence gathering or analysis. Six hours after the Egyptian crossing began, with more than 50,000 Egyptian soldiers already

across the Canal, DIA representatives were still maintaining to the US Intelligence Board that what was happening in the Sinai was not a war, but an 'action/reaction scenario'.

38. Comptroller General's Report, op. cit. (note 35), p. 8.

39. There was a special National Intelligence Estimate produced by the Watch Committee of the US Intelligence Board just prior to the outbreak of the fighting, and transmitted to the WSAG at the White House. The estimate apparently outlined re-supply steps the US might take to assist Israel as and when the war started. The estimate remains classified, however, and the author has been unable to determine its contents precisely.

40. The details of the 'other' airlift, unless otherwise indicated below, were obtained from two primary sources: a senior Air Force intelligence official and a senior staff member of the International Security Affairs section at DoD. Both gentlemen wish to remain anonymous.

41. Gur's request for AIM 9-L's mystified his American counterparts, as the Israeli Air Force had not one F-4 upon which they could be mounted. Unlike earlier versions of the missile, the 'L' required hook-ups for cyrogenic cooling which, in October 1973, none of the Israeli Phantoms carried.

42. Personal interview with Major General Saleh Abdul Halim, Director of Operations of the Egyptian Army, August 1984. Both the sources cited in note 40 have independently confirmed General Halim's story. See also *The Ramadan War*, by Hassan El Badri, Taha El Magdoub and Mohammed Dia El Din Zohdy, T. N. Depuy Associates, Dunn Loring, Virginia, 1974, p. 88.

43. Telephone interview with Ambassador James E. Akins, March 1987.

44. *New York Times*, 12 October, 1973, p. 1.

45. El Shazly, op. cit. (note 4), p. 248.

46. See *Kissinger*, by Marvin Kalb and Bernard Kalb, Dell Publications, New York, 1974, pp. 464–77.

Chapter 7 Middle East Watershed – Egypt's Unilateral Disarmament, 1973–9

1. 'The Arab–Israeli Military Balance', by Brigadier General (Res.) Yehoshua Raviv, CSS Papers No. 7, February 1980, Center for Strategic Studies, Tel Aviv University, p. 26. The following section

comparing Egyptian and Israeli military developments in 1973–9 is
drawn, with permission, from 'Egypt's Unilateral Disarmament: A
Failed Experiment', by Stephen Green and Frank Bonvillain, in
American Arab Affairs, Spring 1985, No. 12, pp. 54–6.

2. Ibid, p. 10.

3. *World Armies*, by John Keegan, New York: Facts on File, 1979,
p. 200.

4. The comparative figures in the following paragraphs for arms
imports, manpower, combat aircraft, tanks and armoured
personnel carriers are derived from International Institute for
Strategic Studies and US Arms Control and Disarmament Agency
statistics cited in *Jordanian Arms and the Middle East Balance*, by
Anthony Cordesman, Washington, Middle East Institute, 1983,
pp. 146–70.

5. This table, also derived from Cordesman, ibid, is incomplete, as it
does not *not* include some $2.2 billion in arms sent by the US to
Israel in the October war airlift.

6. *The Middle East Military Balance 1973*, by Mark Heller, Dov
Tamari and Zeev Eytan, Jaffee Center for Strategic Studies, Tel
Aviv University, p. 89.

7. Personal interview with General Gamasy in Heliopolis, Egypt,
November 1986.

8. Ibid.

9. *Years of Upheaval*, by Henry Kissinger, and *In Search of Identity*, by
Anwar Sadat, Harper and Row, New York, 1977.

10. *New York Times*, 8 May, 1976, p. 4.

11. *New York Times*, 8 September, 1976, p. 14.

12. *New York Times*, 4 April, 1977, p. 4.

13. Recorded interview in March 1986 with a senior US Air Force
officer who was at Tabuk at the time, and witnessed the touchdown.

14. Interview with senior State Department official in April 1986.

15. *Keeping Faith: Memoirs of a President*, by Jimmy Carter, Bantam
Books, New York, 1982, p. 304.

16. Ibid, p. 305.

17. Eitan Haber, Zeev Schiff and Ehud Yaari in *The Year of the Dove*,
Bantam Books, New York, 1979, p. 42.

18. *Camp David: Peacemaking and Politics*, The Brookings Institution,
Washington, DC, 1986.

Chapter 8   Pariahs with Bombs: the South Atlantic Nuclear Test, 1979

1. Transcript of BBC-TV *Panorama* television programme, broadcast 31 March, 1980 at 8–10 p.m. GMT.

2. Personal interview with Gerald Funk, March 1986.

3. The Foreign Assistance Act of 1961. . . (Public Law 87–195), as amended by the International Security Assistance Act of 1977, requires the cut-off of US economic and military assistance or grant, military education or training to any country which manufactures, transfers, receives or detonates 'a nuclear explosive device'.

4. The Vela sighting was made in an area where the ionospheric cap is the thinnest of any location on earth, resulting in that particular location in an unusually high level of natural background radiation. At the time, this was thought to be a coincidence.

5. The full panel included the following: Dr Jack Ruina (Chairman), Department of Electrical Engineering, MIT; Dr Luis Alvarez, Department of Physics, University of California, Berkeley; Dr William Donn, Lamont-Doherty Geological Observatory, Columbia University; Dr Richard Garwin, Thomas J. Watson Research Center for Astrophysics, Harvard University; Dr Richard Muller, Department of Physics, University of California, Berkeley; Dr Wolfgang Panofsky, Stanford Linear Accelerator Center, Stanford University; Dr Allen Peterson, Department of Electrical Engineering, Stanford University; Dr William Sarles, Lincoln Laboratory, MIT; and Dr Ricardo Giaconni, the Space Telescope Science Institute, Baltimore, Maryland. The listed associations were current as of the date of the release of the panel's report in July 1980.

6. Unclassified '*Ad Hoc* Panel Report on the September 22 Event', Executive Office of the President, Office of Science and Technology Policy, Washington, DC, 15 July, 1980, p. 1.

7. *New York Times*, 26 October, 1979, p. 1.

8. Unclassified panel report, op. cit. (note 6), p. 16.

9. Personal interview with a US government official who wishes to remain anonymous, March 1986. See also *Washington Post*, 1 January, 1980, p. 8, and 30 January, 1980, p. 1.

10. *New York Times*, 15 November, 1979, p. 11.

11. Unclassified panel report, op. cit. (note 6), p. 16.

12. *Washington Post*, 2 November, 1979, p. 23.

13. Panel chairman Jack Ruina and panel member Dr Ricardo Giaconni both recalled, in telephone interviews with the author (February 1987) that the political conservatives among the government officials who attended the panel's sessions seemed particularly convinced that a nuclear test had been conducted. Giaconni referred to these people as 'the cold warriors'.

14. Unclassified panel report, op. cit. (note 6), p. 17.

15. *Washington Post*, 14 January, 1980, p. 6.

16. Telephone interview with Dr Alan Berman, January 1987.

17. Ibid.

18. Telephone interview with Dr Ricardo Giaconni, op. cit. (note 13).

19. *Light Flash Produced by an Atmospheric Nuclear Explosion*, by Guy E. Barasch, Los Alamos Scientific Laboratory, LASL Mini-Review 79–84, Los Alamos, New Mexico, November 1979.

20. Unclassified panel report, op. cit. (note 6), p. 10.

21. Ibid, p. 14.

22. Ibid, p. 20.

23. Ibid, p. 18.

24. Telephone interview with Jack Ruina, op. cit. (note 13).

25. Unclassified panel report, op. cit. (note 6), p. 17.

26. 'Navy Lab Concludes the Vela Saw a Bomb', by Eliot Marshal, *Science*, Vol. 209, 29 August, 1980, p. 996.

27. Ibid, and *Washington Post*, 17 January, 1980, p. 11.

28. The London *Guardian*, 31 January, 1980.

29. Telephone interview with Jack Ruina, op. cit. (note 13).

30. The author has confirmed the essential conclusion of the CIA study – that there was a nuclear explosion on 22 September – in a telephone interview with a member of the US intelligence community who participated in the deliberations of the White House panel, but who wishes to remain anonymous. Details of the CIA study are discussed in transcript P568/536 of the *World in Action*, 'South Africa's Bombshell', produced by Granada Television. Transcript was issued 21 October, 1980.

31. Transcript of BBC *Panorama* TV programme, op. cit. (note 1).

32. Unclassified panel report, op. cit. (note 6), p. 1.

33. Transcript of *Panorama*, op. cit. (note 1).

34. In a personal interview with the author (February 1987) John Marcum denied that any agency of the US Government had any non-technical information (i.e. intelligence) that bore materially on the issue of whether the 'September 22 event' was in fact a nuclear explosion.

35. Telephone interview in January 1987 with William Dean Howells II, who at the time was a senior administrator in the Office of Political and Military Affairs within the Bureau of Intelligence and Research, US State Department.

36. *New York Times*, 28 October, 1979, p. 14.

37. The preceding account of how and when the US intelligence community learned of the 22 September nuclear event was obtained from one primary and one secondary source. The primary source is a senior US intelligence official who devoutly wishes to remain anonymous. The secondary source is a former officer in Israeli military intelligence.

38. Based upon telephone interviews with Ruina, Panofsky, Giaconni (who was not part of the sub-group) and a personal interview with John Marcum, op. cit. (notes 13, 34).

39. Ibid.

40. Telephone interview with Admiral Stansfield Turner, February, 1987. Ben Huberman, an OSTP staff member who acted as liaison between the panel and the national Security Council, maintains that a request to CIA for all relevant intelligence *was* made, and that he was the one who made it.

41. *New York Times*, 26 October, 1979, p. 22.

42. Robert Gates was in early 1987 nominated to succeed William Casey as Director of Central Intelligence in the Reagan Administration.

43. See 'Norway is Concerned Israel May have Violated Secret Pact on Atomic Material', *Wall Street Journal*, 10 November, 1986, p. 27, written by John J. Fialka. See *New York Times*, 26 May, 1987, p. 13 on Israeli resistance.

44. Telephone interview with Theodore Taylor, January 1987. Dr Taylor had worked at IAEA headquarters at this time.

Chapter 9 Operation Babylon: the Baghdad Reactor Raid, 1981

1. The Americans were Raytheon Corporation employees working on a Defence Department contract with the Royal Saudi Arabian Air Force, according to a US military official who does not wish to be identified.

2. 'Secret' State Department telegram 01551, from US Interests Section, Baghdad, to Secretary of State, dated 8 June 1981, declassified in response to FOIA request. All sections of the telegram regarding casualties, and other telegrams on the same subject were withheld from release by the State Department 'in the interest of national defence or foreign policy', presumably American.

3. 'Secret' State Department telegram 01558, from US Interests Section, Baghdad, to Secretary of State, dated 8 June 1981. Declassified in response to FOIA request.

4. 'Secret' State Department telegram 01559, from US Interests Section, Baghdad, to Secretary of State, dated 8 June 1981. Declassified in response to FOIA request.

5. *New York Times*, 9 June 1981, p. 8.

6. The identifying term 'Osirak' for the Baghdad reactor refers to the particular type and design, which was modelled on a reactor in Saclay, France.

7. *New York Times*, 9 June 1981, p. 8.

8. *New York Times*, 10 June 1981, p. 1.

9. Ibid.

10. Ibid, p. 31.

11. *New York Times*, 12 June 1981, p. 1.

12. Hearings Before the Committee on Foreign Relations, United States Senate, Ninety-Seventh Congress, First Session, on the Israeli Air Strike and Related Issues, 18, 19 and 25 June 1981, pp. 125–6.

13. Ibid, pp. 131 and 168–9. See also *New York Times*, 18 June 1981. p. 1.

14. Ibid, pp. 132–4.

15. *New York Times*, 18 June 1981, p. 18.

16. 'Confidential' State Department telegram 01568, from US

Interests Section, Baghdad, to Secretary of State, dated 9 June
1981. Declassified in response to FOIA request.

17. *New York Times*, 22 June 1981, 4:3.

18. 'Hearings', op. cit. (note 12), p. 134.

19. *New York Times*, 25 June 1981, 9:1. The CRS study, written by
Warren Donnelly, was entitled 'Possible Contamination of
Baghdad from Bombing of the Iraqi Reactor', and was published
on 18 June 1981, and printed in 'Hearings', ibid, p. 154.

20. *New York Times*, 9 June 1981, p. 7.

21. See 'Hearings', op. cit. (note 12), p. 127, and *New York Times*
editorial by Anthony Lewis, 21 June 1981, IV, p. 23.

22. *New York Times*, 17 June 1981, p. 7.

23. 'Israeli Raid Into Iraq', Archived Issue Brief prepared by the
Library of Congress, Congressional Research Service, dated 18
June 1981, updated 1 October 1981, p. 19. An earlier version of
this CRS report was printed in 'Hearings', op. cit. (note 12), p. 68.

24. *New York Times*, op. cit. (note 19).

25. 'Quotations Regarding Iraqi Nuclear Intentions', by Patricia
Schwartzwalder and Clyde R. Mark, Congressional Research
Service, Library of Congress, Washington, DC, 15 June 1981. p. 1,
printed in 'Hearings', op. cit. (note 12), p. 58.

26. 'Confidential' State Department telegram 01600, from US
Interests Section, Baghdad, to Secretary of State, dated 11 June
1981; declassified in response to an FOIA request.

27. Transcript of press conference broadcast live over Jerusalem
Domestic Service, Kol Israel, at 1605 GMT 9 June 1981.

28. Based upon interviews with Congressional sources who do not
wish to be identified, May 1986.

29. In keeping with CRS's rules of discretion regarding requests for
research from members of Congress, CRS staff members have
declined to confirm whether it was Senator Alan Cranston who
originated the CRS 'quotations' research on Tuesday 9 June 1981.

30. Based on a personal interview with a CRS staff member who does
not wish to be named.

31. 'Confidential' State Department telegram 01674, from US
Interests Section, Baghdad, to Secretary of State, dated 18 June
1981; declassified in response to FOIA request.

32. 'Hearings', op. cit. (note 12), p. 52.

33. Ibid, Appendix 4, pp. 62–3.

34. Ibid, p. 59.

35. 'Tammuz' was the Iraqi Government designation for the reactor at Tuwaitha.

36. The Perlmutter book (Corgi Books, London, 1982) contains several racist references to flawed Arab national 'characteristics', and is replete with inaccuracies on such matters as French and IAEA inspections at the Baghdad reactor, the refuelling of the Israeli fighters in flight, and the presence of anti-aircraft fire during the attack. It is typical of a genre of 'non-fiction' writing on Israeli military exploits which is long on hyperbolized heroism and short on facts.

37. See memorandum from Fred Tipson (Committee Counsel) to Senator Charles Percy, Chairman, Senate Foreign Relations Committee, in 'Hearings', op. cit. (note 12), pp. 93–5.

38. Ibid, p. 45.

39. Ibid, pp. 33–4.

40. Ibid, pp. 125–6.

41. Ibid, p. 134.

42. Ibid, p. 290.

43. Senator Claibourne Pell (R–Rhode Island) did ask one question on this subject, but did not follow up. Two of the expert witnesses did obliquely refer to Israel's nuclear weapons, but could elicit no interest or questions from the senators present.

44. 'Hearings', op. cit. (note 12), p. 23.

45. *New York Times*, 19 June 1981, 10:5.

46. 'Confidential' State Department telegram 01762, from US Interests Section, Baghdad, to Secretary of State, dated 28 June 1981. Declassified in response to FOIA request.

Chapter 10   Helping Lebanon Come Apart: the Bombing Raids of 1981

1. 'Unclassified' State Department telegram from Secretary of State to US Embassy, Amman, No. 150748, dated 9 June 1981.

2. 'Confidential' State Department telegram 03624 from US Embassy, Beirut, to Secretary of State, dated 2 June 1981.

3. *Jerusalem Post*, 7 April 1981, quoted in *Journal of Palestine Studies*, Vol. 44/45, Summer/Fall 1982, p. 29.

4. Ze'ev Schiff and Ehud Ya'ari, in *Israel's Lebanon War*, Simon and Schuster, New York, 1984, p. 31.

5. Ibid, p. 28.

6. *New York Times*, 3 January 1981, quoted in *Journal of Palestine Studies*, op. cit. (note 3), p. 28.

7. Schiff and Ya'ari, op. cit (note 4), p. 35.

8. *New York Times*, 18 April 1981, p. 3.

9. 'Limited Official Use' State Department telegram from US Embassy, Beirut, to Secretary of State, No. 04611, dated 11 July 1981.

10. *New York Times*, 11 July 1981, p. 1.

11. 'Confidential' State Department telegram from US Embassy, Beirut, to Secretary of State, No. 04753, dated 16 July 1981.

12. Ibid.

13. 'Limited Official Use' State Department telegram from US Embassy, Beirut, to Secretary of State, No. 04635, dated 13 July 1981.

14. *New York Times*, 13 July 1981, p. 1.

15. 'Confidential' State Department telegram from US Embassy, Beirut, to Secretary of State, No. 04652, dated 13 July 1981. Dillon's request for a 'forthright statement' was excised from the original cable text released by the State Department to the author.

16. 'Confidential' State Department telegram from US Embassy, Beirut, to Secretary of State, No. 04706, dated 15 July 1981.

17. *New York Times*, 17 July 1981, p. 3.

18. Ibid.

19. 'Confidential' State Department telegram from US Embassy, Beirut, to Secretary of State, No. 04807, dated 18 July 1981.

20. *New York Times*, 19 July 1981, p. 1.

21. *New York Times*, 18 July 1981, p. 1.

22. Ibid.

23. 'Confidential' State Department telegram from US Embassy, Beirut, to Secretary of State, No. 04803, dated 17 July 1981.

24. 'Confidential' State Department telegram from US Embassy, Beirut, to Secretary of State, No. 04798, dated 17 July 1981. This and all paragraphs dealing with Israeli strikes on the US refinery were excised from the documents originally released to the author under the Freedom of Information Act.

25. Telephone interview with Ambassador Robert Dillon, October 1986.

26. 'Confidential' State Department telegram from US Embassy, Beirut, to Secretary of State, No. 04894, dated 22 July 1981.

27. 'Confidential' State Department telegram from US Embassy, Beirut, to Secretary of State, No. 04952, dated 24 July 1981.

28. Interview with Ambassador Robert Dillon, op. cit. (note 25).

29. See, for example, *New York Times*, 13 July 1981, p. 3; 19 July, p 1; 19 July, p. 13 and 21 July, p. 1.

30. *New York Times*, 23 July 1981, p. 1.

31. Interview with Ambassador Robert Dillon, op. cit. (note 25).

Chapter 11   Semper Infidelis: Israel and the Multinational Peacekeeping Force in Lebanon, 1982–3

1. Telephone interview with Brigadier General James C. Mead, September, 1986.

2. United Press International dispatch, 9 August 1982.

3. Interview with marine officer formerly attached to JCS, who is still on active duty and wishes to remain anonymous.

4. Jacobo Timmerman in *The Longest War: Israel in Lebanon*, Alfred A. Knopf, New York, 1982, p. 13.

5. 'Secret' State Department telegram 04285, from US Embassy, Beirut, to Secretary of State, dated 19 June 1982.

6. A survey of the coverage is included in *The Battle of Beirut*, by Michael Jansen, South End Press, Boston, 1983, chs. 2 and 3, and in *Israel in Lebanon: The Report of the International Commission* (the 'McBride Commission'), Ithaca Press, London, 1983, Section II.

7. The London *Sunday Times*, 8 August 1982, quoted in *Lebanon, The Fractured Country*, by David Gilmour, St Martin's Press, New York, 1983, p. 166.

8. Zeev Schiff and Ehud Ya'ari, in Israel's Lebanon War, op. cit.

(ch. 10, note 4), pp. 223–4. David Halevy confirmed Sharon's orders to the author in a telephone interview, September 1986. Halevy was a *Time Magazine* correspondent in Jerusalem at the time, and a former Brigadier General in Israeli military intelligence.

9. Ibid, pp. 224–5. Schiff and Ya'ari list other Sharon objections and demands on these pages.

10. Eric Hammell in *The Root: The Marines in Beirut, August 1982– February 1984*, Harcourt Brace Jovanovich, New York, 1985, pp. 24–5.

11. The text of the US statement appears in the *New York Times*, 17 September 1982, p 8.

12. Ibid, p. 1.

13. Ibid.

14. *The Battle of Beirut*, op. cit. (note 6), pp. 102–5. See also the McBride Commission, op. cit. (note 6), p. 167.

15. The revelations concerning the 'co-ordination' meetings and flares were made during an address by Defence Minister Sharon to the Knesset on 22 September 1982. The other details and public reactions to them in Israel are discussed in Schiff and Ya'ari, op. cit. (ch. 10, note 4), ch. 13, and in the McBride Commission, ibid, ch. 15.

16. Jacobo Timmerman in op. cit. (note 4), p. 167.

17. *New York Times*, 20 September 1982, p. 1.

18. The text of Peres's address appeared in the *New York Times*, 23 September 1982, p. 18.

19. The text of Sharon's speech appeared in the *New York Times*, ibid.

20. 'Confidential' State Department Information Memorandum to the Acting Secretary from INR – Hugh Montgomery – dated 30 September 1982 and citing the Israeli newspaper *Maariv*, issue dated 30 September 1982.

21. Itamar Rabinovich in *The War for Lebanon, 1970–1985*, Cornell University Press, Ithaca, 1985, p. 183.

22. 'Report of the DoD Commission on Beirut International Airport Terrorist Act' (the 'Long Commission Report'), 20 December 1983, p. 35.

23. Based upon September 1986 telephone interview with Lieutenant General Mick Traynor USMC Ret., who was Deputy Chief of

Staff for Plans, Policies and Operations, USMC Headquarters, in September 1982; and with Brigadier General James C. Mead who was Commander of the 32nd Marine Amphibious Unit at that time. See also Hammell, op. cit. (note 10), p. 43.

24. See 'Prohibitions or Restrictions on the Use of Certain Conventional Weapons', by Yves Sandoz, in the *International Review of the Red Cross*, January–February 1981.

25. See 'Weapons that may Cause Unnecessary Suffering or have Indiscriminate Effects', Report on the Work of Experts, International Committee of the Red Cross, Geneva, 1973, chs 1 and 2,

26. Hammell, op. cit. (note 10), p. 41.

27. *New York Times*, 2 October 1982, 8:5.

28. Telephone interview with Ambassador Robert Dillon on September 1986. Dillon was US Ambassador to Lebanon from June 1981 until October 1983.

29. *New York Times*, 30 September 1982, p. 14.

30. Interviews (April 1986) with three marine officers who served in Beirut and Washington during the USMNF's sojourn in Lebanon.

31. Hammell, op. cit. (note 10), p. 48.

32. Interviews with three marine officers, op. cit. (note 30).

33. Attachment to letter from General R. H. Barrow, Commandant of the Marine Corps, to Caspar Weinberger, Secretary of Defence, dated 14 March 1983. See also *The Multinational Force in Lebanon*, by Clyde Mark, Congressional Research Service (CRS), 19 May 1983, Appendix 3, p. 19.

34. Ibid.

35. Ibid; additional details were provided in the interview with three marine officers, op. cit. (note 30).

36. *New York Times*, 25 January 1983, I, 7:1.

37. Attachments to Barrow letter and CRS report, op. cit. (note 33). Additional details provided in interview with three Marine officers, op. cit. (note 30). See also *Washington Post*, 1 April 1983, p. 2.

38. All three incidents are described in the *Washington Post*, 8 March 1983, p. 1, and are cited in the CRS report, ibid, p. 21.

39. CBS Evening News, 2 February 1983.

40. All the inconsistencies are contained in the CRS report, op. cit. (note 33), pp. 22–3.

41. The 'patrol incidents' are detailed in the CRS report, ibid, p. 24. The 'Barrow letter', op. cit. (note 33), describes the incidents of 2 and 12 March.

42. Interview with three marine officers, op. cit. (note 30).

43. This account is based upon a telephone interview with a former member of General Barrow's staff.

44. NBC Nightly News, 6.30 p.m. EST, 17 March 1986.

45. *Washington Post*, 5 February 1983, p. 21.

46. Telephone interview with Brigadier General James C. Mead, op. cit. (note 1).

47. Telephone interview with David Halevy, op. cit., note 8. Ambassador Robert Dillon, whose embassy was the site of the frequent diplomatic confrontations generated by the incidents, states that Halevy's information about Sharon's orders is 'entirely consistent with what we saw'.

48. See Schiff and Ya'ari, op. cit. (ch. 10, note 4), p. 156.

49. Telephone interviews with Lieutenant General Mick Traynor, and Ambassador Robert Dillon, op. cit. (notes 23 and 28).

50. See, for example, *New York Times*, 8 October 1982, p. 6; 13 October 1982, p. 10; 24 January 1983, p. 6; and CBS Evening News, 23 January 1983.

51. Interview with three marine officers, op. cit. (note 30).

52. John K. Cooley, 'The War Over Water', *Foreign Policy*, Spring 1984, 54, pp. 22–23. See also Leslie C. Schmida, 'Israel's Drive for Water', *The Link*, November 1984, Vol. 17, No. 4. Schmida's article reveals that 'Israel's drive for water' in Lebanon continued long after the period with which this chapter deals. In August 1984 Lebanon's permanent representative to the United Nations, Rashid Fakhoury, presented evidence to the UN Security Council that Israel had just dug a tunnel connecting the Litani to a point near the Israeli border.

53. *Christian Science Monitor*, 10 February 1983, p. 23.

54. *New York Times*, 20 September 1983, p. 1.

55. Ibid, p. 9.

56. Telephone interview with a marine officer who wishes to remain anonymous.

57. Long Commission Report, op. cit. (note 22) p. 50.

Chapter 12   War by Proxy: Israel and America Arm Iran, 1980–6

1. The 'Tower Commission' (officially designated the President's Special Review Board) was a three-member panel appointed by President Ronald Reagan in December 1986 to study the operations and staff of the National Security Council and, in particular, to focus upon the NSC's role in the 'Iran/Contra matter'. The panel's final (288-page) report was issued on 26 February 1987.

2. The details of the November 1985 shipment of Hawk missiles to Iran in this and succeeding paragraphs are taken from the Tower Commission Report, Part III, and from the report on the same subject issued by the US Senate Select Committee on Intelligence, issued on 2 February 1987, No. 100–7, entitled 'Preliminary Inquiry Into the Sale of Arms to Iran and Possible Diversion of Funds to the Nicaraguan Resistance'. As a guide to these two documents, the author was greatly aided by CRS report No. 86–190F, 'Iran–Contra Affair: A Chronology', by Clyde R. Mark, published by the Congressional Research Service, Washington, DC, 2 April 1987, updated 29 April.

3. Testimony to the Tower Commission and the Senate Select Committee on Intelligence places the number of promised Hawks variously at 60–120, according to Mark, 'Chronology', ibid, though the number most frequently used is 80.

4. *New York Times*, 30 December 1986, p. 1. Based upon an interview with David Kimche by *New York Times* reporter Stephen Engleberg.

5. Report of the US Senate Select Committee on Intelligence, op. cit. (note 2) pp. 3–4.

6. Ibid, p. 1–2.

7. Ibid, p. 2.

8. *World Military and Arms Transfers*, 1985, ACDA publication 123 produced by the US Arms Control and Disarmament Agency, August 1985, Table I.

9. *US Arms Sales and Security Assistance to the Middle East and*

North Africa, by Dale Gavlak, Congressional Research Service, Washington, DC, 5 October 1981, pp. 8–9.

10. Information on specific weapons in the pipeline is from *World Armaments and Disarmament, SIPRI Yearbook 1980*, produced by the Stockholm International Peace Research Institute, Crane, Russak and Co., New York, 1980, pp. 98–9. The total amount in the pipeline was obtained in an interview in March 1987 with a former DIA official who wishes to remain anonymous.

11. Ibid, p. 98.

12. Interview with former DIA official, op. cit. (note 10).

13. *Israel's Global Reach, Arms Sales as Diplomacy*, by Aaron Klieman, Pergamon-Brassey's, Washington, 1985, p. 158.

14. Ibid, p. 158.

15. Ibid, p. 23.

16. *SIPRI Yearbook, 1980*, op. cit. (note 10), p. 86.

17. Interview with former US DIA official, op. cit. (note 10).

18. The London *Observer*, 2 February 1986, p. 19. Martin Bailey wrote the story for the *Observer*, based upon copies of the documents taken from the Israeli trade mission.

19. Ibid.

20. *Davar*, 29 November 1985.

21. *Washington Post*, 14 December 1986, p. 44.

22. The *Wall Street Journal* (9 February 1979) maintained that at the time of the revolution, Iran provided over half of Israel's energy requirements, but that these negotiations and the resulting purchase arrangements avoided what would have otherwise been an energy crisis in Israel.

23. *Débâcle: The American Failure in Iran*, by Michael Ledeen and William Lewis, Alfred A. Knopf, New York, 1981, p. 126.

24. Gary Sick in *All Fall Down*, Random House, New York, 1985, p. 345n. Sick was Iran desk officer in Carter's NSC at the time of the revolution.

25. Interview with former US DIA official, op. cit. (note 10).

26. *SIPRI Yearbook, 1980*, op. cit. (note 10), p. 99.

27. *The Economist*, 20 July 1985, p. 17. See also SIPRI statistics quoted in the *Jerusalem Post*, 16 February 1986, p. 13.

28. Klieman, op. cit. (note 13), pp. 63–6. According to the *New York Times* (24 August 1981, p. 1–3) by 1981 some 300,000 Israelis, a quarter of the country's labour force, worked in defence-related jobs.

29. *Washington Post*, 12 December 1986. p. 1.

30. 'The Iran Hostage Crisis: A Chronology of Daily Developments', report prepared for the Committee of Foreign Affairs, US House of Representatives, by the Congressional Research Service, Washington, March 1981, pp. 304–5.

31. Ibid, pp. 320–3.

32. Ibid, p. 327.

33. Ibid, pp. 369–70.

34. Ibid, pp. 376–7.

35. State Department Press Guidance prepared 5 January 1981, declassified and released in response to a Freedom of Information Act request.

36. *New York Times*, 22 August 1981, p. 5.

37. Transcript of BBC-TV *Panorama*, broadcast 8.10 p.m. GMT, 1 February 1982.

38. *Washington Post*, 29 November 1986, p. 9.

39. Transcript of BBC *Panorama*, op. cit. (note 37).

40. 'Secret' State Department telegram 12299 from US Embassy, Tel Aviv, to Secretary of State, dated 6 August 1981. The telegram cites the Noticias Argentinias Wire Service on the matter of the ownership of the planes.

41. 'Israel and the Iran–Iraq War', by Shahram Chubin, in *International Defense Review*, Vol. 18, Issue 3, March 1985, p. 304. Chubin was at the time Director of Research, strategic studies programme, Graduate Institute of International Studies, Geneva. See also *SIPRI Yearbook, 1982*, op. cit. (see note 10), p. xxviii.

42. *Washington Post*, 2 December 1986, p. 9

43. London *Sunday Times*, 26 July 1981.

44. The two most complete accounts of the 'Argentinian plane affair' I have seen, aside from the *Sunday Times* story, are the BBC–TV *Panorama* programme (op. cit. (note 37)) and an article entitled '"Tango November": The Israeli Sale of US arms to Iran', by Charles R. Denton, *Middle East Perspective*, October 1981, p. 3.

45. Transcript of *Panorama*, ibid, p. 9.

46. *New York Times*, 24 August 1981, p. 3.

47. *New York Times*, 16 May 1982, p. 9.

48. Ibid.

49. 'Classified' State Department telegram 022031Z from JCS, Washington, to Secretary of State, Washington, dated 2 June 1982.

50. *Boston Globe*, 27 July 1983, p. 4.

51. 'Classified' State Department telegram 231355 from Secretary of State, Washington, to US Embassy, London, dated 16 August 1983.

52. 'Confidential' State Department telegram 232491 from Secretary of State, Washington, to US Embassy, London, dated 17 August 1983.

53. Ibid.

54. 'Confidential' State Department telegram 30643 from US Embassy, Paris, to Secretary of State, Washington, dated 19 August 1983.

55. Ibid.

56. 'Confidential' State Department telegram 04343 from US Embassy, Berne, to Secretary of State, Washington, dated 22 August 1983.

57. *Defense and Foreign Affairs Daily*, 24 January 1984, p. 1, quoted in CRS Report 86–190F, op. cit., p. 6.

58. 'Limited Official Use' State Department telegram 07414 from US Embassy, Bonn, to Secretary of State, Washington, dated 20 March 1984.

59. Ibid.

60. Ibid.

61. *SIPRI Yearbook, 1984*, op. cit. (see note 10), p. 199. SIPRI reported that 40 per cent of Iran's arms imports in 1982 came from North Korea.

62. The 'tank deal' story was obtained from an individual formerly a career US Army officer, who was personally involved, and who fervently wishes to remain anonymous. Personal interviews with the individual were conducted in April 1987.

63. 'Confidential' State Department telegram 232491 from Secretary

of State, Washington to twenty-one US embassies in the Middle East and Europe, dated 17 August 1983.

64. NEA Press Guidance ('taken question') dated 16 May 1984, declassified in response to an FOIA request.

65. Tower Commission Report, op. cit. (note 2), Appendix B, p. 2.

66. Ibid.

67. Ibid, Appendix B, p. 11.

68. Ibid, Appendix B, p. 3.

69. Ibid, Appendix B, p. 11.

70. Ibid, Appendix B, p. 6.

71. Ibid, Appendix B, p. 14.

72. Ibid, Appendix B, p. 16.

73. Report of the Senate Select Committee on Intelligence, op. cit. (note 2), p. 6.

74. Ibid, pp. 6–7.

75. Ibid, and Tower Commission Report, op. cit. (note 2) Appendix B, pp. 19–21.

76. Report of the Senate Select Committee on Intelligence, ibid, p. 8.

77. Tower Commission Report, op. cit. (note 2), Appendix B, p. 30.

78. Transcript of Attorney General Meese's News Conference, *Washington Post*, 26 November 1986, p. 8.

79. *Washington Post*, 26 November 1986, p. 1.

80. Ibid.

81. *Washington Post*, 26 November 1986, p. 1.

82. Thomas Friedman in the *New York Times*, 11 December 1986, p. 20.

83. FBI Report dated 27 January 1949, File No. HQ 2–875, Sections 21–7, declassified in response to a Freedom of Information Act request.

84. FBI Report dated 29 September 1948, File No. 2–875–664, declassified in response to a Freedom of Information Act request.

85. Ibid.

86. 'Secret' military attaché report IR-98-48 from US Air Attaché, Prague, to Air Force Intelligence Directorate, dated 27 December

1948, copy in 'ID File', Office of the Assistant Chief of Staff, G-2, Record Group 319, National Archives.

87. 'Secret' summary of information from 117th CIC detachment, New York Field Office, NYPE, dated 28 December 1948, copy in the Decimal File 091.112 Czechoslovakia, Decimal Correspondence Files, Office of the Assistant Chief of Staff, G-2, Record Group 319, National Archives.

88. FBI Report dated 16 January 1948, File No. LA 2–875–173, declassified in response to a freedom of Information Act request.

89. FBI Report dated 17 March 1950, File No. HQ 2-875-880, declassified in response to a Freedom of Information Act request.

Chapter 13   Near Conclusion

1. The quotations are taken from a copy of the conference materials distributed to attendees.

2. Major General Yaron was also appointed Defence Attaché to the Israeli Embassy in Ottawa. The Canadian Government, however, has taken the unusual step of publicly refusing his credentials, presumably because Yaron, who had been commander of IDF forces in Lebanon during the 1982–3 campaign, had been named by the Kahane Commission in Israel as one of those 'indirectly responsible' for the Sabra and Chatila massacres.

3. Conference materials from the 'R & D Co-operation conference 1987' held in Washington, DC, 26–8 May 1987, prepared by the Embassy of Israel, 'with the support of the American Defence Preparedness Association'.

4. A recent summary of the 'Bryen affair' appeared in the *New York Times*, 22 December 1985, p. 1.

5. Conference materials, op. cit. (note 3).

6. Rex B. Wingerter in 'Israel's Search for Strategic Interdependence and the 1983 US – Israeli Strategic Co-operation Agreement', *American–Arab Affairs Journal*, No. 14, Fall, 1985, pp. 81–94.

7. This MoU was suspended in the following month, December, when the Government of Israel annexed the Golan Heights in occupied Syria.

8. Wingerter, op. cit. (note 6) p. 92.

9. The 'Pollard affair', an elaborate effort by the Government of Israel to steal US military secrets, must be viewed in the context of

the above-listed co-operation agreements. Israel has simply never been denied US military technology or information when it has made the case that sharing was important to its national security interests. And the means by which this sharing is carried out have long since been normalized, formalized and channelled. The extensive 'take' by the Pollard espionage ring in fact did *not* relate to Israeli national security interests but rather, in the main to US – Soviet relations and military capabilities, and therefore to the enhancement of Israeli leverage upon US and Soviet policy in a broad range of fields. But that, I have decided, is another subject, another time, another book.

10. *New York Times*, 27 February 1983, p. E18. The raids may have been more of a victory for American weapons systems than even the generals and admirals realized. On 6 May 1984 Patrick Seale reported in the London *Observer* (p. 6) that a US Air Force AWACs plane, patrolling 150 miles off the Lebanese coast in the Mediterranean, had helped to direct the Israeli air attack by informing the IAF of the location of Syrian planes as they took off to intercept the invading Israeli aircraft.

11. See *Jordanian Arms and the Middle East Balance: Update*, by Anthony Cordesman, Middle East Institute, 1985. A senior US military official working with the State Department verified the information and added details in recorded interviews conducted in April 1986.

12. Dine's testimony to the Armed Services Subcommittee on Strategic and Theatre Nuclear Forces was present on 30 January 1986, and was based upon a paper entitled 'The Threat to Israel by Tactical Ballistic Missiles,' by W. Seth Carus, AIPAC's military analyst.

13. Telephone interview with US military analyst Anthony Cordesman in June 1987.

14. The information on Syrian missile deployments has been confirmed by Ambassador Robert Pelletreau, a senior official of the Bureau of Political and Military Affairs of the US State Department. The primary source for this section, however, was another State Department official who wishes to remain anonymous.

15. 'Guided Weapons (Including Light, Unguided Anti-Tank Weapons)', *Brassey's Battlefield Weapons Systems and Technology Series*, Vol. VIII, by R. G. Lee, T. K. Garland-Collins, P. Garnell, D. H. J. Halsey, G. M. Moss and A. W. Mowat, Brassey's Defence Publishers, Oxford, 1983, p. 180.

16. 'The Near East: The Search for Truth', by Charles Malik, *Foreign Affairs*, Vol. 30, No. 2, January 1952, p. 242. Malik served as President of the United Nations General Assembly in 1958–9.

Index